"Brian Carney and Isaac Getz have use
cept of freedom to serve as a crucial
imaginatively framed ideas in the broader area of commerce.
A most interesting and original work."

—James MacGregor Burns, a Pulitzer Prize
and author of *Leadership* and of
Transforming Leadership

"Brian M Carney and Isaac Getz's book Freedom, Inc. is after
my own heart. Its core idea of empowering employees to lead
organizational growth is the holy grail of corporate sustainability and the only definitive antidote to enterprise rejuvena-
tion. The book is indeed a must-read for all managers and
proprietors who are serious about remaining relevant in the
shifting sands of time!"

—Vineet Nayar, Former CEO, HCL Technologies &
Founder, Sampark Foundation,
author of *Employee First, Customer Second*

"When do you do your best work? When told how to do your
job, or when you know — and embrace—the reason why you
are working? We all know the answer. Carney and Getz help
you apply this fundamental insight to liberate your company,
your employees, and your life. This thrilling book has the
cure for what ails most companies, and perhaps even most
economies."

—Jonathan Haidt,
New York University Stern School of Business,
author of *The Righteous Mind*

"Freedom, Inc. is a revolutionary manifesto for unplanned
dynamism—the root strength of every successful company in
history."   —*Forbes*

"Carney and Getz show that organizations that spend the time, money, and effort on the 'soft' stuff of organization's culture end up with truly empowered workforces."

—*Strategy + Business*

"Messrs. Carney and Getz offer portraits of chief executives who guided their businesses to prosperity by freeing up talent."

—*Wall Street Journal*

"Carney and Getz book's central point: If you give your workers maximum freedom they will lead your business to higher productivity, profits, and growth."   —*New York Times*

"Brian Carney and Isaac Getz take us into companies that have made freedom their lifeblood – companies that trust their employees and liberate them, counting on those employees to act in the best interests of the company, and taking advantage of that passion to achieve enviable corporate financial results."

—*Globe and Mail*

Freedom, Inc.

FREEDOM, INC.

How Corporate Liberation
Unleashes Employee Potential
and Business Performance

BRIAN M. CARNEY
AND ISAAC GETZ

Cover Art © Accent/Shutterstock

Somme Valley House logo © yod67/Shutterstock

Library of Congress Cataloging-in-Publication Data is available upon request.
ISBN 978-0-786-75635-3

Cover Design by James Fletcher

10 9 8 7 6 5 4 3 2

Second Edition

To our children:
Brian's Luke, James, and Aletheia
and Isaac's Elie and Adèle

CONTENTS

PREFACE TO SECOND EDITION

Corporate liberation is not a strategy. It is a business philosophy that leaders around the world are using to radically transform their organizations. Liberating leaders believe that a workplace based on respect and freedom is a more natural environment than one based on mistrust and control. So they acted to align their organizations with these beliefs: They liberated people's initiative and potential and with it, unshackled their companies' performance.

A lot has happened since *Freedom, Inc.* first appeared in 2009. The book itself has been translated to six other languages. In France, it won the best business book award and was the No.1 business/management bestseller on Amazon.fr seven months in a row. More importantly, it has inspired hundreds of leaders to launch their own corporate liberation. The French daily *Le Monde* has heralded the start of a *corporate liberation movement* in France. Since then, the phenomenon has made the cover of leading periodicals, been shown on the evening news of major European TV chains, and been the subject of a 90-minute TV documentary that broke all the records for popularity.

Most liberated companies have been small and medium size—though some have grown tremendously since. Yet increasingly, multinationals

xii   *Preface to Second Edition*

such as Michelin or Decathlon—operating in Europe, America and Asia—are joining the corporate liberation movement that pioneers such as W.L. Gore and USAA began.

Corporate liberation has no frontiers, geographical or industrial. Vineet Nayar has liberated an Indian high-tech giant and David Marquet, a U.S. nuclear submarine. Leaders of organizations of all sizes and types are shedding their hierarchies and bureaucracies and transforming them into respect- and freedom-based workplaces. Every morning their employees go to work, but many prefer to say they go to have fun—pursuing a common dream using their own initiative. Incidentally—or naturally—their organizations routinely outperform the competition. In other words, respect and freedom breed fun and greatness.

Brian M. Carney and Isaac Getz
New York and Paris
September 2015

INTRODUCTION

Freedom works.

In every aspect of our lives—in politics, in economics, in entertainment, and in family life—we demand the freedom to decide matters for ourselves. And yet when it comes to our work lives, far too many people are stifled, constrained, hemmed in, and tied down by bureaucracy and rules that have nothing to do with allowing them to do the best they can in their jobs. These constraints leave people feeling out of control of their work lives, which, in turn, leads to stress, fatigue, and disengagement from work.

Amazingly, all of this is already well understood and has been for decades. As far back as 1924, William L. McKnight, the legendary CEO of 3M, put the matter succinctly: "If you put fences around people, you get sheep. Give people the room they need." With that in mind, McKnight went on to build an environment at 3M that unleashed the creativity and initiative of 3M's people. And yet the culture McKnight built at 3M has been more admired than imitated. Sixty years later, Japanese industrialist Konosuke Matsushita looked across the ocean at his competitors and described a corporate America still in the grip of Frederick W. Taylor's "scientific management," which organizes work by means of detailed procedures that specify narrow, repetitive tasks for everyone, and demands full compliance with their execution:

> We are going to win and the industrial West is going to lose out . . . because . . . your firms are built on the Taylor model. Even worse so are your heads. With your bosses doing the thinking while the workers wield the screwdrivers . . . For you the essence of good management is getting the ideas out of the heads of the bosses and into the hands of labor. We are beyond the Taylor model. Business . . . is now so complex and difficult, the survival of firms so hazardous and fraught with danger, that continued existence depends upon the day-to-day mobilization of every ounce of intelligence.[1]

Notice that Matsushita was not arguing that liberating your employees was a nice thing to do for them, or that it would make them happier or make managers better people. "Continued existence," he said, "depends upon the day-to-day mobilization of every ounce of intelligence." That means every ounce of intelligence in every brain that comes through the door of your company every day. If you are not doing everything you can to take advantage of that brainpower and the knowledge those brains possess about your business, you're not only leaving money on the table, you are putting your company's survival at risk.

As we write these words in early 2009, the United States and the world economy are in a dire state. The U.S. economy is shrinking rapidly, corporate profits are collapsing—or in many cases simply nonexistent—and a half a million Americans a month are losing their jobs. Everyone is afraid. Bosses are afraid that if they don't maintain or restore profitability, their jobs will be on the line. Frontline employees are afraid that their jobs will be cut so that their bosses can keep their own.

We can guarantee you that important opportunities—for the elimination of senseless waste that shows up nowhere on your profit-and-loss statements, for keeping customers, and for acquiring new accounts—lie just down the hall, in the minds of the people you already employ.

But wait—don't walk down that hall and ask them how to save your business just yet. Sit back down and keep reading. If taking advantage of those opportunities were as simple as asking people to raise their hand and speak, you'd have done it already. People respond to the environment in which they find themselves. That's what McKnight meant when he said that if you *put up fences, you get sheep.* The fences turn the people into sheep in subtle ways that they themselves might not even realize.

Now, Matsushita was being a bit unfair—the problems with "Taylorism," with turning your employees into automatons, have been appreciated for a long time, as McKnight's observation shows. At times, trying to address this lack of autonomy has almost become an obsession among management gurus. But for all the ink spilled and all the energy expended in the name of empowering employees, Dilbert's comic-strip world remains depressingly familiar to people inside most companies.

You might conclude from this that bureaucracy, top-down control, and maybe just a touch of George Orwell is simply the cost of doing business in the modern world. We may not like it, but is it possible to live without it?

The liberated companies in this book don't just say that it is—they prove it. In industries that range from high-tech to manufacturing, from services to finance and to heavy industry, these firms have done away with the whole gamut of mechanisms of control that characterize too many businesses—and they've thrived as a result.

Freedom, Inc. is the product of more than four years of research. As we studied these companies, we became convinced of two things: First, they all have things in common that tie their success together with their culture of freedom. And second, if truly liberated companies remain relatively rare even today, it is not because their lessons can't be applied elsewhere. The problem with bureaucracy is a bit like obesity. It's no mystery how to lose weight or avoid gaining it. Study after study has affirmed the basic truth that if you consume more calories than you burn, you're going to pack on the pounds.

We all know this. The evidence is clear, and so, too, is the road to our ideal weight. But more and more people don't travel that road (your authors not necessarily excluded) because it's easier to fall back on habit, even when the habits are bad for you. You may admire the svelte figure of some athlete or model and resolve to look like them someday—and then go back to your desk and sneak another bite of that candy bar.

Well, it turns out that a number of the liberated companies in this book are a bit like that supermodel. Executives come from all over the world to see FAVI in northern France or Harley-Davidson in Milwaukee. Harvard Business School has used Sun Hydraulics in Sarasota, Florida, as its main case study on freedom in the workplace. But while other executives—and even competitors—admire these companies from afar, they don't, or won't, change their own ways. This is not to say, however, that they *can't*. They can. The very diversity of the liberated companies we encountered and studied convinced us of that. If a brass foundry in France, an insurance company in Texas, and a software firm in Pennsylvania could all set their people free; if liberating leaders could change the culture inside companies with decades of dysfunction in their past or build a new *Freedom, Inc.* from scratch; then there were lessons here for any company to use to their advantage.

Those lessons are:

1. *Stop telling and start listening.* Then, remove all the symbols and practices that prevent your people from feeling intrinsically equal.
2. *Start openly and actively sharing your vision of the company so people will "own" it.* But don't do this before Step 1 because people who are not treated as equals will leave you alone with your vision.
3. *Stop trying to motivate people.* That's right. Instead, build an environment that allows people to grow and self-direct—and let them

motivate themselves. If they understand the vision from Step 2, they'll take care of the rest if you let them.

4. *Stay alert.* To keep your company free, become the culture keeper. In this role, as liberating leader Bob Davids says, "One drop of urine in the soup is too much—and you can't get it out."[2] The price of liberty is eternal vigilance.

These principles are universal, but each leader in this book had to apply them to his own unique set of circumstances—and you will, too. In other words, this book cannot give you a formula for applying the above principles to any particular situation. Freedom is, after all, the enemy of formulas—if we knew, or you knew, every situation that would arise and how to deal with it, you would not need freedom—or your employees, for that matter. You'd have all the answers already.

This paradox was captured by Robert Townsend, one of the best, most profound early thinkers on the problem of freedom and organization. Townsend was also a liberating leader in his own right. One of his aphorisms was, "At best, a job description freezes the job. . . . At worst, they're prepared by personnel people who can't write and don't understand the jobs. Then they're not only expensive to prepare and regularly revise, but they're important morale-sappers."[3] Likewise, if your liberation campaign isn't flexible, it's probably a little short on the freedom thing.

Townsend got his start as a leader at American Express in the 1950s, which at the time was a traveler's check company. He introduced charge cards to the business, ingeniously describing them to reluctant top executives as a "cross between a passport and a traveler's check." He also drove AmEx's foray into banking. More important, though, from the moment he became a manager he practiced a kind of leadership based on radical freedom for his subordinates. As he would later say, "As a new manager, remove everything you didn't like when you were a subordinate and implement what you missed."[4] But as the head of only one division at

American Express, Townsend could not transform the whole company. That opportunity came in 1962, when he was offered the chance to become chief executive officer of Avis, which was at the time a moribund company that hadn't turned a profit in thirteen years. In just three years he liberated Avis and unleashed the initiative and action of its thousands of employees. By 1965 Avis had become one of the fastest-growing companies in the United States—its "We try harder" motto comes from those times.

That year ITT, one of the most acquisitive conglomerates of the 1960s, noticed the turnaround Townsend had accomplished and bought the company. Townsend resigned and, five years later, published *Up the Organization: How to Stop the Corporation from Stifling People and Strangling Profits*. The book's aphorisms and advice, arranged in alphabetical order, describe what might be called an early version of a liberation campaign. It opens with "A—Advertising: Fire the whole advertising department and your old agency," and it closes with "W—Wearing out your welcome: Nobody should be CEO of anything for more than five or six years." It would ultimately spend several weeks as a number one *New York Times* best seller and remains in print today. The Wharton Center for Leadership and Change Management at the University of Pennsylvania still ranks it the number one business book "every manager must read." For all that, Townsend's advice has remained somewhat less than universally applied since *Up the Organization* was published.

One person in particular who might have been surprised by this was Douglas McGregor, a professor at the Massachusetts Institute of Technology whose academic work echoed Townsend's practical experience. McGregor's 1960 book, *The Human Side of Enterprise*, is itself a classic on bureaucracy and human nature. McGregor identified two approaches to running a company: "Theory X" and "Theory Y"—clearly, branding was not his strong suit. Each theory, according to McGregor, is based on a different set of assumptions about human nature. The "Theory X" assumptions are:

1. The average human being has an inherent dislike of work and will avoid it if he can.
2. Because of this human characteristic of dislike of work, most people must be coerced, controlled, directed, or threatened with punishment to get them to put forth adequate effort toward the achievement of organizational objectives.
3. The average human being prefers to be directed, wishes to avoid responsibility, has relatively little ambition, and wants security above all.[5]

The "Theory Y" assumptions are different:

1. The expenditure of physical and mental effort in work is as natural as play or rest.
2. External control and the threat of punishment are not the only means for bringing about effort toward organizational objectives. Man will exercise self-direction and self-control in the service of objectives to which he is committed.
3. Commitment to objectives is a function of rewards associated with their achievement. The most significant such reward, that is, the satisfaction of ego and self-actualization needs, can be direct products of effort directed toward organizational objectives.
4. The average human being learns, under proper conditions, not only to accept but to seek responsibility.
5. The capacity to exercise a relatively high degree of imagination, ingenuity, and creativity in the solution of organizational problems is widely, not narrowly, distributed in the population.
6. Under the conditions of modern industrial life, the intellectual potentialities of the average human being are only partially utilized.[6]

McGregor was so convinced of the superiority of "Theory Y" to "Theory X" that in 1950—well before he wrote *The Human Side of*

Enterprise—he predicted the death of "Theory X" organizations within a decade.[7] That didn't happen. Maybe the good Mr. McGregor had never tried to go on a diet.

Dieting is hard because the pleasures of immediate consumption are obvious to our senses, but all the ways in which we are damaging ourselves may be hidden from us in the heat of the moment. It's the same with bureaucracy. As you'll see in this book, overbearing control of one's people comes with all sorts of hidden costs—not just to your bottom line, but even to your health and the health of your employees.

Even so, there are moments when the truth confronts even the most weak-willed dieters. One of the liberating leaders in this book, Jean-François Zobrist, recounted the following story. It occurred during one of those regular visits to FAVI by a CEO who had heard about the company's remarkable culture and performance and wanted to learn more about it.[8] While walking by the supply closet, the visiting CEO was surprised that it not only lacked a lock but that it was missing one of its four walls—there was literally no way to close it securely. Zobrist explained that FAVI, as a liberated company, trusts its people to take what they need for their jobs and that they are free to do so. Just then, a machine operator came over to the closet, so the visitor asked him a question: "What happens if the part you came for is missing?"

"It never happens," the operator replied, "because the guy who takes the last piece in the box goes to the warehouse and brings back a full box."

"Fine," the CEO pressed. "But what if there are no more boxes in the warehouse?"

"Simple," the operator answered. "If the guy sees that he's taken the last box from the warehouse, he lets the operator taking care of purchasing know so that more can be ordered."

"And what if he doesn't do it?" the CEO persisted—this time, surely, the operator would have no more clever answers.

After a pause, the operator told him simply, "It's a question of good manners, *Monsieur*," took what he needed, and excused himself.

The visitor's interlocutor was not simply an uncommonly polite machine operator in a brass foundry. He was the product of FAVI's liberated culture. And what he called "good manners" were, in fact, the norms that serve in the place of top-down rules when a company is free. The visiting CEO might well have left thinking he couldn't entrust his company to "good manners." But then again, even the strictest rules are only as good as people's willingness to follow them. The great intellectual error of bureaucrats everywhere is to assume that because something is called a rule, it's preferable to a less formal arrangement. And yet most of those rules are not only great morale sappers, they're preventing the vast majority of your employees from doing the right thing. The rules become so stifling that the only way for people to do a good job is to go around them—sometimes at great cost. At the same time, they are, as likely as not, failing to prevent the tiny minority of potential malefactors from doing your business harm. In these times, can you afford to continue stifling the vast majority of your people instead of giving them a chance to help your business?

1

"HOW" COMPANIES AND "WHY" COMPANIES

How Not to Run a Business

EVEN IF YOU don't know what Gore-Tex is, you know what it does: It keeps you dry—guaranteed. As a brand, Gore-Tex has been so successful that it sometimes seems in danger of disappearing, of becoming a generic term like "Band-Aid." Since it was invented in 1971, Gore-Tex has given rise to a number of competing products. Some of those boast properties said to be superior to the original. But if you walk into a store and want to know whether a ski jacket is waterproof, the question you'll probably ask is "Is it Gore-Tex?"

It's the kind of brand dominance—over both market share and "mind share"—that marketers dream of, or lose sleep over. The story of how it came to be, and came to symbolize an entire market category, is the story of two radical ideas.

Bill and Genevieve Gore's first idea was that there were market opportunities for a chemical called polytetrafluorethylene—PTFE for short—that DuPont wasn't pursuing.

Today, PTFE is best known as Teflon, that magical polymer that keeps our pans from sticking and our pipes from leaking, among a myriad of other far-flung uses. It is supposedly so slippery that it is the only known substance to which a gecko's feet will not stick. But in 1938, it was an experiment gone wrong for Roy Plunkett, who worked at DuPont. Plunkett was trying to develop a refrigerant for car air conditioners when one of his canisters of gas seized up solid. He cut it open and found that the tetrafluorethylene inside had "polymerized"—that is, turned to a kind of plastic, white and slippery. Three years later, DuPont received a patent on the stuff, but then contented itself with selling it as a raw material to those who wanted to incorporate it into their products. It would be another thirteen years before a Frenchman, Marc Gregoire, stuck it to a pan so that nothing else would.

Bill Gore had other plans for PTFE. He thought it would make a great insulator for electrical cables. But DuPont was a chemical materials company, not an electrical products company, and wasn't interested. So, at the age of forty-six, this father of four quit DuPont, licensed PTFE, and set up shop in his basement with seed money from friends in the Gores' bridge club.[1]

As it turned out, Bill Gore was right about PTFE's potential. But it was his and Vieve's second idea that gave the world Gore-Tex, along with more than one thousand other innovative products, and made W. L. Gore & Associates into a multibillion-dollar leader in markets spanning from aerospace and electronics to energy and health care. Like PTFE, that second idea was borrowed, in a way, from DuPont. But like the remarkable polymer, Bill's insight had to do with what the company he had worked at for years *wasn't* doing.

Bill Gore believed that the way we talk about one another and about our jobs affects the way we think and the way we act. So he replaced his employees with "associates," their jobs with "commitments," and their managers with "leaders."

Of course, it's possible, as George Orwell knew, to change all the words without changing reality. And changing the reality of how people work was Bill Gore's real ambition.

THE END OF "FUNNY" BUSINESS

Les Lewis, today a manufacturing leader at Gore, was one of the company's first associates. He recalled what it was like at Gore in 1965. "It was early on, at a funny time for the company," Lewis explained. "We had [one plant], seventy people, and believe it or not, a dozen 'supervisors.' I was one of them, and I decided to write the first supervisor's handbook—how to deal with back vacations, the sorts of things that a supervisor needs guidelines for."

What Lewis described as a "funny time" is a phase that almost every successful start-up goes through. The company has started to grow; maybe one day you walk in and realize that you no longer recognize everyone who works there and don't always know who does what and how anymore. Sooner or later, someone decides that order needs to be restored, or established. An enterprising manager like Lewis decides he'll share his insights by setting them down on paper, and the first manual is written to tell people how to do their jobs.

If you're one of those managers, this might seem to be an attractive opportunity—a chance to show your quality and pass on your experience. Some people might even think it fun, a bit like setting down the rules of a whole new society that, from now on, will run like a well-oiled machine.

But Lewis's "fun" did not last long. Today, a handbook such as the one Lewis wanted would be unthinkable at this company. But how did founder Bill react to the manual in those early days?

Lewis described Bill Gore's big idea as a product of his experience at DuPont.[2] As Gore explained it to Lewis at the time, "When [DuPont] wanted to work on a project, they would assemble a small team, and that small team would work very much as equals . . . where there was not a hierarchical thing. Everybody worked, everybody brought their skill and knowledge together." This was, for Gore, an ideal way of working. But at DuPont, "once that project got to a certain point, they would all go back to their organizations, in a much more hierarchical chain of command." Gore's notion was simple: If this collaborative, nonhierarchical, liberated structure worked for important projects that needed to get done quickly, why shouldn't a company work that way *all the time?* So once Gore left DuPont and started his own company, he decided to do just that. According to Lewis, Bill Gore "vowed that if he ever had a company of his own, he would want it that way because he thought that it really invited a lot of people's creative skills to come forward." Even so, it took time and experimentation before Gore settled on an effective way to implement his idea.

The discovery of Lewis's supervisor handbook, as it happens, was a clarifying moment for Bill Gore. "He wasn't turned on by it," Lewis said drily, adding, "But when I wanted to introduce a requisition form for shop work, that was the end of it—Bill hated forms."

So Bill Gore decided to take his supervisors out to dinner. Soon the monthly dinners became an academy in the values and principles of leadership. "It was almost a Socratic approach to teaching people to lead," recalled Lewis. "At these dinners, he would talk about how to lead—we wouldn't call it 'leading' then; we were [still] 'supervisors'—and how to 'sponsor'—we didn't call it 'sponsoring' then. He would discuss problems that we had and would ask everyone, 'How would you do that?' We would hear different ideas about how to deal with situations," Lewis explained. "It was absolutely a dialogue. He would never drive his answers to us, [saying, 'This is] what you ought to do.' Instead, he would ask, 'How have you solved this problem? Has anyone else experienced one of these?' Meanwhile, he was also instilling in us values and value judgments."

So the "funny time" ended. No supervisors ever attempted to write rules and policies again, because there were no more supervisors at Gore. And the leaders, who took the place of the supervisors, were busy helping people—instead of telling them how they had to work. But it would take more experimentation and time before Bill Gore fully implemented his second big idea of a radically different way to work.

THE YELLOW BRICK ROAD

Fast-forward to the mid-1980s. Thirteen years ago, Lewis had left the company for greener pastures. After spending this period in more traditional command-and-control companies, he's now decided to return to his native Newark, Delaware, and give W. L. Gore & Associates the benefit of knowledge and experience he's gained about managing big companies. Gore itself had gotten a lot bigger over the years, with several manufacturing sites in the United States and abroad and several thousand associates. The circumstances looked perfect. The plant had just been moved to a brand-new facility and Lewis, a newly minted manufacturing leader had a big corner office, making him feel important: "I was feeling very confident—'I have arrived,' you know?" There was a lot on his plate. Operations were inefficient and the manufacturing techniques people used appalled Lewis: "Instead of computers they were using a columnar pad with numbers they were ticking off to run manufacturing operations by hand."

So Lewis decided to change all that, to instill some discipline, show people that they were working in a backward way, and push them to use a newfangled tool called a computer spreadsheet.

It looked like the right thing to do. Though quite big already, the company lagged behind its main competitors in the use of modern, computer-based operations management. Lewis's proposed course of action was unimpeachable and would have been accepted in any other company. What Lewis couldn't see is how different Gore had become since he'd left.

His efforts lasted six months and the only result was personal—he was ready to leave the company again. And it wasn't because of then-president Bob Gore's—Bill's son—hatred of computers ("Bill hated forms, Bob hated computers," Lewis explained) but because no associate would ever listen to him, never mind follow him. "I was using the techniques that I had been practicing for thirteen years elsewhere. More power, more influence, more whatever, and suddenly it dawned on me—an epiphany: 'You know what the Gore organization is like. You were in it. Why are you trying this top-down kind of a way?'"

And so Lewis rediscovered the values and principles of leadership Bill Gore had taught him and others at their Socratic dinner meetings. Lewis dubbed it the "yellow brick road."

"You ask your associates 'Where do you want to go?'" Lewis told us. "And they say, 'To the Emerald City.' So you don't tell them, 'Follow the yellow brick road,' the road your own knowledge dictates is the right one," Lewis explained. "You don't, because all they will say is, 'You're crazy. We're going off through the woods.' So you take your bricks and go with them, and throw them one by one in front of them—not giving the answer, but ideas, information, letting them find their own answers. And with every new brick they step on, [your] credibility goes up." Lewis summarized: "I had no credibility, but little by little each of those bricks brought my credibility up."

Lewis had rediscovered that, with all his responsibility for leading a big plant, all his knowledge and experience about how to run operations better, associates wouldn't follow him until he filled what he called his "credibility bucket." He was learning that a "leader" is not just a manager with a different title. A leader is someone whom others follow *naturally*. At Gore, when Lewis returned, that culture was already so strong that he ran into it face-first, and it nearly drove him back into the command-and-control world. But even at more traditional companies, this same dynamic holds. It's just that at traditional firms, all the tension is under the surface. As Gore's CEO, Terri Kelly, explained, "What you find in a lot of companies is that if there isn't true support for the decision, it gets undermined along the way. In fact, it may never come to fruition. So on the one hand you've made a very quick decision—'We're going to go to China'—but then you've got all kinds of resistance."[3] So in those companies, the employees may not go into open revolt—most of the time. But if they are not sincerely consulted by their manager, or if they think he lacks credibility, your company will quietly leak productivity every day—and perhaps even sink.

The difference at Gore is that the associates there are *genuinely* consulted—and they are free to choose. This freedom is one of the hallmarks of all of the liberated companies in this book. And by exercising their choice not to follow the Les Lewis who had returned from the outside world, Gore's associates were actually doing him a favor. They were providing him with valuable information about how he was doing his job that allowed him to change tack and become a more effective leader. The all-too-familiar alternative—each of us grumbles to himself, his family, or his coworkers, but keeps his head down and does enough work to avoid attracting attention—may be one of the invisible but profound reasons your company isn't performing the way you think it should.

OK, you may say. But how do you get everyone to row in the same direction without a boss at the helm? What guides people's freely chosen actions and prevents them from pursuing their own interests at the company's expense? Gore has a way of thinking about these challenges. And unsurprisingly, it's just a little bit different from the way most companies do. Gore people live the company's four principles: The first is "freedom." But along with it are "fairness," "commitment," and "the waterline." The thing to know about these principles is that, unlike the mission and values statements at many companies, associates actually think about and *live* them. Fairness, commitment, and the waterline make freedom work for Gore.

"FORMULA FOR FAILURE"

Fairness is about being fair to others—both inside and outside the company. According to Lewis, W. L. Gore & Associates wants to treat its suppliers and its customers as equals. But fairness has an internal component as well—it's about treating your colleagues with dignity and as equals. Lewis, in fact, once needed a little help to understand the fairness principle.

Back in the mid-1960s, when Lewis was a young supervisor, the company was scraping by and still working out the kinks in its production of PTFE-coated cables—its only product at the time. When a batch went bad, Lewis came up with what he thought was an enterprising way to save money by stripping the bad cables so the materials could be reused. "So, I got these three women in the back of the plant and I gave them a wire spool each to sit down on," Lewis explained. "And I put these spools of cable that had to be stripped there, and I gave them some kind of a knife or something to strip it, and they are sitting back there in the bowels of the Earth like a coffee klatch, stripping this wire off." Lewis thought to himself: "'All right. I am set up. Man, we are getting this stripped off and getting it recoated; we are going to save all this.' Back then we couldn't afford to throw stuff away." Needless to say, Lewis was pretty pleased with his economy and enterprise. Bill Gore, however, thought that Lewis needed some help.

Lewis left the women to their work and went back out onto the shop floor, where Bill found him. Lewis continued the story:

"'Do you have a minute?' Bill Gore said.

"And I said, 'Sure.' So we turn around and walk out of the shop and into the only office in the plant, where the only blackboard was in the whole plant, and he shut the door and said, 'Have a seat.'

"And I sat down, and he wrote up on the board, '*Formula for Failure*,' and underlined it."

Underneath, Gore listed a series of bullet points:

- Provide inadequate lighting
- Provide uncomfortable seats
- Provide tools that give blisters.

"He listed about eight things. Honestly," Lewis said. "And then he said, 'Are *you* responsible for that wire stripping in the back?'

"I said, 'Yes sir.'

"He opened the door and walked out."

Fairness means, above all, that human dignity is not subordinated to bottom-line considerations. Lewis may have thought he was saving money for a struggling start-up with a dwindling bank account. Instead of frugality, Bill Gore saw short-term thinking that would lead to long-term failure.

But there was an even deeper lesson for Lewis in Gore's "Formula for Failure." Lewis had a problem—how to save some money on the defective wire. And he imposed a solution on his employees that, he thought, would solve it. He was not the one who had to strip the wire or sit in the dark on old spools, so the obstacles that he had erected to those people doing their jobs did not even occur to him until Gore pointed them out. Lewis never asked whether they had any ideas for how to salvage the wire or what tools or conditions they'd need to get the job done. He never even asked himself whether the problem he was trying to solve was the right one. He never treated his fellow associates as intrinsically equal, as people who are paid to know how to do *their* jobs as well as he knows his.

If his company was going to be different from traditional companies, Bill Gore could not afford leaders who treated people unfairly. That, too, was a formula for failure.

"ALL IN THE SAME BOAT"

At Gore, associates have commitments instead of jobs. This, again, is more than mere semantics. A job is something a boss gives *you*, something framed in a box on an organizational chart. A commitment is *freely* entered into, and is a promise of sorts made to those working alongside you. Commitments are more fluid than jobs. Depending on one's workload and capacity for new projects, an associate may have one, two, or several commitments simultaneously. An associate may flow in or out of a commitment as the work requires. New hires are not assigned a job but encouraged to seek out commitments where they feel they can best employ their talents, skills, and experience.

In this sense, a commitment is the opposite of a job. It is something chosen, rather than something imposed. It is another sense in which Gore associates are set free from the demands of a traditional hierarchy.

But that's a recipe for anarchy, not for freedom, you may think. Today a person may like some activity and commit to it. But tomorrow, he may like another activity more and just "recommit" there, leaving his current team with a huge hole to fill. Without some discipline, this freedom of commitment will quickly fall apart. This is where the credibility bucket comes in.

A drop goes in the bucket every time an associate keeps a commitment, from one to finish a memo by tomorrow to seeing through a multiyear project. The credibility bucket also gets a drop added every time an associate helps somebody. Commitments are voluntary—but once a commitment is made, you'd better keep it. If you don't, your credibility bucket will drain quickly, and with that your ability to work with other associates dries up. Leaving your current commitment without first discussing it with your team, finding a way to reduce your involvement gradually, and avoiding disrupting your colleagues will not only blow a hole in the team's activities. It will also blow a huge hole in your credibility bucket and, with that, your chances to work in a new team. W. L. Gore & Associates' culture doesn't use discipline to avoid anarchy. It relies firmly on self-discipline.

The waterline principle is another way that W. L. Gore & Associates uses self-discipline to keep freedom from becoming anarchy. A "waterline decision"—another local code word—is one that could sink the "boat." If an associate feels that a decision is important enough that it is make or break—either because it involves a large financial outlay or it could have broad ramifications for the business—then he must consult with leaders and other associates with better knowledge or authority to guide him to the right decision. Corporate freedom is not a blank check, and the waterline helps ensure that freedom is used in a responsible manner at Gore.

The authority to help make those waterline decisions, however, does not come from organizational charts, as Lewis found out when he first returned to Gore—which has no org charts anyway. One of the ways that a leader at Gore acquires the authority to lead is by filling his credibility bucket. Lewis's was empty upon his return, which explains why people wouldn't listen to him.

One could imagine how the waterline, if interpreted broadly enough, could become a covert mechanism of control. But the waterline is not invoked very often in most associates' daily lives. Individual initiative and risk taking have always been strongly encouraged at W. L. Gore & Associates. Bill Gore was known for asking associates on his daily plant tour: "Have you made any mistakes lately?" And if the answer was "No," he would say: "You haven't been taking enough risks." Needless to say, if the risk is that you might fail to keep a commitment, you should warn others immediately. If you don't, you'll punch a hole in your credibility bucket.

For Gore's associates, the result is a company where they feel uniquely free to pursue their own interests within the framework of a fulfilling job—or, rather, commitment. But for the company as a whole, the proof is in the results. And the company has been eating its freedom pudding for fifty years now. It still tastes as great as ever. In the early days, Bill Gore started out with an unloved little compound called PTFE and one product—coated wires and cables. Today, Gore takes more than $3 billion in sales and and has averaged better than 10% annual growth over the past decade. It not only makes the most famous waterproof membrane in the world, but it continues to innovate in ways that no five-year plan could foresee.

ONE THOUSAND INNOVATIVE PRODUCTS

Take Gore's foray into guitar strings, where it is, unbeknownst to most of the world, the market leader. The story of how it got there is surprisingly typical of the way that Gore has grown for decades, without planning. Elixir guitar strings are a premium product, selling for three times what ordinary strings can command in the market. But they came about, like Gore-Tex itself, through a happy accident of the sort that the company has stumbled into over and over. One of Gore's associates in the medical devices division, Dave Myers, was a bicycling enthusiast who was unhappy with the performance of the cables used to shift gears on his bike.[4] So in his spare time, he set about to see whether he could improve them by coating the metal cables with PTFE. It worked, but the product itself, Ride On bike cables, was something of a bust. In the meantime, however, Myers had moved on to another commitment—PTFE-coated wires for giant marionettes (don't ask).

While working on the marionette wires, Myers hit upon the idea that would bring Gore into a whole new, and more profitable, line of business. Guitar strings age because they oxidize; dirt and grime from the players' fingers accelerate the process. Coating them with PTFE might be just the ticket. Myers didn't play guitar, so he tapped the experience of a colleague, Chuck Hebestreit, who did, and Elixir—a guitar string that sounds better and lasts up to three times longer than an ordinary string—was the result. Gore had no idea how to break into the market, and its initial—traditional—efforts flopped, so it resorted to a giveaway, including sets of strings free with the purchase of guitar magazines. The product took off; today Gore controls a third of the market.

As for Gore-Tex itself, it, too, was discovered by accident, by Bill's son Bob. In 1969, Bob was trying to stretch PTFE into strands thin enough to be woven into a fabric. It wasn't going well. In frustration, Bob took a piece of freshly extruded PTFE and yanked on it. It stretched into a thin, flexible, strong form that, when made into sheets, was both breathable and waterproof. In this way, expanded-PTFE, or ePTFE, for which Bob Gore would be granted a patent in 1976, was invented. The rest is sportswear history.

As impressive as Gore's record is, there's no denying that founder Bill Gore had certain advantages. He started the company and was able to shape it from its earliest moments. He could hire people with the attitudes and values that fit the culture he was building—although he occasionally had to deal with managers' penchants for developing "formulas for failure." He could let them find the roles where they were willing to contribute most. He could impose a principle that no facility could exceed 150 associates, in order to keep communication fluid. More generally, he could use his privileged position as founder and CEO to prevent even one drop of command-and-control culture from poisoning his corporate well—the uniquely free environment he was building in his company.

But what if you don't have those advantages? Halfway across the world from Gore's Delaware headquarters, Jean-François Zobrist faced exactly that problem when he took over a brass foundry called FAVI in April 1983.

THE CHAIN OF COMMAND

FAVI is as old-economy as they come, manufacturing brass plumbing fixtures and gear forks for cars. It was family owned, and Zobrist was parachuted in as CEO. Actually, he was helicoptered in. FAVI's owner liked surprises. So after taking Zobrist on a one-hour helicopter flight to a destination unknown, the proprietor touched down at the plant and offered Zobrist the top job in a most unusual way. When they had landed, the owner gathered all the employees and informed them all—including Zobrist—that Zobrist was their new CEO. FAVI's owner then left as suddenly as he had arrived. For three weeks Zobrist heard nothing further from him, until one day his phone rang. The owner asked Zobrist, "They haven't wolfed you down, have they?"[5]

"No," Zobrist replied.

"Well, then you can stay," he said. After a short pause, he added: "Your charge: Make me money and don't go to jail."

Familiar with the owner's penchant for extreme language, Zobrist translated this charge as "You have all the freedom of action you want, within the limits of law." That suited Zobrist. But he soon realized that the rest of FAVI's employees were not so free. Zobrist got an early taste of this one day while walking past the supply closet. There he saw an employee, Alfred, waiting in front of the closed window.

"What are you waiting for?" Zobrist asked.[6]

"I came to exchange my gloves," Alfred replied. He hastened to add, "I have a slip from my boss and my old gloves."

And so Zobrist learned the policy: When a worker wore out his gloves, he would show them to the head of the workshop, who would give him a slip for exchange. He would then cross the workshop floor—chatting with others and perhaps visiting the bathroom, before ringing the supply closet's bell, waiting for the keeper, and giving him the slip and the old gloves. At that point, he could get his new gloves and go back to work. The process could easily take a good ten minutes—assuming the closet keeper was present and answered the bell promptly.

So Zobrist posed a question to the accounting department, which informed him that it cost FAVI the equivalent of one hundred dollars an hour to run the equipment on which Alfred worked. That worked out to more than fifteen dollars lost every time a pair of gloves needed to be exchanged—nearly twice what the gloves themselves cost. The *real* cost of the gloves to FAVI was so high that if they were freely distributed, the company would actually save money, even if some workers took home an extra pair for their gardening every now and then.

Of course, as in most companies, accounting had a line item for glove purchases but kept no track of the productivity lost to glove policing. In reality, FAVI was losing thousands of dollars by keeping the gloves under lock and key, Zobrist discovered, but on the official ledger, it would be recorded as a gain.

And the gloves were only the beginning. The more he looked around, the more of these bureaucratic false economies he discovered. Based on these early observations, Zobrist concluded that if FAVI remained set in its ways, it was headed for extinction—or to China. And, in fact, that is precisely what happened to much of the old-line manufacturing in Europe during the time that Zobrist ran FAVI. But Zobrist had other ideas.

And under his leadership, the company has thrived where others have failed.

He eliminated the time clock because employees "should work to make products, not hours."[7] At the same time, he eliminated overtime pay while raising salaries to the level of one's total pay over the previous year, for the same reason. Zobrist captured his leadership philosophy with a distinction. There are, he said, two kinds of companies: "*Comment*" in French, or "how" companies, and "*pourquoi*," or "why" companies. "How" companies spend their time telling workers *how* to do their jobs—where to place the machinery, when to come to work and when to leave, and so on. This has two consequences. The first is that you end up judging employees by everything except what counts, which is whether the job gets done and the customer is happy. The second is that it becomes difficult, if not impossible, to change any of the myriad rules about *how* to get things done. You want to move that cart to a different spot on the shop floor? You need clearance from your manager, who may have to ask *his* manager, and so on, creating a never-ending "chain of *comment*." The result, as Zobrist put it, is that it becomes impossible to get the work done without disobeying somebody in the chain of command.

A *pourquoi* company is different. It replaces all the myriad "hows" with a single question: Why are you doing what you're doing? The answer is always the same: to keep the customers happy. As long as what you do satisfies that commandment, Zobrist doesn't worry about how you do it. Freedom at FAVI meant replacing the chain of *comment* with a single *pourquoi*.

Getting there wasn't easy. Zobrist smiled when he recalled how his newly liberated employees still gazed wistfully as they passed the blank space on the wall where the time clock used to be—and where some of them used to hang out in advance of the shift-ending bell so that they could be the first to punch out and head home. But even more than the shop-floor workers, Zobrist had problems with the middle management. He tried winning them over, but they—conscious that with everyone set free on their own initiative, they'd have little left to do—wouldn't budge. Eventually, he dispensed with middle management altogether, moving supervisors to other roles more beneficial to the company while leaving their salaries intact. He eliminated the human resources department, too—because, he said, humans aren't resources, they're people.

In place of the supervisors, he organized the shop floor into what are essentially self-directing teams of two dozen or so. Those teams each serve a particular customer with a particular product, allowing them to become intimate with the needs of the clients they serve and to see directly whether they are happy—or not. And they approve candidates for the leader's role, whom they can also depose. Those leaders report to Zobrist—about as flat an organization as you could ask for.[8]

The results have been extraordinary. For twenty-five years, FAVI has been able to reduce prices by 3 percent a year on average and has never been late with a delivery, allowing it to remain competitive in an age of globalization. It remains a European leader in its sector—half of all cars built in Europe contain gearbox forks from FAVI, an unheard-of market share for an auto-parts supplier. It has bought out its last remaining competitor on the Continent, introduced breakthrough brass products, such as electric rotors, in totally new markets, and—unlike its now-extinct European competitors—FAVI actually *exports* parts to China. And FAVI came out of the economic downturn in 2009 it with a 70 percent market share in gearbox forks in Europe because a number of its international competitors have been wiped out by the bad times.

Many CEOs have great things to say about their companies' corporate cultures. Many also claim to believe that their people are their greatest assets. We suspect that somewhere there is a top-secret executive seminar for CEOs where they are trained to tell their employees that they shouldn't be afraid to bring problems to their bosses' attention, and that if they walk into a room with their fly down, they expect an employee to tell them right away.

But the fact is, most employees don't believe a word of it. Sometimes it's the little things that give the bosses away. The CEO will say she's open to new ideas. And then she'll direct employees to a special-purpose internal website—a high-tech "suggestion box"—where those ideas go to die, to be read by an assistant charged with sending a respectful reply and ignoring the recommendation, or wind up examined, filtered, and mostly rejected by some duly appointed "suggestion committee."

FAVI and the rest of the companies in this book really are different. They prove it—to their people most of all—in ways big and small. When Zobrist says that your only job is to keep the clients happy, he proves it by eliminating the measurement of everything else. The results, as seen in the foundry's performance numbers, are remarkable. But when viewed from "down below," through the eyes of those employees, the effects are astonishing.

THE JANITOR WHO IMPRESSED A CLIENT

It was 1985, two years after Zobrist became CEO. Christine, a night janitor at FAVI, was doing her job after everyone else had gone home when, at 8:30 p.m., the phone in the plant rang. Christine didn't know it, but the man at the other end of the phone was an auditor from Fiat, an important new customer for FAVI. He had just landed at the airport in Paris and was expecting someone from FAVI to pick him up and drive him up to Picardy, ninety minutes away, where he had an appointment at FAVI first thing in the morning to ensure that the plant was meeting Fiat's quality standards.

Christine, upon hearing that the man on the other end of the line was a visitor expecting a pickup at the airport, arranged a meeting point and hung up the phone. Zobrist picks up the story: "I had waited until 7 p.m. on the evening the auditor was due to arrive, thinking that he perhaps had some difficulty. And then I went home. Imagine my surprise when I saw him waiting in my office the next day at 8:30 a.m. He said, 'Something very strange happened to me yesterday.'" [9]

The Fiat auditor explained that, being in a hurry, he had not been able to call in advance (there were no cell phones back then). When he arrived at the airport and found no one from FAVI waiting for him, he called the company. To his surprise, a feminine voice answered. He explained that he was late, but that in principle the company had told him someone would pick him up. The woman who had answered the phone came, retrieved him from the airport, drove him to his hotel, and wished him good night.

"The funny thing," the auditor told Zobrist, "is that she was very kind, very polite, but she didn't seem to have the slightest idea who I was or what company I was from." Even funnier, though, was that Zobrist could not for the life of him figure out who the mystery chauffeur of this important visitor was.

After the meeting, the CEO called a few people and tracked down Christine. When she had heard the man's story, Christine had simply taken the keys of one of the company cars—keys that always hang near the entrance to the plant so that they are available to any employee who needs a car. She then went to the airport, brought the visitor to the hotel—and came back to finish the cleaning she had interrupted three hours earlier.

What's more, she had seen no need to tell anybody about her trip. She was an employee with a job of her own to do, who had nonetheless taken three hours out of her evening to drive to the airport and back. She took a company car on a two-hundred-mile round-trip journey without seeking anyone's approval simply because it seemed like the right thing to do. The company had offered this man a ride from the airport and there was no one else available to fulfill the obligation, so she did it herself, without hesitation and without seeking credit for what she had done.

This is the difference between a "how" company and a "why" company. Christine, a night janitor who had probably never taken a company car on company business in her life, saw a chance to do some good for the company, and she took it. As Zobrist put it, "Facing a company problem, she is not a 'janitor,' she is 'the company.'" Most companies hope in vain for that attitude to take root among their employees. In fact, on the off chance an employee at a "how" firm *had* gone to those lengths on the company's behalf, one of two things would likely have happened. In the worst case, Christine would have been sanctioned for unauthorized use of company property, not to mention leaving her assigned duties. But only slightly better is the alternative, in which the company, so surprised at the lengths to which this janitor went, makes a hero out of her. Zobrist did neither. "When you neither punish nor reward people's actions, those actions become normal, banal," Zobrist explained. "She didn't think she was doing something exceptional. Everyone here facing a problem and having a solution, just goes and does it. No need to tell, either before—for permission—nor after, for thanks." Then, with a satisfied smile, Zobrist added: "By the way, thanks to her initiative the auditor increased our quality rating by 10 percent!"

The time between Zobrist's encounter with Alfred outside the supply closet and Christine's impromptu nighttime drive was just two years. But in those two years, Zobrist had already achieved a remarkable turnaround in the habits of many of FAVI's employees. The subsequent years have seen innumerable acts of everyday heroism by FAVI's liberated employees. There was the time that an order could not be delivered because the truck needed to deliver the products did not arrive. The employees in question—together with Zobrist—hired a helicopter to get the order to the customer as promised. Or the worker on the factory floor who told us that when one of *his* customers had a problem with a product, he, together with a coworker, immediately left the factory and drove to Germany to address the issue—without prior authorization, *bien sûr*. When we asked him why, he shrugged. It seemed like the right—even normal—thing to do.

Most companies say they dream of people who can develop high-margin, innovative products in their spare time, or who look for creative ways to satisfy customer demands without thinking twice about it. But the truth is that these people are all around you right now—the technician who seems unconcerned with product quality, the sales rep who appears uninterested in clients' innovative suggestions, and, yes, the janitor who looks like he's never been interested in anything—who looks invisible, even. They just need to be set free from the bonds that hold them back. Our liberated companies have discovered the secrets to doing just that.

By freeing the initiative and gifts of every single employee on their payroll, they have succeeded where their competition has failed; they have taken on entrenched incumbents many times their size and have, in many cases, grown beyond their founders' wildest dreams. Some, like six-hundred-person-strong FAVI, are relatively small. Others, like the insurance giant USAA, with twenty-six thousand employees, are much larger. They exist in services and in the industrial sector. Some, like Harley-Davidson, are publicly traded and are dominated by unionized workforces. Surprisingly, Harley's main reason for going public in 1986, according to then-CEO Rich Teerlink, was to be able to launch a liberation campaign, which would otherwise have been blocked by the banks that controlled the company at that time: "I'd rather face shareholders than bankers, any day," Teerlink said.[10] In 1998, Sun Hydraulics, a world leader in hydraulic valves, also went public, many years after building its liberated culture, and a decade later it hadn't lost an ounce of its unique culture. And still others, like the Richards Group, the largest independent advertising agency in the United States, are still private—and will remain so forever.

Though very different, all of them had leaders who were unwavering in their commitment to the creation of a corporate culture that freed up the initiative of everyone on the payroll. Bill Gore and a series of leaders he helped nurture manifest that commitment by small daily acts—offering help and encouragement when associates' actions live up to the company's principles and asking, as Bill Gore did with Lewis, "Do you have a minute?" when their actions violate them. Some, such as Stan Richards of the Richards Group, have literally broken down barriers. Richards changed the physical geometry of his Dallas office so that nothing stood in the way of face-to-face human contact. Each of these responses reflects the unique challenges posed by their particular fields and their starting points. But whether they were built from the ground up to be different, like the Richards Group, Gore, and Sun Hydraulics, or were transformed after a long period of underperformance, like USAA, Harley, and FAVI, they all hold lessons on the power of freeing the potential that inheres in one's people.

Freeing that potential isn't easy. It requires a firm commitment to the idea that, taken together, your people know a great deal more about what your company is capable of than any single employee or—for that matter—CEO ever could. If you believe that, then it becomes easier to understand what Jean-François Zobrist meant when he said that his goal as CEO is "to do as little as possible." But to fully understand what is wrong with the "how" companies' approach to running a business and whether it's possible to change it, it helps to understand how we got here.

2

ARE YOU MANAGING FOR THE "THREE PERCENT"?

*Exceptional Companies Do Not Confuse
the Exception with the Rule*

WHAT JEAN-FRANÇOIS Zobrist calls "how" companies are also known as hierarchical, bureaucratic, or command-and-control companies. And, unfortunately, they are known all too well by too many of us. These terms describe, with slightly different emphases, the structures that are common to most large organizations—the (sometimes long) chain of command, procedure-driven decision making, or top-down control. But those structures, in turn, emerged in support of the real core of "how" companies: the assumption that the people on the frontlines need to be controlled and told how to do their own work. Underlying this core assumption are deep beliefs held by management about human nature. When management—often implicitly—believes that people don't want to work or to learn much, it will naturally assume that people have to be told and controlled. Given this assumption, it makes perfect sense to put in place hierarchies that give authority to the superiors to "tell" and control. And from there, it's only natural to routinize much of this telling and controlling through policies and procedures.

This "natural order of things" emerged—as we'll see in the next chapter—during the Industrial Revolution, when firms had to employ mostly illiterate workers with rural backgrounds. But it's important to acknowledge that this type of organization permitted many "how" companies to perform well, not only back then but throughout the past two centuries.

Indeed, in many ways the performance of "how" companies has been remarkable. According to the economic historian Angus Maddison, these traditional organizations helped propel newly industrialized nations to rates of economic growth that were unprecedented in human history. This growth, in turn, allowed a substantial portion of the people in these countries to live the materially comfortable lives that had previously been reserved to a tiny elite throughout the world.[1] And on a smaller scale, there's no question that these traditionally organized "how" companies have given the world many of the material advancements and innovative products that shape our lives every day.

To the early-twentieth-century German sociologist Max Weber, the success and dominance of the "bureaucratic organization" was perfectly logical. It was, he argued, the result of its "technical superiority over any other form of organization." He claimed that the demands of the "capitalist market economy" could be met only by a "strictly bureaucratic organization" that was capable of discharging its "official business . . . precisely, unambiguously, continuously, and with as much speed as possible." Other forms of organization would only slow down the fast-moving world—of 1922.[2] And to this day, some management scholars continue to think that companies have to be bureaucratic tyrannies to perform well. "Of course they do," one author wrote recently, "if we want speed, flexibility, and above all profit in a competitive world. Our ability to create wealth depends at least partly on managerial authority. Top-down power and its potential abuse are here to stay in corporate America. It is foolish to think otherwise."[3] But since Weber's day, a long line of management thinkers have come forth to dispute this view and argue against bureaucratization.[4]

Critics of capitalism are right that the unprecedented economic growth achieved by traditional companies has come at a price—a human price. In the early years of the Industrial Revolution, the working conditions in all but a few of these traditional "how" companies were akin to those currently found in the sweatshops of the world's poorest countries—with child labor as its inevitable consort. But even after basic workers' rights and working conditions were protected, the human price remained high. Frequent friction between labor and management, work stoppages, and even wildcat strikes and deadly violence are still around. Of course, militant unions and arrogant management may explain some of this conflict, but not all of it. Neither compliant unions—or no unions—nor less arrogant management can change the day-to-day experience of too many people who are constantly told how to do their jobs and compelled to comply.

There is a reason, in other words, that the television show *The Office* has been a hit on two continents, and *Dilbert* has become a cultural touchstone. At the same time, the idea of humanizing large corporations is not new. A whole host of management theorists and gurus have come forward over the years with this or that proposal to ease employees' senses of futility and alienation.[5] The continued existence of the cottage industry devoted to reforming companies is proof that much still remains to be done. But even so, these efforts have not been totally without effect. Highly efficient, yet "humanized," mainstream companies do exist.

Take Toyota. When you enter one of its plants, you are struck by the way everything there ticks like a Swiss watch. Identically dressed employees know exactly what procedure they must follow to accomplish their tasks in the most efficient way. These procedures may entail pedaling a tricycle to deliver specific parts at precise times to particular operators, or detail which bolt to use on a given type of wheel and even with which hand to drive it home—all operators are trained to be ambidextrous and have two pneumatic screwdrivers available at any moment. A procedure may even specify eye—yes, eye—movements, so that operators will not unnecessarily turn their heads hundreds of times per day and risk straining their necks. Everything is performed according to standard procedures in which employees are well trained and everything is measured and controlled.

Thousands of industrial companies have adopted a similar Japanese-born procedure-based approach, known as "lean manufacturing." Lean manufacturing reduces waste, inventory, space, human motion, the tools needed, and product development time. And many industrial, service, and distribution companies have adopted another Japanese approach called "Total Quality Management"—or TQM—which relies on the participation of all employees in the reduction of every process variation to common standards in order to guarantee complete customer satisfaction. Not all of them can boast, as Toyota does, that they don't need to check their final product before delivering it to the customer, so sure are they that their standardized procedures will guarantee quality. But many have very good results. Not much affected by turbulence, they steadily deliver high-quality products desired by customers at competitive prices, showing continuous growth and robust profits in all kinds of industries.

But there are no infallible procedures, and even the best process can't account for the unforeseeable. Although Toyota and other successful procedure-based bureaucracies may seem to run like a Swiss watch, they don't. Because of the inevitable problems in complex manufacturing, service, or distribution processes, they stop and break down quite often. At the best of these companies, many of these stoppages are not caused by problems but are initiated by the employees themselves or by the management.

On a Friday at noon in January 2001, just three flawless weeks after opening its first small-car plant in Europe, Toyota's management in Valenciennes, France, ordered the assembly line stopped. Facing the astonished operators, the managers explained that this break was voluntary, would last half an hour, and was called to allow operators to put in place their ideas to improve the existing procedures. At Toyota, as well as in many other successful bureaucracies, procedures are not designed to tell underskilled or undermotivated people how to perform their tasks and to control them as they carry them out. No, the procedures are designed to capture the *best known way* to accomplish routine tasks. So, unlike in so many companies, rare is the Toyota employee who complains about "this dumb procedure." If he does he can simply change it.

At Toyota, it is not the foremen, or group leaders, who determine whether operators follow the procedures. It's the operators themselves. If the results are not up to standards, most often the cause is the operator's action, which he self-corrects. But sometimes the operator is conforming to procedure and the cause is the procedure itself, which is no longer adequate and has to be improved or replaced by a better one. That's why lean-manufacturing procedures coexist with teams that enjoy substantial autonomy to reorganize their work, and standard-enforcing TQM coexists with continuous improvement and idea-management systems, which are the opposite of idea-killing suggestion boxes because they ensure that ideas are quickly and efficiently implemented. This encourages everyone to suggest useful improvements. This flip side—the procedure-challenging, reorganizing, and improving side—is as important as the standard procedures themselves, and perhaps even more so. Without it, employees won't commit themselves to the standard procedures handed down to them by managers or industrial engineers. In fact, at Toyota they don't even have a job title of industrial engineer. In order for employees to respect the procedures, they have to be involved in their design, control, and improvement. In short, the standards have to be *theirs*, not management's or the engineers'.[6]

That's the paradox most companies that rushed to copy lean manufacturing and TQM did not understand. So it's no wonder that according to one study, two-thirds of the TQM projects at American companies have not met expectations.[7] But there is no real paradox. They focused on the tools and ignored the deep assumption that Toyota's management holds about its workers. In a way, Toyota's workers—in spirit—resemble pre-Industrial Revolution artisans in charge of what they do.

For all that, in many ways Toyota is still a traditional bureaucracy, with the accompanying hierarchies, policies, and procedures. And yet Toyota has a dramatic—but often overlooked—advantage that distinguishes it from most other mainstream companies and has helped make it one of the best manufacturing companies in the world: Toyota believes in people's willingness to do a good job and to learn. As a result, the company organizes its managerial practices around the assumption that standard procedures convey the *best known* way to perform a task—but the people on the frontlines know better what works. So they are constantly encouraged to question and improve these procedures. Toyota's people, in other words, are given efficient ways to perform their assigned tasks, but are not told to stick to them if they discover a method that works better. And rather than employ the traditional tools of corporate control, Toyota provides its people with tools to monitor themselves. This allows them to see for themselves whether current procedures are still efficient or need to be improved. This is dramatically different from the experience of people in most mainstream companies. No wonder Toyota has never endured labor strife in the United States.

Indeed, despite numerous attempts to organize Toyota's plants, the unions have never attracted enough support. More dramatically, at its first U.S. plant—NUMMI (New United Motor Manfacturing, Inc.), built at a former General Motors truck plant in Fremont, California, Toyota did inherit the United Auto Workers, and with it a rather rough labor history to boot.[8] GM had closed the plant several years earlier and no wonder: One depressingly typical year had featured four thousand grievances, 20 percent absenteeism, and wildcat strikes. It was there that GM offered Toyota the chance to build its first American plant, which was to be jointly owned but run solely by Toyota. To the surprise of GM's management, the plant became the most productive auto-manufacturing facility in the United States within just a few years, inundating the market with high-quality, affordable Geo-model cars. But what's more, labor relations were exemplary at NUMMI under Toyota's control.

Kiyoshi (Nate) Furuta, who negotiated at NUMMI with UAW president Dick Shoemaker, described the gap Toyota wanted to close:

> Once they [the UAW] agree to a production standard they cannot change it. If management wants to change it, there is a struggle. That is a very rigid system. When we develop the original standard work, we want the team member involved. We then want the team member involved in improving the standard. We need multiskilled and not single-skilled workers. We say we do not need so many job classifications—too many . . .[9]

And Furuta succeeded spectacularly. Although sales were 30 percent below target the first year, NUMMI management kept the entire workforce—there were no layoffs, which would have been routine in the past. Instead, they developed a major training program, launched team members' workshops to improve standards, and provided extra vacation days. The trust NUMMI management had developed with the union allowed them to agree to the most liberal contract the UAW ever signed, including just two job classifications, the ability to move workers around based on capability rather than seniority, and even the right to use temporary workers.

Not surprisingly, GM's management started to fly in planeloads of executives to the plant to discover what magical management tools Toyota had employed to pacify the facility and make it so productive. And they did try to apply what they learned back in Detroit. But according to NUMMI's former CEO, they didn't get it, even after spending days at a time at the plant trying to uncover its secrets.[10] It wasn't the management tools that they couldn't comprehend; it was Toyota's assumption that people were willing to do a good job and to learn, if only they were allowed to. The "magic" could not be found in any particular manufacturing technique or procedure. It lay in the freedom of Toyota's people to continuously improve the procedures with which they began. GM copied the procedures but left out the freedom, and instead focused on trying to enforce strict adherence to these new procedures. Needless to say, GM's pilgrims to NUMMI never could figure out why Toyota's manufacturing techniques didn't work at their plants. They had borrowed the procedures but left the "magic" behind in California. In sum, although on the surface it looks like a traditional "how" company, Toyota is closer in spirit to the freedom-based companies.

Toyota's performance is impressive, but it is possible to go much, much further than it has done—as we shall see. Even so, its very existence is a standing rebuke to the executives of other automakers who argue that they are doing the best they can with the tools and the people they have.

The companies in this book compete in a wide array of industries, from manufacturing to services and technology. Each of them is proof that, whether you are in insurance, manufacturing, software, or some other field, you can set your people free and reap the rewards of their knowledge and initiative. If, like GM, you have the misfortune of competing against a world beater like Toyota, you may already feel the pressure to understand what makes them "great" while you are merely "good."

But if there is no Toyota or Gore or FAVI breathing down your neck—or leaving you in the dust—you may suppose that the old, supposedly proven ways of managing people and businesses are just fine. After all, there are plenty of profitable and even growing companies out there that no one—least of all their employees—would call "free." It's fair to ask whether, at the end of the day, there is anything wrong with that. To answer that question, we need to take a closer look at the performance of these traditional firms.

THE HIDDEN COSTS OF "HOW" PERFORMANCE

Great Britain's Royal Mail is the oldest and most famous post office in the world. In the early 2000s, on any given day, 10,000 of its 170,000 employees were absent without any valid reason. Desperate to reduce absenteeism, the post office offered raffle tickets to employees who bothered to show up for their jobs for six months without missing a day. The prizes included thirty-four $24,000 cars and sixty-eight $4,000 holiday vouchers.[11]

We can assume that this lured back at least some of the malingerers. But we're willing to wager that the managers of the missing ten thousand employees would have been just as happy if they'd stayed home. In offering enticements totally extraneous to their work—on top of, you know, paying them—the Royal Mail was engaged in an extreme version of treating the symptoms rather than the disease. It must have seemed far easier to the Royal Mail's top management to offer prizes than to examine why they had such a terrible absentee problem. Dave Ward, the local union official, offered them some free advice: "The company needs to get to the root of the problem, which is low morale, poor pay and conditions. That is the cause of sickness and absenteeism." Now, union officials always say that more pay will mean more-productive workers. That's their job. But by bringing in low morale—disengagement—Ward was on to something, even if it is a subject that management wants to talk about even less than low pay. Increasing pay is, at least in principle, something management can easily do if it wants to. But improving morale is a lot harder than signing a check—because it requires management to examine their role and the structures they put in place that contributed to the problem in the first place. Far better, then, to ignore the causes and attack the symptoms—in the case of the Royal Mail, bribing employees to do what they had already legally contracted to do.

The Royal Mail's "solution" was extreme, and this institution, in many ways, is incomparable to better-performing companies. Most good firms, especially private ones, are motivated by profit and never allow things to get quite that bad. Absenteeism cost the Royal Mail $500 to $700 million a year; few private firms can afford a deadweight loss like that—as even GM has recently discovered. But all around us, every day, most of our organizations, large and small, instead of addressing the disengagement problem, prefer to treat its "symptoms"—not through extravagant bribes but through the establishment of rules and procedures meant to catch the malingerers.

Gordon Forward, the former CEO of Chaparral Steel, calls this "managing for the 3 percent."[12] Many managers have a tendency to address a small problem—sometimes a problem confined to a single "nonconforming" employee, or a couple of them—by creating even more drastic rules for everyone. One CEO at a small company explained to us that because he caught one secretary dipping into the office supplies for her kids' back-to-school needs, he issued a regulation that no office supplies could be ordered during the summer. "In that way," he explained, "there will be nothing left on September first for her to take." Of course, by then there might not be any office supplies for anyone else either, but by golly, he showed that secretary, didn't he?

"Management for the 3 percent" is inevitable in "how" companies because simple controls are always outwitted by that 3 percent. Naturally, new, more drastic ones are introduced to catch them. In addition to the ordinary bureaucratic overhead incurred through the accumulation of these "corrective" policies, managing for the 3 percent imposes dramatic hidden costs on businesses by contributing to the disengagement of the other 97 percent.

But this kind of rule making, as silly as it looks from the outside, does have a number of advantages if you're a manager. There's no awkward confrontation with the pilfering employee, no embarrassed denials or outward resentment. Instead, the manager gets to fall back on the last refuge of bureaucrats everywhere: "That's the policy!" And so the regulations live on, far beyond whatever usefulness they once had, even years or decades after the single, awkward circumstance that they were designed to address has passed out of memory. All the while, these "useless" rules nevertheless have far-reaching consequences. They reliably contribute to the malaise of the 97 percent, who find themselves treated with suspicion and crushed by seemingly arbitrary company policies.

But more and more "how" companies go even further than simply casting a generalized control and suspicion over the 97 percent. Still unable to catch the 3 percent who usually find ways to outwit the bureaucratic police, these companies try to enroll the 97 percent in policing.

We happened to encounter two managers from one large American company who had been placed in precisely that situation. They had received a new company policy document on "how we conduct business." Every employee was expected to read, agree to, and sign the document, which included a commitment to call a hotline and blow the whistle on any malfeasance of which he became aware. One of the two objected to this—he didn't want to be a snitch. He threatened to refuse to sign the policy. His colleague suggested that, instead, he just sign it and not adhere to it, as others would do. The two men then proceeded to debate whether it was better to object to the policy openly or pretend to abide by it.

The point is not which course of action they chose in the end; that these two were even having this debate demonstrates that the objector, at least, had enough integrity to take the policy seriously. The 3 percent at whom the policy is aimed, by contrast, won't hesitate to sign and ignore the policy while the rest of the employees will feel alienated by the humiliating ritual of promising to act as informers on their colleagues.

You may think that disengagement problems like these are rare in "how" companies—that in the majority of traditional companies, a very small proportion of employees is disengaged. Otherwise, how can we explain the unprecedented growth that the developed world has experienced since the Industrial Revolution? This argument would be plausible if we didn't have some statistics on the matter. Gallup regularly conducts broad surveys on the engagement of American workers. Its results are always similar. In 2013, only 30 percent of employees at the average company were "engaged," while 52 percent were "not engaged," and 18 percent were "actively disengaged."[13] To picture active disengagement, imagine that in an eight-man rowboat, you and another leader in the two front seats are rowing energetically. The five in the middle periodically dip their oars in the water just enough to make a little splash. The last man, meanwhile, is rowing energetically—but in the opposite direction from the rest of the crew. And you wonder why, for all the splashing, your company seems stalled?

Our rowboat is a metaphor, but it highlights an important literal issue: Do traditional bureaucracies, with rules and procedures designed to substitute for lack of skill or motivation, make up for the weight penalty of all that control with better results? It's time for a deeper consideration of this question. Let's first take a look at the top line—the revenues—and then at the costs.

DO "HOW" COMPANIES SHOW GREAT ORGANIC GROWTH THROUGH INNOVATION?

As we discussed earlier in the chapter, there are many examples of traditional command-and-control bureaucracies that have had long spells of admirable revenue growth. Pharmaceutical giants Merck and Pfizer are two good examples. How much of that growth is organic and how much is driven by acquisitions is not always easy to sort out, given the rate at which these companies reshuffle divisions and business units. But in those firms where there has been real, organic growth, one feature is usually present—innovation. When it is mentioned, most traditional bureaucracies put two cards on the table—their substantial research and development budgets and their patents. Unfortunately these plays don't have numbers to back them up.

Many companies talk up a large R&D budget, which has the same relation to innovative product sales as the scouting budget of the New York Knicks—the NBA team with the largest payroll—has to its dismal performance between 2002 and 2009. In the United States, big pharmaceutical companies have the highest R&D budgets relative to sales of any industry. Between 1991 and 2001, total research spending rose to $30.3 billion from $9.7 billion, while at the same time the number of new drugs introduced each year dropped to twenty-four from thirty.[14] Money can't buy you love, and a big budget alone can't buy you the next Viagra. As a matter of fact, Pfizer's R&D budget couldn't even buy the *first* Viagra. The drug's benefit was discovered by pure accident when a number of patients in a heart-disease drug trial—all of them male—reported a strange, but not unpleasant, side effect. Thus a multibillion-dollar industry was born.

Then there are patent portfolios. Research shows that patents themselves have no effect on a company's revenue: Only 5 percent to 10 percent of patents have any market relevance, and only 1 percent of them actually bring in any profits.[15] Even though it might seem counterintuitive, what really matters when it comes to patents is the number of times they are cited by others. Having a portfolio of *frequently cited* patents does correlate with sales of innovative products.[16] Think of it this way: A patent is like a pass in basketball. By itself, it doesn't help your team win. But a patent that is valuable to others, as shown by the number of times people cite it, is like an assist—a pass that leads to a basket. Those do help your team win in a direct way. Only those company's patents that are cited by *other* firms' patent filings have some business value in their eyes, and vice versa; if a patent is never cited by other firms, it can be intriguing for science but of no value to business. But while the NBA carefully tracks players' assists, few companies measure the citation rate of their patent portfolios, preferring to trumpet the size of the portfolio itself. It's as if Stephen Curry, the NBA's best point guard in recent years, went around bragging about how many passes he made the night before. In the late 1990s, IBM boasted the world's largest patent portfolio. But when measured by citations, its relevance to profits was below that of start-ups acquired by Cisco or even of a smaller company, such as Micron Technology.[17]

R&D experts are very important, but organizing their activities into large, often isolated, bureaucracies, providing them with big budgets, and hoping it will lead to profitable innovations at competitive costs hasn't worked very well. Twenty years ago, Richard Florida and Martin Kenney, authors of *The Breakthrough Illusion: Corporate America's Failure to Move from Innovation to Mass Production*, asked why the Japanese seemed much better than American companies at turning scientific research into profitable and innovative new products. Their conclusion: "White-collar scientists" in the United States were "arrogant toward shop-floor workers." As a result, "most [American] corporate R&D labs retain [a] specialized, assembly-line model of organization," which leaves them deaf and blind to ideas that don't come from the "right" places.[18]

In sum, besides a costly—and bureaucratic—R&D program and a big patent portfolio, most traditional bureaucracies have little to show in terms of effective innovation. Even at companies such as Intel and the consulting firm Accenture, it takes real guts for an employee to push their ideas if they fall outside a small number of officially sanctioned R&D projects.

Jay Hedley was a junior consultant at Accenture who had a blockbuster idea with the potential to bring in tens of millions of dollars for his company and possibly even more far-reaching benefits for the U.S. economy.[19] He had designed—and would eventually patent—an electronic system for assessing tolls on cars traveling at highway speeds without installing transponders in the cars. And yet at nearly every step, he was blocked or turned down in his quest for support for the project. If it wasn't for his tenacity—he is a U.S. Air Force Reserve pilot who has served tours of duty in Afghanistan—his wit, and his good relations with many executive assistants, his idea would have never been tried. But when, through good fortune and the good offices of those vital assistants, he got it started, and when a top manager, by chance, learned about it over a beer in a bar, the idea was named the innovation of the year at Accenture. Hedley went on to become the company's innovation hero—and all the official obstacles he'd faced before being discovered were quietly forgotten or brushed aside.

Organized around structures that tell people how to do their work and control them while they do it, "how" companies are fundamentally hostile environments for the ideas proposed by their frontline people—the vast majority of the workforce. One of the first managers to whom Hedley submitted his idea told him dismissively, "You're supposed to chop wood. Later, you will tell us where the wood is."

As Gordon Forward—who has a doctorate from MIT and worked in research and development before leading Chaparral Steel—told us, "Good ideas die every day" in command-and-control companies.[20] Asked whether their current job "brings out their most creative ideas," only 17 percent of those "not engaged" and 3 percent of "actively disengaged" employees answered affirmatively.[21] Recall that together, these two groups of employees make up 70 percent of the American workforce.[22] It's no wonder that, despite plenty of talented people on their payrolls, many traditional bureaucracies have to rely on innovation "heroes" or on special "creativity" programs and platforms to ensure that ideas are heard and transformed into innovative products and services. When a company's structures broadcast to the vast majority of people that their ideas don't matter—that they are supposed "to chop wood"—it comes as no surprise that it will resort to extraordinary measures "to find where the wood is." Some companies don't even do that and are forced to buy innovation from small, creative companies—from which we get the all-too-common strategy of growth by acquisition.

Liberated companies such as Gore have long understood the limits of a closed and elitist approach to innovation. So instead of confining innovation to exclusive in-house units pursuing a limited number of R&D projects that have been sanctioned at the highest levels, they encourage innovation for everyone. This has led to a continuous flow of Skunk Works-type projects and low-cost experiments, some of which, such as Elixir guitar strings and Glide dental floss at Gore, have gone on to become leaders in their segments.

Like Elixir, Glide was launched with a guerrilla marketing campaign.

Gore associates knew that floss made from PTFE had great potential, but they knew nothing about selling dental floss, so they didn't try. They gave it away instead—to dentists. Patients loved it so much that they asked their dentists for some more for their family and friends. When Gore convinced some drugstores to carry it, they could barely keep it in stock. And, yes, we are talking about dental floss.

Few "how" companies have Gore's reputation for organic growth powered by outstanding capacity for innovation. Some, such as Hewlett-Packard, Sony, Samsung, and Procter & Gamble, have had long spells of innovation, but they aren't many. If there were more, we wouldn't hear 3M and Apple repeated every time that innovation and organic growth are discussed.

But if bureaucracy does not produce great innovation and organic growth, perhaps it's at least good at keeping costs under control. After all, cost containment is something most traditional "how" companies care deeply about. Repeated waves of rationalization—from "delayering" and downsizing to "reengineering" and outsourcing—have regularly trimmed the corporate body fat—sometimes leading, ironically, to lay-offs for the people who designed and supervised the myriad procedures and layers of control in the first place. The argument that traditional bureaucracies have a good record—appreciated on Wall Street—of keeping costs in check would be easy to accept but only on one condition: that we stick to the costs measured by accountants and stock analysts. But these costs are not the end of the story. There are other costs, swept under the proverbial rug. Welcome to the under-rug costs—or the underworld.

THE COSTS THAT YOUR ACCOUNTANT IS NOT TELLING YOU ABOUT

There is one kind of cost that all "how" companies have, one that never shows up on the books. It's the cost of all the things that didn't get done because of the stifling effects of Zobrist's "chain of *comment*," the chain of "how." These *unaccountable* costs—the forgone revenue, the missed business opportunities, the creeping inefficiencies—are the *real* toll that "how" structures take on a business.

The largest of these unseen costs stems from what we might call the low "execution capacity" of a top-down firm. Whether working on a mundane task or a major corporate initiative, employees who aren't engaged—and more so the *actively*disengaged ones—don't go the extra mile that is so often critical to meeting deadlines or avoiding penalties or the loss of a customer.

"Culture eats strategy for breakfast": so said a banner hanging in Ford Motor Company's "war room," from which the company was plotting an ambitious change strategy to save it from near-bankruptcy in 2005. And for those who didn't get it, the plan's czar, Mark Fields, would add: "You can have the best plan in the world, and if the culture isn't going to let it happen, it's going to die on the vine."[23] Sure, companies can find ways to coerce, or "bribe," their employees—and many do—into executing what they are ordered to, but corporate history is full of stories of how badly such workers accomplished their appointed tasks.

By their nature, the precise cost of lost opportunities brought on by disengaged employees is hard to measure directly. But there are some indirect ways of quantifying the losses. One cross-industry study showed that 73 percent of customers who abandoned a company attributed it to an indifferent or bad attitude from customer service employees.[24] And a 2001 study of mergers and acquisitions showed that, contrary to the expected boost in revenues and reduction in costs that most mergers aim for, "83 percent of all mergers and acquisitions failed to produce any benefit for the shareholders, and over half actually destroyed value" due to a weak execution culture.[25] Finally, a large study across the world's ten leading economies compared companies with *high* employee engagement with *low*-employee-engagement firms. It found that over a three-year period, the first group *increased* their operating margin by 3.74 percent and net profit by 2.06 percent on average. The second group *decreased* these bottom-line indicators by 2.01 percent and 1.38 percent respectively.[26] These differences are substantial. But they still don't give a full accounting of how exactly all these disengaged employees translate into lost revenues and increased costs. And, indeed, all this may look like a necessary cost of doing business, something akin to the accidents that accompany ownership of a fleet of corporate cars. This interpretation would be easier to accept if we knew nothing about the costs of one major disengagement-related phenomenon. To discuss it will require a detour to the world of psychiatry.

HOW MUCH YOUR STRESSED-OUT PEOPLE COST YOU—BEYOND THEIR SALARIES

Anecdotally, workplace stress has become a redundancy. But is this ubiquity backed by numbers? Unfortunately, yes.[27] According to the National Institute for Occupational Safety and Health, stress affects 40 percent of American workers and is the number one cause of worker disabilities. We will describe in a moment what the sources of workplace stress are, but one thing is clear: Most of the symptoms are highly unpleasant, and we react to them with the instinctive impulses of flight or fight.

We try to flee the people and events causing us stress. Hence the absenteeism and lost productivity. We fight back by striking out (albeit usually not physically) at what we believe to be the causes of our stress—whether those are coworkers, managers, or even the entire company. That is what Gallup's *actively* disengaged 18 percent are doing. This, once again, leads to lost productivity—$328 billion per year for the U.S. economy according to Gallup's estimate.[28] And when we are unable to literally flee *or* fight, we may "escape" by smoking, drinking to excess, and even abusing drugs. All this flight and fight is accompanied by the evolution-conditioned responses of elevated adrenaline secretion, blood pressure, and heart rate. But while all three are momentarily good if you happen to be fleeing a saber-toothed tiger, they damage our health when they become chronic companions. Unsurprisingly, workplace stress is recognized today as a key contributor in 75 percent to 90 percent of all primary-care doctor visits. And the longer these stress responses persist, the more damage is done to our health.

In the short term, workplace stress leads to mundane "modern" diseases, such as stomach disorders, back pain, musculoskeletal problems, headaches, skin problems, loss of sleep and energy, and emotional distress. Because stress weakens our immune system, it even makes us susceptible to catching colds. And if stress persists over a long period, the problems get less mundane and often lead to heart disease.

The conclusion is grim: Stress-related problems are not only expensive—even if mostly unseen today by traditional accounting systems—but also lead to avoidable human suffering. So what causes workplace stress?

Decades' worth of psychological research provide us with a good understanding of the mechanism. It all begins with events and situations in the workplace that we perceive as either physically or psychologically threatening. Psychologists call them "stressors." Among the stressors are such things as increases in the amount of work or of work demands, or uncertainty about what needs to be done. In addition, stressors include all the constraints and interpersonal conflicts that prevent employees from doing a good job. The reader will, we fear, recognize many of them below:

- Someone interfered with your work.
- Others took resources or information you need for your job.
- Someone took credit for your work.
- Someone made a negative comment about your intelligence or competence.
- You were a target of rumors or gossip.
- You were excluded from a work-related or social meeting.
- You were given the silent treatment.
- Others failed to warn you about impending dangers.
- You were denied a raise or promotion without being given a valid reason.[29]

All the big and small stressors trigger negative emotional reactions in us, most often anger or anxiety. From there, the road to the stress symptoms—called strains—is all downhill. Sometimes, it is true, stress leads to constructive actions aiming to cope with the stressor, such as getting the needed information from somebody else. But most often, the reaction is destructive—flight or fight. And right alongside come those "bad" companions—increased adrenaline, blood pressure, and heart rate—and the health damage that follows. In some corporate cultures, it is normal to belittle those who react badly to what some consider "ordinary" work-related stress. But this is a serious mistake: Research has shown that stressful work incidents are even more damaging to our well-being and health than major stressors in our personal lives.

So what's the bottom line on stress for the economy? Studies estimate the cost for U.S. businesses could be $150 billion to $300 billion a year or more from stress-induced absenteeism, lost productivity, and health expenditures. And the hidden cost to your business? According to the U.S. Bureau of Labor Statistics, the annual cost of stress is $10,000 per employee.

Fortunately there is one extremely important potential ameliorating factor for workplace stress: the perceived control an employee has over her work. First, when a person believes she has a high degree of control over an event or situation, she judges it as less stressful, even as simply "challenging." Military fighter pilots don't typically report seeing their flight missions, even in combat, as stressful—because they have complete control over their jobs. In fact, training flights may be more stressful than real missions because trainees do not yet feel totally in control of their aircraft or tasks. Second, this perception of control minimizes a person's "emotional reaction" to the stressor. For example, facing a sudden upsurge in clients, a salesperson who feels in control of her work will be confident that she'll find a way to adjust and keep the workload manageable. Hence, her emotions, instead of becoming negative, may even bring a positive feeling of challenge. Finally, high perceived control may lead to the search for constructive responses to the stressful event.

Why is this important? Because for a person with a low level of control over her work, the reaction is quite different. Not believing that she can change the way she does her work, she'll engage in the destructive actions of fleeing or fighting to reduce her emotional distress and feel better. Three psychologists, Hans Bosma, Stephen Stansfeld, and Michael Marmot, spent five years studying the stress levels of more than ten thousand British civil servants. And what they found was that men who *feel* that they have little control over their jobs—whether that is true or not—are 50 percent more likely to develop heart disease than those who feel as if they are in control of their jobs. For women, it's even worse—the risk is 100 percent higher, presumably because they often work in positions that have even less job control than men. Bosma and associates suggest that such control and freedom of choice may be a universal human need. But they say more: "Especially in bureaucratic organizations, this need may not be satisfied for those at the bottom of the hierarchy. . . . In such strongly regulated organizations, control may be especially relevant, because persons with control can possibly more easily escape from bureaucratic procedures and more often may know the manifest and latent rules concerning the distribution of rewards."[30]

This is one way to escape stress and its consequences—available, of course, to a minority, the higher-ups. But there is an alternative, much more dramatic, way the hidden stress-related costs can be reduced—for everybody. Give people real—and perceived—control over their work, stop telling them how to do their jobs, and the stress will go down. Absenteeism will go down; hidden costs will go down. Engagement will go up. All this, of course, is hard to accomplish in "how" companies. As we will see later, the perception of self-control is the key to the free corporate environment that liberating leaders aim to build. There is more good news: Freeing a company's people to act not only eliminates many hidden costs—it also dramatically boosts its innovation and organic growth, as we've seen with Gore.

In sum, although traditional "how" companies are omnipresent and some report organic growth and good margins, their performance could be better—it could be *great*. What prevents this is the so-called 97 percent, many of whom are disengaged, stressed out, ill, or even absent. The damage doesn't show up in the official accounting but is hidden in the costs of turnover, workplace stress, and conflict-ridden labor relations. It also shows up in lack of innovation and slumping organic growth. In the NBA, a team on which players are late or absent from training or even games, who snipe at one another and quarrel with the management, can't dream of going far in the play-offs or even reaching them. In the NBA, teams can't hide their problems. Their performance consequences are out in the open for everyone to see at the next night's game. In the corporate world, however, many companies succeed in keeping their failures out of the public eye for a long time. But even official accounting can't hide these costs forever—think of the legacy airlines or the Detroit three.

The issue we turn to next is when these "how" companies emerged, and why—despite all the underperformance and hidden costs—most firms still organize themselves this way. Then, we'll discover whether it's possible for a "how" company to change its culture.

3

FROM ARTISANS
TO AUTOMATONS

The Origins of the "How" Culture

THE BUREAUCRATIC, "HOW" approach to running a business seems natural today. But it hasn't always been that way. It emerged during the Industrial Revolution to address two specific problems: The first was the perceived need to regiment the work habits of artisans accustomed to keeping their own hours and working at their own pace. The second was the need to obtain uniform, reliable output from the mostly illiterate rural workers who were hired into factories in large numbers in the late eighteenth and early nineteenth centuries.

Nowhere was this transformation seen more clearly than in the city of Birmingham in the British Midlands. In 1776, in "the city of a thousand trades"—as Birmingham was known at the time—war in some far-off colonies was the last thing on most people's minds. Birmingham was busy with a different kind of revolution—an economic one. Since 1769, when James Brindley's canal from Wolverhampton to Birmingham was opened, the place had been booming.[1] Overnight, the canal had transformed Birmingham into an inland port, and the incomparable superiority of water transportation over roads had had a dramatic impact. The price of coal had dropped by half. Flour and bread were much cheaper, thanks to the demise of local grain monopolies. Raw materials from other areas were abundant.

Since 1774, local entrepreneur Matthew Boulton's factory had been running full speed manufacturing a unique and revolutionary product— James Watt's steam engine. Watt patented his steam engine in 1769, but after an earlier venture failed, Boulton made the steam engine a commercial success. The first generation of steam engines had been employed primarily in pumping water out of coal mines. But Watt's new engine was four times more efficient than the older designs, making them practical as a power source for the cotton, corn, and malt mills that had previously relied on water wheels—or horse power.[2] Coal-fired steam engines had been around since about 1704, but they had caught on only slowly. Now Watt's patented improvement on the old Thomas Newcomen engine was transforming entire industries.

One industry in particular had benefited from both the new source of power and the canal—pottery manufacturing. Among pottery manufacturers, Josiah Wedgwood stood out both for the way he capitalized on industrialization and for the economic and social contributions he made. Despite having no formal scientific education, he made many improvements in pottery production that allowed the mass production of high-quality green- and jasperware. A great proponent of the canals—some people even called him their "king"[3]—he foresaw how they would reduce his costs for clay while providing a far more reliable delivery system for his finished products; he could avoid the frequent breakages that came with using the rough, rutted roads. And Wedgwood's vision was validated in full: The freight costs to and from potteries would fall by more than 80 percent after the completion of the Birmingham-Wolverhampton canal. Wedgwood even discussed with Boulton the idea of building previously unheard-of steam-powered canal boats.

That kind of visionary thinking was encouraged in the Birmingham Lunar Society, of which Wedgwood and Boulton were both members. Founded in the 1750s, the society met regularly—on full-moon nights so members could find their way home—to discuss new, often dramatic, projects and ideas related to their industrial and economic times. Perhaps it was after one of these discussions that Wedgwood decided to go beyond improving production methods and delve into improving the organization of work itself.

Whatever the genesis of the idea, Wedgwood implemented a system of organization that, in 1776, Adam Smith dubbed the "division of labor." Every worker was trained "in detail" so that he was able to respond to the "growing demand for new shapes, glazes, and clays." Commodity articles were produced by workers different from those producing ornamental items. Such was the extent of this scheme that in Wedgwood's Etruria plant—built in 1769 on a canal he had helped to plot and on a site he named in honor of ancient Greek and Etruscan pottery traditions—all but five of the 278 workers had a specific assigned task.[4] However, "with a view to the strictest economy of labor" Wedgwood didn't stop there in his search for efficiency. He placed foremen over the line workers to ensure that productivity was maximized. The flexible working hours that had been inherited from the artisanal tradition were banished and replaced by strict, regular schedules. Wedgwood was so unrelenting in his pursuit of efficiency that he even installed a time clock. His business prospered. Patrons and orders flowed in, including from Queen Charlotte, who appointed Wedgwood a queen's potter, and Russian empress Catherine II, who ordered 952 pieces in 1774. His wealth also increased dramatically—at his death Wedgwood left behind a fortune of £500,000 (the equivalent of perhaps $100 million today), a thriving business, and a daughter, Susannah, the mother of Charles Darwin.

British industrialists greatly benefited from the Industrial Revolution that unfolded in the Midlands, Scotland, and elsewhere around the British Isles. Economic growth during this period was such that even though half of British industry's export market was lost due to American independence, growing internal demand quickly took up the slack. However, not all participants in this revolution benefited equally from it.

In 1795, a local clergyman memorialized Wedgwood's death with the following poem:

> *Such the true patriot, from whose gates each day*
> *A crowd of healthy workmen make their way*
> *Whose rare productions foreign courts demand*
> *And while they praise, enrich his native land.*
> *View his Etruria, late a barren waste*
> *Now high in culture, and adorn'd with taste.*[5]

Wedgwood's workers did indeed have decent housing at the idyllic site, but that was not the case for most of the working class. This new way of working created conditions for workers that were very different from those experienced by craftsmen a quarter of a century earlier. We will not dwell on the despicable use of child labor and the scandalous poverty that most lived in; today's Third World poor remind us how it was back then in much of the West. But even in the rare places that didn't employ children and that offered decent salaries, housing, and even health care, how did the laborers feel inside these mills and plants?

According to the University of Chicago philosopher Richard Weaver, the author of *Ideas Have Consequences*, they felt shocked.[6] For the first time in their lives—and in the lives of their parents and grandparents—they could not see or control the final result of their work. Before, the peasant farmer would determine what was necessary to bring the harvest in and saw everything through to the end. The craftsmen—who acquired their skill through years of apprenticeship—decided how they needed to work to make the perfect product. Now, the simple act of following one task through to fruition was neither possible nor expected of the factory worker. It was not possible because he was in charge of a small, specific part of the production process. It was not asked of him because there were procedures—and foremen to enforce them—that determined how to do things. All the worker was asked to do was to arrive at a specified time, to execute specified operations for a specified number of—long—hours, and to leave. Indeed, in overcoming an independence that stretched back centuries, Wedgwood's main difficulty was not training people to do this repetitive work, but to stop them from wandering around, taking unauthorized "holidays," and even drinking on the job.[7] The new division of labor, as Adam Smith described in *The Wealth of Nations*, had great advantages for productivity. But it came at a cost that was harder to measure than was output in terms of pins per hour. Lack of control over one's work, over its purpose—and, as a consequence, lack of involvement in the final results—led to a loss of respect for the procedures. This, in turn, led to more supervision from the foremen, the introduction of time clocks, and other control mechanisms. The result: even greater disengagement of the worker from his work's final purpose. The seeds of the "how" bureaucracy had thus been planted.

Over the past two centuries, that apparatus of control has been tuned, adjusted, and updated. But its basic form and underlying assumptions would be recognizable to Wedgwood even today, were he around. In fact, there are factories in England right now in which Wedgwood would feel very much at home. Northampton, England, is fifty-four miles southeast of Birmingham and looks for all the world like so many nineteenth-century industrial towns in England. More important for Northampton, though, is that it is only sixty-seven miles from London, the main market for its traditional industry—shoe making. The town's association with shoe making predates industrialization: Its artisans made boots for Oliver Cromwell's army in the seventeenth century. The local folklore has it that Cromwell thanked Northampton's cordwainers for all those boots by never paying his bill. By the early nineteenth century, more than a third of the men in Northampton worked as cordwainers, the traditional term for those who make shoes—unlike a cobbler, who *repairs* shoes. At that time, cordwainers still worked as artisans in their own homes, even if they worked for a larger concern. But beginning in the 1850s shoe making became industrialized. By the late nineteenth century, it employed half of the town's working men.⁸ The Northampton tradition of shoe making continues today; if you're fortunate enough to own a pair of "Made in England" men's shoes, with its model and size still written by hand on the inside, there is a strong chance they were made in Northampton.

In 2008, we visited one of these factories, housed in a nineteenth-century redbrick building that seemed little changed since it was built. For that matter, the way the company and its work were organized also seemed untouched by the passage of time. There are still more than a hundred steps involved in making a pair of shoes, each step done by hand with the help of rudimentary machines. All this handwork helps ensure the shoes' outstanding quality. But in following this whole manufacturing process step-by-step, from cutting the leather with special knives (a process called "clicking"), to the hand waxing and polishing of the finished shoes, the similarity to nineteenth-century industrial organization was unmistakable. Every person worked at a specific position, repeating the same small operation the whole day, day in, day out, on a timeworn, noisy, and rather dirty shop floor. These highly skilled workers, making some of the best men's shoes in the world, looked surly and depressed. Many were overweight. The only enthusiastic workers we saw were a new hire, who had asked to master several positions so that he could regularly switch to escape the monotony, and a couple of shoe waxers who—although uncomfortable—were sitting next to each other and chatting a lot.

The CEO of this plant, who runs it for an international corporation that now owns the shoe company, explained that he was fully aware of the situation. He knew of sophisticated machinery to replace the aging equipment in the plant—equipment for which spare parts are impossible to obtain because no one makes them anymore. He was aware of all the modern shoe-making methods, of lean manufacturing and continuous improvement, used, for example, seventy miles north, at Toyota's Burnaston facility. But he couldn't change anything, he said, as he was

blocked by the opposition of local managers and fear of disrupting production even for one day.

Whether these reasons were true or just excuses for his indecisiveness,
the fact is that *exactly* the same type of organization that Wedgwood and
other British industrialists implemented during the Industrial Revolution
is perpetuated today in some companies that have the best products in
their industries. It's true, of course, that modern machinery, computers,
and a cleaner environment have made their way into many other companies. But in most of them the key principle of Wedgwood's organization
has survived: People are told *how* to do their work and are controlled and
judged on how well they succeed in following orders. Companies have
structures to support telling and controlling, and the inevitable "management for the 3 percent" to catch the few who evade the controls. Thus,
they create the employee disengagement and incur the hidden costs and
under-performance that stand in the way of greatness.

But if the "how" culture is subpar for both business and people, and
business is cutthroat, with competitors seeking advantages wherever they
can find them, how could such a flawed form of organization persist for
so long? Why hasn't the pursuit of best practices, such as Toyota's, long
ago eliminated the excesses introduced by men like Josiah Wedgwood?

WHY THE "HOW" CULTURE PERSISTS

A famous experiment involving five macaques and a banana—which admittedly may or may not have happened—offers a clue to help unravel
this mystery.

The macaques are in a cage. A banana hangs from the ceiling, with
stairs leading up to the tasty treat. But the moment the first macaque
starts to climb toward the banana, the researcher sprays him—and all the
other macaques—with cold water. The macaques quickly get the message: Reaching for the banana—or even letting anyone else do so—is a
bad idea. Once they've learned their lesson, the researcher replaces one
of the five macaques with a newcomer. Sure enough, the rookie spots the
banana and heads for the stairs—whereupon he is tackled by the other

four, who remember and fear the cold-water treatment. Frightened, he stops his initiative.

Once the newcomer has learned his lesson, another veteran of the water hose is removed and replaced by another neophyte. The process repeats itself, with the first replacement joining in the beating of the new guy without even knowing why he must be prevented from climbing those stairs. One by one, the original macaques are replaced, but each newcomer learns the rule—don't go for the banana—even though none of them, by the end of the experiment, have ever experienced the cold shower that the first group got. If the macaques could speak, they'd probably just report that going for the banana is against company policy or that "this is how things are done around here"—call it monkey bureaucracy.

This experiment has been described, with minor variations, in hundreds of books and thousands of presentations. It may well be apocryphal. But whether those five macaques ever got the hose or not, audiences love the story because they instantly recognize the phenomenon it describes.

Indeed, this story suggests a plausible explanation for our earlier quandary—how a senseless and even damaging order of things can persist for so long. Giving a "cold shower" to those who attempt to take the initiative can have long-lasting effects. People learn from the harsh treatment that results from their "banana mistake" and then act strenuously to prevent others from trying to do the same. This is the way that corporate cultures are born, sustained—and eventually quash all attempts at change.

For many people, negative reinforcement from managers is a daily experience that broadly discourages taking the initiative, which, ironically, is precisely the sort of thing that a well-run company should hope its entrepreneurial people would do in order to retain a client, solve a problem, or deal with an internal conflict. Just one person in a group receiving negative reinforcement when attempting to show initiative may be sufficient to convince others that they themselves shouldn't show initiative. Moreover, it also encourages them to prevent others from making the same "mistake." Here is a sample of familiar yet "mistaken" initiatives an employee may prevent others from attempting:

- agreeing to reimburse an unhappy client during his first call about an issue (one is supposed to seek authorization first);
- immediately leaving to visit a client who has a problem with the company's product (same "mistake");
- spending a small amount of one's own money to solve a problem and asking for reimbursement later (same "mistake");
- holding one-on-one discussions with all concerned colleagues about a major problem (one is supposed to write a memo and call a meeting);
- directly reaching out to a concerned colleague (instead of going through "channels");
- publicly giving bad news to everyone (bad news is for management only); or
- communicating lavishly but only orally (one is supposed to keep written track of everything).

Depressingly enough, the odds are that you recognize at least some of these transgressions from your own experience and could even add to the list yourself. For the cold-showered employee, getting authorizations, keeping written track of internal discussions, following the policies—*how* the job is done—has become more important than *why* the job needs to be done or what you are trying to achieve. What's more, a freedom-discouraging environment does not even have to be installed by the top guy—one employee in a small group is all it takes to turn the people around him into a bunch of "banana-fearing monkeys."

For this reason, the odds of bureaucratization increase the longer a business—even a small one—has been around. A company that starts out with a strongly entrepreneurial culture will inevitably hit a rough patch, at which point someone will decide that it's time to bring in some "real managers" to get the situation "under control." Because control is their mandate and because their experience—which qualifies them as "real managers"—has not prepared them to deal with a liberated company or its uppity people, freedom is usually the first thing to go. "What this company needs is some discipline!"—read: procedures and policies. And the larger a company grows and the longer it's been around, the greater the danger of being infected by the "how" bureaucracy virus.

Recall the experience of Les Lewis upon his return to Gore in chapter 1. After several years away, he became a carrier of the bureaucracy virus, and it was only the strength of the culture that Bill Gore had instilled in the company that rejected his virus and prevented him from infecting everyone around him.

Perhaps it was also easier for W. L. Gore & Associates to reject attempts to institutionalize telling and controlling because the firm had been built around freedom from the very beginning. Most companies, by contrast, don't see anything wrong with telling and controlling, and even when their business becomes so inefficient and the human price rises too high to be hidden, they don't question their "how" organization—they just try to "reengineer" it. Indeed, it's tough for an existing "how" company to change, but it can be done. In the following chapters we will discuss several examples—FAVI included—but we acknowledge that each has particular circumstances. Their industries, sizes, histories, or locations may be very different from companies you may be familiar with. But there is one fundamental phenomenon that illuminates the question of whether an existing hierarchical, domination-, and control-based social culture can ever change, and if it can, then how. To explore it, we'll have to make an unusual detour to the world of primates—this time, real ones.

OUR PEACEFUL BRETHREN

At first, studying primates may seem like a strange way to learn how to run a business. But if primates can change their social habits, ingrained in them over millions of years, it's possible that humans, too, can learn how to change their work habits, developed over just a few generations.[9]

Common chimpanzees, unfortunately, don't provide much encouragement. Not only do they live in extremely hierarchical societies, but they are also violent, murdering and even eating one another from time to time. Primatologists do not have evidence of common chimpanzees changing their cruel and despotic ways. But there is another variety of chimpanzee, pygmy chimps called bonobos. And, boy, are they different from their robust brothers and sisters. Their males are not very muscular; they share food; and if there is domination, it's not by males but by females. Bonobos resolve social tensions in a pretty unusual way, too—with sex. In fact, in captivity bonobos have sex with everyone—related or not, with any number of individuals, and in a variety of ways that seem to defy Newton's gravitational laws. Want to say hello, or need to resolve a conflict, reduce stress, or celebrate a good meal in good company? Have sex. This is not a nature film you'd like your kids to watch on the Discovery Channel—it goes far beyond back-scratching.

Unfortunately, it's also not the way most of us would like to see our businesses run—office romances can quickly go bananas. Besides, bonobo society is still hierarchical, which causes many problems, for which the bonobos have just one, X-rated, solution. In the wild—the dense, remote Congolese rain forests—the sex, in all its charming diversity, was accompanied by violence. Males pull, slap, hit, and bite other males to increase the aggressors' opportunities for sex. Females do the same to their "sisters" to increase access to certain males and, joined by other females *and* males, also regularly head gang attacks on males who tried to force sex. So, though bonobos may show that both love and war are ways of life among our primate brethren, pygmy chimps are out, too. Censored!

So much for chimps. Luckily, researchers have also studied Anubis baboon societies living in the East African savanna. At the beginning there was not much to hope for, as far as we're concerned. Males frequently fight to gain rank in the despotic hierarchy and regularly hit innocent bystanders, too. Females' ranks are hereditary, so they don't fight. Unlike males, which transfer between troops at puberty, females stay where they are born, and the high rate of "affiliative" behavior—such as grooming—between females is perhaps the one gentle aspect of their otherwise tough lives. Males rarely affiliate with females, and never with one another. The whole troop spends time foraging for food in the open savanna.

So how is this relevant to the question of changing existing hierarchical cultures? Witness the surprising transformation the researchers stumbled upon while following one specific Anubis troop that scientists named "Forest Troop."

In the early 1980s, this troop started spending the night in some trees about half a mile from a tourist lodge with a large, tempting garbage dump. Another Anubis troop, dubbed "Garbage Dump Troop" by the researchers, had already taken control of it and were sleeping in the overlooking trees. In the early mornings, the most aggressive, asocial Forest Troop males—those particularly uninterested in the early morning male-female grooming ritual—would challenge the Garbage Dump males and raid their place. The food never ran out in the dump, but one day in 1983, Garbage Dump Troop's luck did run out when some of the baboons ate tuberculosis-infected meat. Tuberculosis is extremely fatal to baboons; by 1986 the entire Garbage Dump Troop was dead. What's more, Forest Troop's most aggressive baboons—nearly half of all the males in the troop—also died. And here's where the story gets *really* interesting.

Two things changed right away in Forest Troop. First, the surviving male baboons found themselves with two females apiece. Moreover, the males who remained were the least aggressive ones, which meant there was less aggression from dominating males over lower ranking ones, more tolerance to occasional reversals of hierarchy, less hitting of innocent, female bystanders, and finally, more inter-sexual grooming. There were even several cases of male-to-male grooming—unheard of among other Anubis in the wild. Hence, males and females alike had it better in the new, accidentally improved Forest Troop. But more changes followed.

The biggest beneficiaries of the new Forest Troop ways were

newcomers. As mentioned before, male baboons transfer to other troops when they reach puberty. And when they enter a new troop, they are "nobodies"—low-ranking targets of the dominant males and ignored by the local females. But the new Forest Troop was different. In ordinary troops, a newcomer had to wait an average of sixty days before the first female presented herself sexually to him and two weeks more before she started grooming him—yes, in that order. In the new Forest Troop, newcomers typically waited only eighteen days to enjoy sex and a mere two additional days to be groomed. In sum, newcomers were quickly inundated by female attention. But even more amazing is that this friendly way of life continued long after the original batch of "sensitive" males had gone. By the early 1990s, none of the original males remained in the new Forest Troop, but their legacy continued, as it has to this day. The old hierarchical society had irrevocably changed into an egalitarian one. And it all happened because the oppressive top males were taken out of the picture, allowing the remaining baboons to shape a more egalitarian culture.

This shift from dominating and aggressive to egalitarian and relaxed is not unique in primate research. Another study showed that violent rhesus macaques, once removed for five months from their despotic hierarchical societies to live with the egalitarian stump-tailed macaques, came back and maintained a totally changed, relaxed, and nonviolent behavior once reintroduced to their fellow rhesus macaques.[10] Here, too, it was the absence of oppression by a dominating few that led to a lasting transformation of their behavior.

MONKEY DO, HUMAN DO

If a monkey can durably change his behavior when taken out of an oppressive system, we reckon people can do it at least as well. But moreover, the primate experiments illuminate the *causal mechanism* behind this change.

In the case of the Forest Troop baboons, the disappearance of the most aggressive members relaxed the others—primarily females, in the Forest Troop—who were more willing to reach out to the newcomers. The latter, though "programmed" to be treated badly, were pleasantly surprised. They relaxed, too, and became low-aggression males themselves, thus perpetuating the new culture. A similar mechanism was behind the transformation of the rhesus macaques.

The fundamental lesson for hierarchical "how" companies is simple: Change has to start from the top. The leaders must radically relax their ways so that the "subordinate" members—now treated as equals—become relaxed too. And interestingly, once they are treated as equals, primates relax exactly the same way that humans do. Researchers traced how the change in the Forest Troop's social habits influenced members' stress and health. And their findings were strikingly familiar.

Anubis baboons are typically known as a highly stressed species. Indeed, the chronic psychosocial stress of subordination and aggression leads to the continuous secretion of adrenals, accompanied by high blood pressure and elevated heart rate—the "bad three" pattern we see in humans—leading to such health problems as adult diabetes and impaired growth, slowed tissue repair, and infertility. But in the new Forest Troop, with its relaxed ways, subordinate males didn't show any increased level of adrenals, nor its poor health consequences. The same good health consequences are observed when stress decreases in humans—one more reason to consider carefully the lesson that primate studies provide.

The good news is that people are not monkeys. It took an outside intervention to change the behavior of the baboons and the macaques—in one case, disease, in the other, manipulation by researchers. But people can decide to change on their own. We don't recommend poisoning middle management, but a liberating leader must, nevertheless, free her people from the oppressive culture of the "how" company. Once she does, she'll notice that the behavior of the rest of the "troop" starts to change, too—from complacent to free and proactive.

4

FREEDOM IS NOT ANARCHY

A Liberated Company Must Have a Shared Vision

I'm gone for eight months. . . . If you feel that it's critical to contact me, that I get involved in your problem, what I want you to do is to lie down. When that feeling goes away, I want you to get up, solve the problem, and then send me an e-mail with the solution.

—BOB DAVIDS[1]

WE ARE IN the Bahamas—at least, Bob Davids is.[2] Davids is the owner of Sea Smoke Cellars, a young 350-acre vineyard in the gorgeous Santa Ynez Valley of central California. But he spends eleven months of the year elsewhere, whether that's in Reno, Nevada; Bali; or fishing in the Bahamas. His goal is nothing less than to produce "the best Pinot Noir humanly possible" from his vineyard. He says he scoured the world to find just the right spot for it, and having found it, he stays away from it as much as he can.

His quest to build a world-class winery began in earnest in December 1997, when Davids, founder and CEO of Radica Games—then the world's third most profitable toy maker—announced to the board that he wished to resign so that he could make wine. The reactions were, well, mixed.

The first to react was Robert Townsend, whom Davids had considered a mentor since they first met in 1981 and whom he convinced to join the board after Radica went public in 1994.

"You cannot leave the company. You *are* the company," Townsend told him.

"But your book," Davids retorted, referring to Townsend's best-selling *Up the Organization*, "says that the board's job is to replace the CEO every five years and I have been here seven years already."

"Not if the CEO is doing a good job," Townsend shot back.

"Well, that last part is not in your book," Davids sniffed.

Then, board chairman Jon Bengtson offered his own, Townsend-like, reaction.

"Do you know the best way to make a small fortune?" he asked Davids. Davids shrugged. "Invest a *big* one in a winery," Bengston offered. Davids let that one go. He wasn't getting into the wine business to lose money, however. One of his credos is, "If you have 1 percent hobby in your business, it becomes 100 percent hobby."

Despite this lukewarm reaction, Bob Davids, after doing his best to pass the reins at Radica, retired, bought the land, started the winery, and, in 2001, put his first bottles on the market.

Two years later, on this summer day in the Bahamas in 2003, Davids got a call from the winery's general manager, Victor Gallegos.

"I've got to talk to you," Gallegos said. "We're having a problem with the 2003 fruit."

"Okay," Davids replied laconically.

"Well, we've got to do a drop," Victor announced, referring to the technique of prematurely cutting a portion of the grapes from each vine so the remaining fruit, having been endangered by suboptimal weather, is given a better chance to reach full maturity.

"Well, you're the viticulturist, why are you calling *me?*" Davids asked.

"Well, it's a problem," Gallegos answered.

"I'm not a viticulturist. I can't help you," Davids repeated.

"Well, we're going to have to drop a lot of growth," Gallegos warned.

"Okay, what's going on?" Davids demanded.

"Well, we're having all these issues." Gallegos flailed. Davids began to understand the real problem.

"How much fruit do you have to drop?" Davids asked.

"A lot."

"'A lot' doesn't answer my question," Davids retorted.

"About 1.8 million dollars' retail," Gallegos finally admitted, presenting Davids—as he explained to us later—"with the opportunity to make this decision" for Victor.

But Davids didn't take it. Instead, he said, "I'm going to give you your charge again. Your charge is to grow the very best grapes humanly possible from that site."

"But it's 1.8 million dollars," Gallegos replied, clearly in agony over the magnitude of the decision.

"I'm going to repeat your charge," Davids said. "It's your charge to grow the very best grapes humanly possible from that site. I'm not a viticulturist. I don't know how to do that. Your charge is to grow the very best grapes humanly possible."

"But it's 1.8 million dollars!" Gallegos implored.

"I'm not going to take your monkey. I think this phone call is over."

Gallegos cut the grapes.

And no, the monkey Davids referred to wasn't some exotic pet or anthropological experiment. Davids believed that Gallegos was trying to take the proverbial monkey off his own back and put it on Davids' by giving him responsibility for the big grape drop. Davids refused to take it.

What did Bob Davids gain in sacrificing his power to tell Victor Gallegos what to do? Worry-free time to enjoy fishing in the Bahamas? No, Davids sacrificed it because it's good business. "If Victor didn't do that, then he didn't complete his charge to grow the very best wine," Davids said. "He couldn't sleep, he was uncomfortable with the 1.8-million-dollar decision, but if he never gains experience with such decisions, how is he ever going to make them?" Davids clearly explained his business philosophy and vision to Victor and every other employee he hired right while interviewing them: "I don't have the skill to make wine," he would tell them. "I'm going to give you all the tools and the ability to make the best product humanly possible you could make . . . all you need so you do not have an excuse to come back to me and say, 'I could have done it better if only you had allowed me to [fill in the blank].'"

Perhaps, you think, Sea Smoke is a unique company—a winery—with unique problems. Most existing companies are not like that. It would be easier to agree with this if Davids hadn't also done what he's doing at Sea Smoke at the eight-thousand-person Radica Games and several other companies he has headed—build a freedom-based environment.

Sea Smoke is a small and relatively young company, and its story illustrates the first two key steps to building such an environment. First, telling people how to do their job is fundamental in "how" companies, but a freedom-based business is founded on *not* telling your people what to do—even if they want you to. This has to start at the top—with the owner, chairman, or CEO.

However, you can't just say, "Do whatever you want," or even, "Do whatever you think is best"—that way lies anarchy. Without appropriate guidance, you'll have everyone doing what they believe is best for the company, even if those actions conflict with the company's vision or with the actions of the people around them. Or, worse than that, people will act in their own self-interest, not the business's.

Freedom in the workplace is neither *hierarchy* nor *anarchy*.

The phrase "ordered liberty," from political philosophy, comes close to capturing the best way to think about it, even though freedom in the workplace is not political freedom. It is a highly disciplined—actually, self-disciplined—form of organization. And its main disciplining element is the company's shared vision of world-class performance—the second key step of building a freedom-based company. What Bob Davids conveyed to his people—from the moment he interviewed them for the job—was that Sea Smoke's vision is to produce world-class Pinot Noir. It is to achieve *that* vision that he has set them free to take the best actions they can.

Did these newly hired people believe that they were really free to take actions they deemed the best? We have all heard leaders of "how" companies promise freedom of initiative and autonomy of action, only to be asked to submit for approval the first idea we aired. But Davids was not building a "how" company.

Sea Smoke's chief winemaker, Kris Curran, was dubious at the beginning, too. "I chuckled and said 'Yeah, Bob, we've heard that a million times before. And then the owner puts twenty thousand dollars more into landscaping and doesn't allow me to buy an extra two-hundred-dollar wine hose that I need.'"[3] Even after she accepted the job, Curran remained skeptical until the day Davids asked her to get the project off the ground and told her to start with all the equipment she needed for an absolutely perfect winery. So Curran took him at his word and drew up "a just outrageous list of things." When she was ready, Davids came in and went through the list item by item, discussing "every last clamp, pump, and barrel."

It took six hours. But in the end Davids said to her, "OK, so when do you start buying all this stuff?"

Curran, still skeptical, answered, "You're not going to knock anything off?" just to hear Davids repeat his freedom philosophy again.

"No, I believe your arguments that this is going to make better wine, and therefore I'm going to give you everything you need so you do not have an excuse to come back to me and say, 'I could have done it better if only you had allowed me to . . .'" Did *this* convince Curran that Davids's business philosophy and vision for Sea Smoke was not just blowing smoke?

"I was blown away," Curran said, "because I had been in the industry for eight years at the time, and I had never seen anybody that I had worked for and anybody that I knew that really stood behind what they said." At that moment, Curran realized that Davids would follow through with what he said in her job interview and that she would be able to take the actions she thought were best for the winery. Davids put this freedom-building block down for her—or so he thought.

But as much as people bristle at being told how to do their jobs, it can still be hard to jump right in and accept one's own freedom and the responsibility that comes with it. Victor Gallegos accepted his freedom in certain situations, but he stumbled when a large sum of money was involved. Curran, on the other hand, wasn't shy with her initial list of equipment for making a world-class wine; as she admits, she was testing Davids, trying to call his bluff by making a list she was sure he would balk at. But whatever psychological obstacles people may face in embracing their own freedom, this is still the easy part—freedom can be scary, but it's nice to have. Getting people to emotionally own the company's vision is much harder. As a matter of fact, Kris Curran found herself on the wrong side of the line between anarchy and freedom early on.

Several years into producing Pinot Noir, Davids—who says his main role in the business is brand building—came up with the idea of making a great white Chardonnay on an area of the vineyard's soil that was ill-suited for Pinot Noir. He explained to Curran and her assistant Katie Kennison—today marketing and direct sales manager—that the plan was to use the Chardonnay to *promote* the Sea Smoke Pinot Noir in the marketplace and the media. In other words, he planned to give the white wine away. He even had a name for the wine—Gratis. Curran and Kennison, still getting used to Davids's ways—and perhaps thinking that this small Chardonnay production was marginal and not a part of the great Pinot Noir vision—didn't argue much, though as winemakers they profoundly disagreed with the idea that you should ever give away your wine.

Months passed and on one of his occasional visits, Davids entered the winery and saw Kennison rolling out a row of used barrels. "Katie, where are those barrels going?" he asked, surprised.

"We're doing the Chardonnay," Kennison answered.

"I thought we were using one hundred percent new barrels," Davids asked.

"No, we're putting it in used ones this year," Kennison explained. Davids asked Curran, the chief winemaker, to step outside.

"Kris, I thought we'd always been using new oak?" he asks.

"No," Curran explained. "I'm not going to use new oak on a giveaway wine. If it was my pocket, I'd even use stainless," Curran replied, referring to a cheaper way of aging wine: stainless steel tanks.

"Did I ever ask you to save me money?" Davids asked.

"No," Curran admitted.

"What barrels will make the best quality Chardonnay? You choose," Davids said.

Curran went back to the cellar and told Kennison, "We're going to use one hundred percent new oak."

This didn't make the assistant winemaker very happy. "Oh, dang it," Kennison said. "I already washed all these barrels."

You may object here that Davids didn't really stop telling Curran how to do her job. He simply chose to tell her indirectly, making his wishes known without giving an order in so many words, as so many bosses are wont to do. "Do what you like," such a boss might say. "But if I were you, I'd do this . . . ," leaving the listener in little doubt about what was necessary. This brings us again to the issue of freedom and anarchy.

Freedom begins by not telling people "how" to do their jobs. According to Davids's principles, Curran was free to decide how to make the Chardonnay. At no point did Davids tell her directly or indirectly how to produce it. Nor did he insist on vetting her decisions on it. It is true that his persistent questioning of the decision to use old oak might well have been interpreted, in a traditional company, as a tacit order to change course. But that was not Davids's intention. He freely admits that he doesn't know how to make Sea Smoke's wine—that is why he hires a winemaker. What he did want to ascertain, however, was whether the decision to save on the barrels was being made for the right reasons—for reasons, in other words, consistent with Sea Smoke's vision.

Freedom and trust can't be given out piecemeal. If they are, people will immediately see the strings attached and reject the offer as a sham. But this does not mean that the owner—or any colleague, for that matter—has to turn a blind eye when he notes by chance that some action is *not* in the best interests of the company's vision. That is the road to anarchy, not to freedom.

In fact, sharing and communicating the company's vision is a key role for a liberating leader and the second building block of freedom. This is especially true when faced with evidence, as Davids was, of a failure to fully understand and own the vision. If the leader doesn't fulfill this role, some people will likely fall back on what *they* believe is best based on their experience—of highly controlled "how" environments. And one experience that we all have is that saving a buck is always a good thing, especially in a downturn. There is nothing wrong, of course, with avoiding needless expenses in any company. A liberated company in particular will be attuned to the perils of hidden costs and false economies, instead of fixating on photocopying and travel expenses. And the best action to take should *not* simply depend on particular experiences or current conditions but on one single thing—pursuing the company's vision. Cost-saving actions should definitely be considered best if the company's vision is low-cost market leadership, as it is for Southwest Airlines. But they won't necessarily be as important at W. L. Gore & Associates, whose vision has always been—in good or bad times—market leadership through outstanding products and fair customer relations.

Gore's Les Lewis was disturbed a few years back when he discovered that on-time delivery performance was slipping.[4] He made some inquiries and learned that some newer people, those with experience at companies with a different vision, had decided that 80 percent performance was acceptable if getting to 100 percent would mean going over budget. Lewis did not view on-time delivery as an economic decision at Gore. It was one of its core principles and an element of its corporate vision—fairness to the customer. The numbers revealed a vision-sharing problem, which Lewis then set about correcting by reminding the associates in question how fairness fit into Gore's vision: "The success of our enterprise in making money and having fun rests on our ability to invent, sell, and service products our customers value." *Always* delivering on time is part of the value that Gore provides to its customers. Lewis, of course, had learned the same lesson himself years earlier when Bill Gore sat him down for his impromptu lecture on the "Formula for Failure"—when all he wanted to do was save a buck.

Freedom inside a company isn't anarchy when it is bounded by what Davids calls his people's "charge," or by Zobrist's "why" question. Both amount to the same thing—the company's strategic vision, which employees bring to fruition through their best actions. A liberating leader's first two tasks are to build a corporate environment in which all the people are free to make decisions, while ensuring that they understand, own, and aim toward that vision. This second task—as we saw with the Chardonnay—is a tougher one for the liberating leader.

OWNING THE COMPANY'S WORLD-CLASS VISION

Getting people to emotionally own a corporate vision is a long—indeed, never-ending—task for a liberating leader. Fortunately, in freedom-based companies the vision is *always* world-class—a dream which facilitates its acceptance. As Zobrist put it, people desire and own dreams more easily than mundane goals—no one jumps out of bed enthused by the goal of increasing market share by 2 percent. The task starts with the first encounter with a prospective employee.

First, Davids—like other liberating leaders—makes sure that every applicant knows the corporate vision before she is hired. That way, if she doesn't agree with it she can opt out right away. Sometimes, in her zeal to land the job, a person will agree with everything, vision and all, without really thinking it through. Vertex is a Berwyn, Pennsylvania-based nine-hundred-employee-strong company whose vision is global market leadership in advanced tax software and related services. To make sure that all his new hires think this vision through, Jeff Westphal, the company's co-owner and CEO, tells them on their first day, "Welcome to Vertex. You are free to leave." And it works.

"One of my most wonderful days at work was saying good-bye to one of our best employees," recounted Westphal.[5] "I gave a speech years ago when we were working on our vision for the first time, and there was a woman who had been a long-time employee, a wonderful woman and a fine employee. After we talked about this and she engaged in the vision process, she came to me and said, 'Jeff, I have to go. I want to carve birds, it's my hobby, but that's what I love to do. I like working here, but I love that more and I want to try to make a business out of that.' And I said, 'Kathleen, God bless you.' I gave her a big hug, had a little lunch for her, and off she went. Because I knew I was serving her true needs, not our self-interest to trap her here against her will." Kathleen exercised her freedom to leave to pursue her own vision, which had become more important to her than that of Vertex.

Tony Hsieh, the CEO of Las Vegas-based Zappos.com, takes it even further than Jeff does—he continues to hammer home a similar message even after people start work, or at least paid training.[6] Zappos sells shoes online, but is, like USAA, essentially a customer-service business with a big call center, and has been growing fast. Still a young company, its revenue was more than $ 1 billion in 2008, up from zero ten years earlier. And so it hires a lot of people to work in its call centers and distribution hub. Hsieh, the company's founder, guards its vision and internal culture zealously and carefully screens new hires for compatibility with both. But even so, he recognizes, as he says, "Zappos is not for everybody," and some people will realize that, too, as they go through the training pro-cess. So, after putting them through four weeks of paid training, Hsieh makes them an unusual offer: Quit now, and not only will we not hold it against you, but we'll pay you to leave. Until mid-2008, this quitting bonus was $1,000, but Hsieh doubled it to $2,000 because, he told us, *too few* people were accepting it. He wants to make sure his employees are there because they share Zappos's vision, and so he is willing to pay the would-be timeservers to hit the road. Getting people to own the com-pany's vision emotionally can demand not only real effort but also real money.

But communicating and sharing the company's vision doesn't end on day one or during training—that would be too easy. Most people, espe-cially if they've gotten the macaques' proverbial "cold shower" at previ-ous jobs, have trouble accepting that a vision is more than something to be put on the walls, pasted into the annual report, and otherwise forgot-ten. So getting them to share it and emotionally own it takes time and vision-reinforcing effort. Let's take another look at the Chardonnay.

Curran, the winemaker, agreed with Davids's vision of making a great Pinot Noir—she was even thrilled by it. But until Curran was asked by Davids to draw up the winery equipment list, making great wine re-mained *Davids's* vision—*not* hers. Davids had set her free to draw up a wish list of equipment to make his strategic vision a reality. And she used all her experience as a winemaker to compile her "outrageous" set of demands. But only when Davids approved her list in full did she begin to believe in his vision and make it her own—at least as far as the Pinot Noir was concerned. But in the case of the free Chardonnay, she didn't connect it to the world-class Pinot Noir vision. Seeing the goal as sim-ply making a great-but-free wine, she made the decision—reasonably, in light of her understanding of the goal—of saving the company money on what was, after all, a promotional product. Davids stumbled on it by chance. As the vision keeper, he then took the time to explain to Curran that saving money on the Chardonnay would conflict with the vision of

Sea Smoke as a maker of world-class wines. But he did so in a manner that still relied on her to draw her own conclusions and make her own decision. Case closed.

Ownership of the company's vision—dream—and the freedom to act on one's own initiative to pursue it are not, as they may at first appear, two separate, distinguishable things. Many companies communicate their visions and try to make people "buy in." But the results are usually disappointing. People start emotionally owning the company's vision only when they are free to make *their own* decisions in pursuing it. Being free to do A or B forces them to think of the criteria for choosing between the two—to ponder the company's vision. In "how" companies, on the other hand, where people are told to do C and then D, there is no need to ponder the vision. In fact, pondering it becomes a big distraction from following orders. People who are free to act come to know why they did A rather than B, and this "why" becomes their own. The vision stops being an abstraction for them, something touted by management for a while and then forgotten. They start to own it emotionally. That's why, as Davids says, he wants people to shake off the feeling that he can make their decisions. This is not to say that it is easy for people to start using a corporate vision to guide their choices. Groomed in "how" companies, many employees are prone to interpret "what is best" from their own perspectives, based on their particular jobs, skills, or experiences. It falls on the liberating leader to patiently overcome these individual perspectives without telling people how to do their jobs.

Instead, the liberating leader must continuously provide employees with information relevant to the strategic vision along with the means necessary for them to do their jobs. When needed, the leader may check that someone facing a big choice understands the likely consequences of that decision. At first, this checking-up may have to be done often, so that the liberating leader can verify both that he has provided the necessary information and means to those employees, and that they have used it all in their decision making. Davids spent those six hours with Curran reviewing her equipment list not because he was looking for ways to cut costs, but to ensure that she had made her choices with the right "why" in mind—"to make the best wine humanly possible."

Once a liberating leader is convinced that his people have all that they need and are making decisions that best fulfill the vision, he leaves them to act on their own. And even when they ask him to tell them "how" to act, he refuses to take their monkeys off their backs.

At other times, a leader may run into a questionable decision face-to-face, as Bob Davids did when he encountered the used barrels into which Kennison and Curran were getting ready to pour the Chardonnay. Needless to say, people can make questionable decisions that run *contrary* to the company's vision. This is no cause for despair, but it is a signal that a leader has more work to do to make those employees own the vision. A leader can't *force* people to emotionally own the company's vision; he can only seek to create the conditions—freedom of action—in which they are *convinced* of it themselves. As Zobrist explained, trying to impose the vision leaves a leader in the position of a locomotive engine that has lost its cars because the cars don't feel like going the locomotive's way.

A liberating leader's ongoing role is to communicate relentlessly and "lavishly,"[7] constantly feeding people new information about the corporate vision. That vision, though, is never static. Markets, technology and the business environment continuously evolve, and more so in our VUCA (Volatile, Uncertain, Complex and Ambiguous) world. Companies that don't question and renew their corporate visions are bound to encounter rude shocks—especially during tough times. Even a shift in a corporate vision, however, can't simply be imposed from on high. Here, too, people must have the freedom to question it and may or may not take ownership of it. Resistance should be met with even more lavish provision of information—*telling* them how to do their jobs *at this stage* is even more destructive than at the outset, because people will feel betrayed by the denial of a freedom that they have by now come to expect and enjoy. That said, if the opposition is strong enough and resists your best efforts to communicate and explain the change in vision, there may be good reasons. If you come to believe that your employees are right and that the change isn't feasible, you need to be prepared to change course or return to the former one. One of the great advantages of a liberated company is that it doesn't wait until customers, volatility, or a downturn have called a vision into question—by the time that happens, it's usually too late. Free employees are free not only to act, but to question those big strategic turns—and to do so while there is still time to change course.

Bob Davids seeks this kind of consultation when he goes out to the vineyard between brand building and bonefishing—which, he said, he does simultaneously. "I go out on the Atlantic Ocean and go fishing for days and days and days. And I go out there with my rod in my hand, throw in, and just think. What I'm thinking about is, 'What are we doing for long-term brand recognition?' So I'm able to think about things three or four years ahead while Victor is down [at the vineyard] clubbing the daily dragons." Davids then offers his new ideas, "from a free thinker who has time to think," to Gallegos and the team. He spends enough time to give them all the information he can on how these ideas comport with his evolving vision for making and selling a world-class Pinot Noir. Sometimes he gets his new ideas across internally right away; sometimes his in-house experts need more time or more information to evaluate his bonefishing branding brainstorms. Even then, some ideas—such as giving away the entire production of Chardonnay every year—are so contrary to a winemaker's instincts that Curran and Kennison resisted, no matter how clear the rationale was to Davids. This resistance to link it to the company's world-class vision, in turn, precipitated their attempt to save money with the used barrels, which made Davids realize that he hadn't fully explained the thinking behind Gratis.

Sacrificing the power to tell workers "how" and sharing your world-class vision—your dream—with them are not easy to do. But they are also just the beginning—it takes more than that to truly transform and liberate a company, as Davids can attest not just from his time at the small Sea Smoke Cellars, but from his previous life at big companies.

We visited Smoke Sea Cellars in its first decade and, so far, it has succeeded both in cultivating its freedom culture and in fulfilling its world-class wine vision. But then Davids also succeeded in growing his previous start-up, Radica Games, into the third most successful toy company in the United States, after Mattel and Hasbro.[8] Not only did he continue not to tell his Radica employees—all eight thousand of them by the time he handed over the reins—what actions to take during all that growth, even after the company went public, he also did it with a workforce that lived under an oppressive political autocracy—94 percent of Radica's employees resided and worked in mainland China. None of them had ever seen a liberated leader before in their lives. Later we'll explore some of the methods Davids used to instill this culture in a company that was growing like mad and whose employees had even less experience with freedom—at work or elsewhere—than most in the West enjoy.

A leader's particular tactics for changing people's habits and assumptions depends on whether employees' resistance or skepticism comes from work experience at other firms, cultural factors, or just plain personality. Different types of businesses likewise require different methods. Bill Gore's approach to his engineers was different from Zobrist's with his machinists or Davids's with his wine experts. But one thing is always true: This change has to start with the leader himself. It's crucial for a would-be liberator to completely refrain from telling because everybody watches to see whether he will "walk the talk," as it were. Liberating leaders must live the values they want to instill in their businesses. What drove this group of leaders to start doing so is the subject of the next chapter.

5

WHY THEY DID IT

Two Triggers of the Liberation Campaign

I N THE PREVIOUS chapter we described a leader's first tasks in launching a liberation campaign. However, before we discuss the next steps these leaders took to liberate their companies, we want to focus on *why* they did it.

This issue is easily overlooked, but it is worthy of examination. It is exciting to follow a story of achievement, such as becoming a great sports champion or even losing sixty pounds. But unless one understands what triggered people to engage in their lengthy efforts and stay the course, reading about what they accomplished will be of little help for anyone wishing to replicate the feat. Seeking world-class performance and possessing freedom values are both necessary conditions required in order to liberate one's company, but it was two specific types of experiences—*exasperation* and *admiration*—that triggered our leaders to launch their liberation campaign.

World-class performance means nothing less than market dominance and financial results that are the envy of one's competitors. Aspiring to this level of performance is a necessary condition for building a liberated company. This aspiration provides a vision an inspirational vision that people can emotionally embrace. True, most leaders, once they are in charge of a company's destiny, worry about its performance. However, there is an important gap between worrying about performance and the desire to become world-class. Take an example from the world of sports.

Some NBA coaches, even if they would never admit it, coach to have a good team—and franchises that are merely "good" still make a lot of money for their owners. For example, Lenny Wilkens, who has more wins—and more losses—than any other coach in the NBA, "is known for his quiet, sensible, and optimistic coaching style."[1] But "his career was marked by consistent records rather than by championship cups." Other coaches, such as Phil Jackson, the Los Angeles Lakers coach who has won eleven NBA titles, want to build championship teams, to make basketball history—and they leave if the owners or the team don't share this goal. Jackson did exactly that in 2004, when he walked away from his job with the Lakers. When he was ready to return to coaching, several teams, including the New York Knicks, tried to hire him. But Jackson returned to the Lakers in 2005—not out of sentimentalism, but because he believed that they were a team that could win the NBA championship, even though they weren't playing very well at the time. In 2008, he nearly succeeded, going all the way to the finals, and in 2009, he won his tenth title—the most in NBA history.

Many good corporate leaders are like Lenny Wilkens. This is no insult—Wilkens won one championship, in 1979, with the Seattle SuperSonics. They compile solid records of achievement and do fine by their stockholders. This, however, is not the same thing as world-class performance.

The desire to build a world-class company is only one of the two necessary conditions required to launch a liberation campaign. The other is what we call "freedom values." Sure, a world-class-seeking leader could just as well apply other approaches and see if those worked. Robert

McDermott, who as CEO liberated the insurer USAA, tried different tactics at the Air Force Academy, when he led that organization. And Jim Collins's book *Good to Great* describes several now-famous cases of leaders taking their organizations from good to world-class. None used a radically free approach. But our liberating leaders didn't try to achieve world-class performance by trying to restructure a "how" company. Though aware that "how" companies can be made world-class, their freedom values made them lose faith in this type of culture. They believed that a radically different—freedom-based—environment was needed. What they lacked was a particular experience to trigger their break with the "how" culture and drive them to start the liberation campaign. Our research revealed two such triggering experiences: One was exasperation with the consequences of trying to manage the "how"; the other was admiration for other liberated companies.

KITCHEN-TABLE LESSONS IN LEADERSHIP

Jeff Westphal always believed in the importance of freedom but couldn't envision how to apply his values to his business, even after becoming, in the early 1990s, a senior executive of a small tax software company owned by his father. An eager reader, he familiarized himself with many approaches that questioned the "how" environment, including Stephen Covey's *Seven Habits of Highly Effective People*. But he didn't apply any of them to his company until, in 1993, a key software-development project turned into a fiasco. While preparing to use his executive power to tell the team that they had "to redouble [their] efforts, step back, reorganize, and . . . go right back at it,"[2] Westphal suddenly found a solution to a different, more personal, problem—with his wife.

At the time, he couldn't understand why his wife never seemed to want to go on an impromtu camping trip with him, just the two of them. He took it personally. He was so exasperated that he even questioned her sanity to himself. But one night, sitting in the kitchen with her, he remembered something Covey had written, and he tried it. He attempted to set aside all judgment and just imagine himself in her place, to just listen to her. "And then," Westphal told us, "this huge epiphany hit me: She cares more about the children's safety than our romance." Her reluctance had nothing to do with him or their marriage and everything to do with her concern for their children. But Jeff had been too wrapped up in his own interests and desires to see it.

"I realized I had never gotten it," Westphal continued. "And it, literally, just totally changed my world. Because I thought I understood everybody, and I realized in that instant that I never really understood anybody. I understood what I wanted to understand about them, rather than who they really were and what their needs were. And my second thought was, 'Oh my God, how many times have I been wrong before?'"

This is not the way a typical CEO begins a conversation with visitors who have come to learn about his leadership. But just as we began to worry that he'd mistaken us for itinerant marriage counselors, he tied it all together. "The application to business was this: 'Whoa! I'm walking around thinking I get it. But I don't get it. And other people are walking around thinking they get it, but *they* don't get it.'" With each person, or each department, in a company operating from its own self-interest, conflicts are inevitable and unsolvable, so it *seems* natural to install someone above them—a boss—who can referee disputes between these competing interests, calling it coordination. But the boss is trapped within *his* own frame of reference, unable to listen and used to telling, giving rise to gamesmanship and the interoffice intrigue that we all know all too well. "Once you know that basically everybody is walking around not really understanding the people that they are relating to, you know that you *have* to do something about that," Westphal said. "You can't *not* do something about it; you have to. Because now you can imagine the superior business performance you could achieve by having people who actually understand each other," and who can, by working together, achieve things that none of those involved could have accomplished while trapped in their own narrow perspectives.

"The very first 'program' that we implemented," Westphal continued, "was for me to change *my* behavior. I started *listening*, I started actually involving people in my decision making." Westphal realized that it was his top-down approach, telling people how to do their jobs, that made them stick to their individual perspectives and make choices that fit their self-interests and breed conflicts, instead of communicating and deciding among themselves on the best action to advance the company's vision. So, instead of "tell, tell, tell," he decided to try something different: "I came to work the next day after the experience with my wife and I started listening." It was not so long afterward that this first and, apparently, small step of building a free environment delivered a huge result.

During a meeting to assess how to move forward with the failed software-development project, one manager observed how the tax-software field seemed to be moving in a different direction from the one their project was pursuing. Enterprise resource planning, this person argued, was the future of their business. Westphal recalled, "After this failed project I thought we should redouble our efforts . . . because I tended to be goal-target focused. But then I started to listen. And Gerry Hurley, who is our marketing VP today, had noticed that circumstances were changing in our core sales-tax software business. And I said, 'What should we do?' We were a pretty small company then, sixty or seventy employees. And he said, 'We have to shift gears and we have to put our priority over *here*, because if we don't pay attention to this we are going to be in trouble.' I listened and agreed."

Westphal accepted the idea that opened the path to the company's growth. He admits that if they had revamped the failed project as he initially wanted, Vertex would have been ruined: "It's a darn good thing we did, because we barely got ourselves into a position in time to seize the growth opportunity in ERP that really put the company on the map. Had we not done it, we probably wouldn't be in business today."

Of course, that insight came later. But at the time, how did he feel leaving a major strategic decision to his team? "I was not diminished because it wasn't *my* idea," he explained. "My measure is the net performance of the organization, so we can either get an itty-bitty bit of leverage out of the incremental power of my little pea brain or we can get a ton of leverage with the incremental power of six hundred brains. It's not about who has the best idea, it's about *us* having the best idea. But it was hard at first because you feel vulnerable."

Note that listening, by itself, did not trigger Westphal's decision to launch his liberation campaign. Rather, it was the reality Westphal discovered after he started listening that exasperated him and triggered his decision.

Seeing Vertex's performance improve, Westphal—now emancipated both from the telling "how" style and his ego—began to see clearly that the environment inside his company was what he called the "rule of the jungle." It encouraged people to stick to their own perspectives, to push decisions favoring their own interests and thus create permanent conflicts, and then to go to the "boss" to resolve these conflicts. It was a hierarchical, conflict-ridden environment with all the stress and disengagement that entails. Similar to the exasperating issue at home, Westphal saw that the never-ending conflicts at the workplace stemmed from telling instead of listening. He decided to transform the "how" company into a liberated one, encouraging people to listen to one another, to agree on a common business purpose reflecting the company's vision, and to come up with the best decisions and actions to achieve this shared purpose.

After fifteen years of effort, Westphal figured that Vertex's culture was more than halfway to his ideal but needs "another ten or fifteen years" to reach it. Yet, despite this severe self-appraisal, he was eager to provide an illustration of how far he had already traveled on the road to freedom: "I remember feeling like I had to have . . . the right answer all the time. And now . . . I know that I just have to have the right question. It doesn't matter where the answer comes from."

Many of our liberating leaders experienced similar moments of exasperation with the "how" culture. Stan Richards, the owner and CEO of the Dallas-based Richards Group, the largest independent ad agency in the United States, reached the point of exasperation with the way the environment in traditional agencies stifled creative ideas and produced interdepartmental strife. The sectarian conflict between "accounts" people and "creatives" was so bad that Richards compared it to Northern Ireland, where physical walls were built in the middle of streets in Belfast to keep Protestants and Catholics apart. These firms, Richards says, were like "Ulster, with regular business hours." That experience made him quit the world of traditional ad agencies and start his own freedom-based company.

Bob Koski was the founder and longtime CEO of Sarasota, Florida-based Sun Hydraulics, a leading manufacturer of high-performance hydraulic valves. But he started Sun only after he became exasperated by the antagonistic labor relations at his previous job. Koski would spend a lot of time walking around the plant hearing the concerns of the workers. When he predicted that the workforce would vote in favor of unionization because the rank-and-file had lost faith in management, he was laughed at. In the end, the union won ten to one, and Koski struck out on his own—not because the union won the vote, but because he was fed up with the rest of management's denial about how disengaged—in, fact, actively disengaged—the workforce was. Robert McDermott became exasperated by a different consequence of "how" management: As CEO-in-waiting during his first six months at USAA, he saw how the company's bureaucratic ways made it impossible for its customer service reps to serve USAA's customers.

What sets these leaders apart from others is that they were not simply critical of their companies. They actually could not stand it anymore. Not content to just criticize their employers, or complain about what didn't work while actually doing nothing, they were moved to action. The distinction between being critical and being exasperated is not just psychological hairsplitting. After all, when businesspeople are critical of something, they quickly act to ameliorate it. Right?

Not so fast. We know one division head at a famous American corporation who loves to tell internal audiences a story about his father, a crane operator. One night at dinner, the story goes, his father told him that a new boss had come in and said that the company's goal was to improve productivity by 30 percent.

"Will you do it?" his son asked.

"Hell, no," the father replied.

"But do you know how to do it?" the son persisted.

"Sure I do," the father answered, showing his deep disengagement with the company and its "how" bosses and his unwillingness to help them. If they want to tell him how to do his job, well then, his attitude is, fine. But don't ask me how to do it better. The father in the story was resigned to the idea that management didn't value his ideas anyway, so he saw no reason to try to help them.

The executive who tells this story around his own company is convinced that people have the golden keys to improve performance, and he is critical of the "how" environment that prevents them from putting these keys to use. But he, himself, despite being critical of his company's performance—where the annual turnover among salesmen has hit 40 percent—is not *exasperated*. Besides sharing this tale from his childhood, he has done little to create an environment that frees people in his own company. Telling people that they hold the keys to great performance is still, after all, a form of telling. Liberation demands more.

Yet, like this executive, thousands of CEOs and key players who experience poor performance and criticize their "how" environments, don't change them. Instead, many row twice as hard. They blame certain employees or certain corporate fads—or, worse still, factors external to the company. Hence, the many periodic bloodlettings and fad "diets."

Others don't even row harder. Instead, they spend time criticizing and waiting for some instant alternative. Meanwhile, they don't lead the necessary transformation so that the right boat can be built to take the company to a world-class destination. As the eminent leadership scholar and former executive Robert Greenleaf wrote:

> So many . . . having taken their firm stand against injustice and hypocrisy, find it hard to convert themselves into *affirmative builders* of a better society. How many of them will seek their personal fulfillment by making the hard choices and by undertaking the rigorous preparation that building a better society requires? . . . Criticism has its place, but as a total preoccupation it is sterile. . . . If too many potential builders are taken in by a complete absorption with dissecting the wrong and by zeal for instant perfection, then the movement so many of us want to see will be set back. The danger, perhaps, is to hear the analyst too much and the artist too little.[3]

What did this hard choice concretely imply when the "artists," the "affirmative builders" of the freedom-based companies, decided to act, to take the first step of the liberation campaign? For most, it was to restrain themselves from telling a subordinate how to solve a problem that didn't properly belong to them. Instead, they shifted to a question: "What do *you* propose?" And if the subordinate had no ideas—though often she does but won't share them because she isn't used to being asked—the liberating leaders would say: "You're the one who has competence in this matter. I'm sure that if you take a bit of time you will find the solution."

Even showing this restraint is hard. As Albert Camus once wrote, winning your own freedom requires "accept[ing] whatever happens."[4] And doing this leaves one vulnerable—as Westphal acknowledged. Camus advised that we should "fear nothing." Still, the first time you leave your subordinates free to make $1.8 million decisions for a fledgling company, you may have a knot in your stomach. And as Camus warned, there is no one to help you with it.

FROM ADMIRATION TO EXECUTION

Exasperation with the consequences of the "how" environment has been a key trigger for many liberating leaders. But simply doing the opposite of what you would have done in a "how" company is a fuzzy action plan.[5] There are a few leaders—such as Zobrist—who were inspired by the writings of management theorists. Much more common is the case of Bob Koski at Sun Hydraulics, who translated his exasperation with "how" companies into a plan for liberation based on what he had learned about alternative management approaches at companies he admired.

"Starting Sun with three employees (John Allen; my wife, Beverly; and me) and believing that the company would grow to employ several hundred people, I thought we had a golden opportunity to minimize the destructive effects of politics and egos."[6] That's how Bob Koski described the initial trigger for starting the freedom-based Sun Hydraulics in 1970, now publicly traded and repeatedly ranked among *Fortune*'s 100 fastest-growing small public companies in America and *Forbes*'s 200 Best Small Companies. Bob Koski wanted to create a company without those "destructive effects," a company where employees would feel respected and free to act as they choose. Koski recalled one of the first meetings with his colleagues at his new business: "I said very coyly, 'I don't know what to do but I sure know what *not* to do.'"[7] He thought of his former company's workplace and labor conflicts, largely caused by the big-ego managers telling people how they have to do their jobs, constantly controlling them, and not listening to them—even after people voted, as mentioned earlier, ten to one to unionize their company. But to launch this project, Koski needed to craft the appropriate plan, because for him, as for other liberating leaders, the freedom he aimed for did not mean anarchy but "a highly orchestrated, disciplined environment that sought to tap into the strengths and intelligence of people."[8]

During a year of planning and reading, one organization attracted his attention: the DuPont labs of the 1920s and '30s. These labs had no formal organizational charts or titles. They were run by small, self-managed teams of scientists who shared leadership and had the freedom to make decisions, accompanied by the obligation to inform other team members. There was fluid movement of scientists from one project to another. Koski noted how this freedom had led DuPont to world-class performance: "The DuPont Chemical Company prospered. DuPont's talent pool was highly regarded. DuPont's position in the chemical world grew rapidly."[9] Without realizing it, Bob Koski was describing exactly the same features that led Bill Gore to wonder why a whole company couldn't be organized along the same lines.

Inspired by the environment of DuPont labs, Koski designed the environment for his own company and described it, along with his financial and business arguments, in a thirty-four-page handwritten business plan (see its "soft" part on the next page). Only then did he pull the trigger, sending it out to local banks and other potential investors. Surprisingly, the banks didn't throw out the plan, convinced by its hard data and projections and, perhaps, skipping over the soft subjects. Bob Koski didn't take offense—he took the money from one of them, which was the most important thing at that moment—and with some family and friends as other investors, launched the business. But since the company's first days, Koski never stopped emphasizing the importance of the soft over the hard, that is, of freedom as a condition and a guarantee of continuous outstanding performance:

> A most useful way for shareholders to evaluate the quality of longer-term investments in companies like Sun Hydraulics is to gather clues about how a company tends to think and behave. . . . Personally, I think manufacturers that manage solely with hard asset numbers are making a big mistake. Companies that manage by nurturing soft assets, like corporate knowledge and relationships, will do better in the long term. . . . We believe that our competitive edge is based in the creativity, skill and commitment of our employees.[11]

THE PHILOSOPHY OF SUN HYDRAULICS, CORP.

To Obey The "Golden Rule" In All Relations Both Within & Without The Company No Matter How Difficult This May Seem At The Time.

To Respect The Dignity Of Every Individual And To Be Courteous At All Times.

To Honestly And Fairly Make And Meet Our Commitments With Customers, Distributors, Employees And Suppliers And To Establish Stable Relationships With Them.

To Be A Leader In Our Chosen Fields Of Activity And In The Development Of Our Industry & Community.

To Be A Growing Company So That Employees Are Continually Provided An Opportunity For Additional Responsibilities.

To Constantly Improve Our Products & Services So That They Are Worth More To Our Customers And To Constantly Improve Our Operational Methods So That We Can Afford Higher Than Average Wages.

To Provide Steady And Continuous Employment For Persons Hired With Reasonable Working Hours And Safe Working Conditions.

To Encourage Employee Self-Improvement And To Promote From Within Whenever Possible.

To Keep Employees And Stockholders Informed Of Company Policies, Procedures & Plans.

Sun Hydraulics' philosophy in the company's original business plan.[10]

These are the opening lines of Sun Hydraulics's 2003 annual report for investors, though the company called the report by a different name: *Observations from Bob Koski and Clyde Nixon* (the chairman of the board at the time). Knowing that words are not enough to convince potential investors, Koski asked them to come and see for themselves: "If you are, or, might wish to be, a serious 'investor' in Sun Hydraulics, come to Sarasota, Florida, Coventry, England, or Erkelenz, Germany, and meet your investment: the people that are the heart and soul of our company."[12] Personal observation is what Koski believes to be the best way—as opposed to the cold numbers—to evaluate his company's soft assets. Admittedly, though, it is not easy for shareholders scattered around the continent or even the globe to visit personally, which explains the lengths and effort that Sun Hydraulics takes to describe these soft assets in the company's annual report.

Bob Koski did not experience the benefits of the freedom-based environment in DuPont himself. He'd merely read about it. Like him, many other liberating leaders learned about this environment from other companies, admired it, and used the lessons to trigger their own freedom-building action plans. Bob Davids, for example, befriended Robert Townsend—the former CEO of Avis—and carefully studied his experience, which he then used in liberating his own companies. Jeff Westphal visited Gore and Harley-Davidson and used his observations to plan his liberation campaign at Vertex.

Harley's Rich Teerlink, though, had an even stronger connection to a freedom-based company than simply visiting one: He worked at one. While an executive at Herman Miller, the furniture maker, he observed its freedom-based environment every day—and could discuss liberating leadership with Max De Pree—the CEO and an eminent author on the subject. After Teerlink became Harley's CEO and successfully transformed it from an almost bankrupt company assaulted by Japanese bikes to a Wall Street darling, he analyzed the reasons for his success. Armed with his freedom values, he determined that it was not simply

Total Quality Management or the Kaizen tools that turned the company around but the freedom that its frontline people had to take quality and improvement actions. We will explore how Teerlink liberated Harley-Davidson in chapter 6, but his firsthand admiration for Herman Miller's culture was instrumental to his decision to build a similar environment at Harley.

Bill Gore's case is more puzzling at first. The company that inspired Bob Koski—DuPont—was the origin of both Gore's exasperation and admiration experiences. Exasperation because—as we mentioned earlier—after working for DuPont for seventeen years in the 1940s and '50s and experiencing its dysfunctional bureaucracy, he decided to leave to build his own company. But also admiration, because when DuPont needed to spur innovation, it would set up a temporary freedom-based organization similar to the one that Bob Koski had read about. So both exasperation and admiration—in his case for the same company's practices—triggered Gore's decision to build his own company around freedom.[13] But he also went beyond business organizations and groups and read up on animal behavior, primates, primitive groups, and tribes.[14] From Robert Ardrey's *The Social Contract*, Gore learned how friendship-based emotional interactions led to the highly efficient early human groups that eventually evolved into *Homo sapiens*. And from thinking about the key roles of communication, trust, and understanding within these groups, Bill Gore developed the most important challenge for "The Lattice Organization," his "philosophy of enterprise":

> Cooperation between two people is relatively excellent. . . . With increase in the number of cooperators, communication becomes more complex, less efficient, and limitations arise in the kinds of possible communications. A precipitous drop in cooperation appears as the group size becomes large enough so that everyone no longer "knows" everyone else. At this point one hears the "we" decided, or did, or believed, etc., become "they" decided, etc. This

precipitous drop in cooperation is difficult to forestall in groups larger than about 150 persons. Beyond some such level, it becomes necessary to impose rules, regulations, procedures, and the like that dictate how the cooperation shall be done.[15]

Other principles of the lattice organization that Gore defined were: "no fixed or assigned authority; sponsors, no bosses; natural leadership defined by followership; person-to-person communication; objectives set by those who must 'make them happen'; tasks and functions organized through commitments."[16] At the very beginning his company had supervisors, but as Les Lewis recounted, the development of the lattice organization principles triggered Bill Gore's decision to build a more radically freedom-based environment there.

PILGRIMS AND DOUBTERS

The decision to liberate is neither simple nor obvious—even to those who are aware of and admire the performance of liberated companies. Hundreds of executives have made pilgrimages to Harley-Davidson and France's FAVI, which hosted them in meeting rooms that employees have now jokingly dubbed the "chapel," the "cathedral," and the like. They realize that, from the outside, FAVI is seen as cultlike and Zobrist as a savior of their "lost souls." So many people visited Harley that it started charging visitors for the time. But whether they've paid for the privilege or not, the vast majority of these excellence seekers come back from these visits and don't change anything in their "how" environments, because they are not armed with freedom values. The visits become merely a "benchmarking" exercise—they admire Harley's performance but don't understand its freedom.

Bob Koski, surprised at the widespread faulty reasoning among businessmen, once remarked, "I have to wonder what they teach at business schools." In fact, among many other things, they teach about *his* company and its freedom environment. Sun Hydraulics is Harvard Business

School's primary case study on the freedom-based environment. Despite Sun's story being taught at one of the preeminent business schools in the country, Richard Arter, Sun's head of investor relations, is not aware of any company that has been modeled on Sun's "organizational structure—or lack thereof" as a result. In fact, Bob Koski and other executives occasionally appeared in person at Harvard, taking the stage in class to prove to skeptical MBA students that Sun was a real company and not just some hypothetical case.[17]

The Harvard case study is all about Sun's values. But making the leap that connects these values with world-class vision is the real intellectual breakthrough that a liberator needs. In fact, only leaders who deeply valued freedom themselves could see during their visits—or through their readings and studies—that world-class performance is the *consequence* of the company's freedom, and use this understanding and admiration to trigger freedom building in their own companies.

When asked about Sea Smoke Cellars' outstanding performance both as a wine and a business, Bob Davids said, "If the environment is right, then we do the product right and we make a ton of money and have a blast. You can't force making money and having a blast." He added, "In this culture, there is zero tension. And there is absolute trust. Katie trusts Kris to make the wine. I trust Don to handle the barrels. Kris trusts Katie to do all the right selling and make all the right decisions. Everybody trusts everybody to do their job."[18] Remembering the episode with Katie and the used barrels, we noted with satisfaction Bob's trust of the new assistant winemaker—Don—to handle the barrels, which is one and the same with trust in Don's ownership of the company's world-class-wine vision. The winemaker, Kris Curran, also connected freedom to world-class performance: "We could have the best fruit in the world. But if you're working in miserable conditions, you're not going to make great wine. It's culture, it's conditions, it's being able to make certain decisions on your own and have that freedom in order to express your art, your craft, and your passion."[19] Perhaps it's the first time in wine history that freedom has been linked so directly to wine greatness. But then, it's the first time in history that a winery—which made the best new wine in the United States in 2006, according to *Food & Wine*—made *Wine Spectator's* list of the hundred best wines in the world in its first year of its existence and then for four years straight—including in 2003, when Victor decided to drop $1.8 million worth of grapes. That vintage, in fact, came out particularly well—*Wine Spectator* ranked it number fifty in the world, Sea Smoke's best-rated vintage. So far.

Unlike many of their counterparts in traditional companies, the liberating leaders don't believe that world-class performance can be forced. It results from the right environment—a free one. But the first years of building a free environment are not easy. Not all leaders who launch a liberation campaign succeed. How the successful ones accomplish it, and—because they can't do it alone—how they convince others to join the liberation campaign, is recounted in the next chapter.

6

WHAT'S YOUR (PEOPLE'S) PROBLEM?

Building an Environment That Treats People As Equals

All human beings are born free and equal in dignity and rights. They are endowed with reason and conscience and should act towards one another in a spirit of brotherhood.
—ARTICLE 1 OF THE UNIVERSAL DECLARATION OF HUMAN RIGHTS, UNITED NATIONS, 1948

TODAY, TELLURIDE, COLORADO, is a picturesque mountain resort, but in the early 1900s it was a gritty mining town, wracked by the labor strife that was all too common at the time. A plaque on the main street attests to this violent past, describing a deadly clash between striking miners and strikebreakers.

Such times are a distant memory in the modern Telluride in which Rich Teerlink, the retired CEO of Harley-Davidson, makes his home several months a year. But the lesson, for him, is fresh. "Look," he said, as we drove through town, "when management treats people like dirt, they sometimes go to extremes."[1]

Teerlink knows something about management-labor relations. When he joined Harley-Davidson in 1981, it was floundering, bleeding market share and on the verge of bankruptcy. By the time he stepped aside in 1999, it was back on top, earning more in profits than it had total revenue when he came on board. Its market capitalization surpassed that of GM, even before the car maker's twenty-first-century woes. Like GM, Harley's workforce was organized. But unlike those mine owners and workers a century ago, Teerlink and his workforce found a way to turn the motorcycle maker around together. This fact goes a long way toward explaining Teerlink's surprising sympathy with the miners commemorated on that Telluride plaque. He knows from personal experience that when labor-management relations go sour, management often deserves at least a share of the blame. He also knows that treating people as equals is one of the keys to setting a liberation campaign in motion.

What happened in Telluride in 1901 and the following years was extreme, even by the standards of the day. Beyond the shootout between the strikers and the strikebreakers, management and labor had become locked in a vicious, self-destructive conflict. Two months before the shooting broke out, the miners had gone on strike to demand three dollars a day in pay and an eight-hour workday. But when the Smuggler-Union mine decided to play hardball, it hired strikebreaking miners—for the same three-dollar, eight-hour days that it refused to concede to the union. The result was not just the deadly shooting on July 3, 1901, but years of labor strife in Telluride. And it began with a pay concession that the mine granted its own strikebreakers right off the bat. More than three years after the first strike began, the mine owners finally broke the union.[2]

But to no end. In those days, there was no shortage of militancy on both sides of the labor-management divide, and no shortage of violence, either. A century later, the violence is a thing of the past and the right to strike and to organize is more widely recognized. But the legacy of that old-time antagonism still haunts the labor relations of many firms, with unions and management alike falling too easily into a lose-lose trap of trying to squeeze as much as each side can out of the other.

This is not unique to unionized workplaces, either. It is, in fact, depressingly common. A company tries to goose performance and cut a bit of fat by implementing a set of controls and norms of how people should do their work and how much work they have to do. Those controls might be designed to act as a floor on performance, but in practice they become the ceiling. Everyone starts to "work to rule," in the union phrase. That phrase, by the way, is extremely revealing. Technically, unions negotiate all those work rules in order to have clear definitions of how to do their jobs. But unions and management both understand that "working to rule" can bring a business to its knees. Both sides are negotiating over rules that neither side plans to honor except in a larger dispute—and then the rules become weapons wielded against one side or the other. Management and labor both know that, whether vindictively enforced or quietly ignored, those rules are no way to run a business.

Even in less severe cases, it is all too easy for these rules and performance standards to become, or be mistaken for, the business goals themselves. As Jeff Westphal of Vertex put it, you need to fill the gas tank to get to Big Sur, but you don't drive to Big Sur just to keep filling the tank. Or, to borrow another phrase, because you get what you measure, your measurement becomes the performance. And before long, rather than boosting your firm to ever-faster growth and ever-higher profitability, you have people busy "making the numbers," a creative game that they love to play because it's a great outlet for expressing hostility toward a "how" company, as well as to undermine its performance more subtly than a strike would.

Teerlink, in a way, was fortunate. When he first came to Harley in 1981, the company was in dire straits. As he recounts in *More Than a Motorcycle*, most people he knew thought he was crazy to take a job at a company that seemed doomed. By the time he stepped aside in 1999, he and his colleagues could claim credit for one of the most dramatic turnarounds in American manufacturing, although Teerlink, a mild-mannered, Chicago-born man, is too modest to do so. Still, the facts speak for themselves:

Within a few years, Harley had gone from the brink of bankruptcy to 30 percent-plus profit margins—performance you're more likely to see at the best software and technology firms than in American manufacturing.

One of the keys to Harley's reversal of fortune was a total rethinking of labor-management relations, which then transformed workplace relations overall. And it began with an idea as radical, in its way, as the notion of an eight-hour workday in 1901. "Life is nothing more than a series of relationships," Teerlink said. "Why shouldn't you have a relationship with the head of the union? Not just a meaningless relationship, but a true, human relationship?"

Thanks to Harley's near-collapse in the late 1970s and early 1980s, the unions and the executives worked closely together for several years after Teerlink's arrival because both sides knew that the company's very survival was on the line. But after the crisis had receded and Harley, now profitable and growing again, had taken its shares public in 1986, Teerlink began to worry. If the company slipped back into its old ways and a not-my-job mentality, another crisis would be inevitable. He wanted to use the moment he had to drive a permanent transformation of the company, one that would survive the now-subsiding sense of crisis that had driven the earlier collaboration.

His first idea was to develop a gain-sharing plan, which was promptly rejected by the union. After consulting several professors and experts, it appeared that much deeper corporate transformation was needed, and it had to be done together with the unions. Lee Ozley, a management consultant, told Teerlink and his team early on that people will resist having things imposed on them—even if they'd willingly do those same things if they felt it was up to them to decide. Teerlink would later adopt the idea and often repeat "people don't resist change; they resist *being* changed," but it's a permanent truth. Recall how the Smuggler-Union mine had no problem paying three dollars a day for an eight-hour day—but the owners didn't like having those conditions imposed on them by the striking workers.

So, in the same spirit, Teerlink and Ozley and the executive team did two things. First, they reached out to the unions to try to explain what their goals were. Some of the unions weren't interested—the union at the York, Pennsylvania, plant, in particular, wanted no part of the transformation.[3] So, for the moment, Teerlink let that go and focused on finding willing partners at the plants in Wisconsin.

Teerlink took an additional step in 1988. In a few months, Harley's current three-year contract with the unions would expire. Rather than present the union leaders with the traditional list of demands about changing the work rules here and improving productivity there, Teerlink came to the negotiations with just one request: Work with us for a year on developing a joint vision for Harley-Davidson. Sit down with us, and let's try to figure out what we all want this company to be and to do. Instead of negotiating another three-year deal, he wanted to renew the expiring agreement for one year, focusing in the meantime on how to start transforming the company.

This proposal accomplished two things: It broke the cycle of trading goodies for sensible improvements in work rules—and it signaled to the unions that management really wanted to try something different by working with them. By giving up its own traditional demands at the start of a labor-contract negotiation, management showed that it was prepared to pay a price itself to get the process started. Harley's leadership tried to break the competition for material goodies by, first, giving up some of its traditional prerogatives voluntarily.

Rich Teerlink's focus on building a "true, human" partnership with his unions was not born out of a United Nations-like idealistic belief in the brotherhood of all men. His focus is not universal, even in the corporate world. It reflects the realities of a large, heavily unionized organization in which a liberating leader usually can't overcome people's mistrust, and develop genuine relationships with them, until he has done the same with their unions. Conversely, in nonunion incumbents, not to mention small companies and startups, a liberating leader can start building genuine relationships with people by treating them as equals "in dignity and rights" from the outset.

THE LEADER AS BLOCKING BACK

Don't print and circulate organizational charts. They mislead you and everybody else into wasting time conning one another. . . . The head of the mail room or the chief telephone operator may hold your destiny someday. Figure out who's important to your effectiveness and then treat him (or her) that way.

It wouldn't hurt to assume, in short, that every man—and woman—is a human being, not a rectangle.

—ROBERT TOWNSEND, 1970[4]

To convince people that they will be treated as equals, a would-be liberator must break down the barriers of distrust and status that exist in most companies. We have already discussed how important it is for the liberating leader to stop telling and start listening, but that's only the initial step. Bob Davids has started or run seven companies in his life. When asked what is required of a leader in order to begin a liberation campaign, he replied, "To be able to subordinate himself to his employees." By this he didn't mean only listening. He also meant cleaning the floors of his latest start-up, Sea Smoke Cellars, himself because it needed to be done and because his employees had more important work to do. It also meant literally getting down in the dirt and digging a ditch alongside his fellow employees at his former company, Radica Games. In both cases, Davids was applying the advice of Robert Townsend, a friend, mentor, and eventual board member at Radica. The former Avis CEO held that a leader is like "a blocking back whenever and wherever needed—no job is too menial to him if it helps one of his players advance toward his objective,"[5] and a water boy "who carries water for his people so they can get on with the job."[6] Because subordinating oneself to one's people is the opposite of using one's power and authority, it's a way to build a genuine—"egalitarian," as Davids and Townsend call it—relationship with them.

Seen in this way, it becomes only natural that liberating leaders, the "blocking backs," the servants of their people, do not display the material signs of privilege.[7] Mahogany executive floors and big corner offices with expensive furniture, company limousines and personalized reserved parking spaces are some of the symbols of unequal status that they avoid.

Even doors can be wielded as a sign of status in a company. At Harley, for this reason, they decided that even "open doors" wouldn't do the trick of facilitating genuine relations. So if you walk into their legendary redbrick headquarters in Milwaukee, you will find no doors at all—they removed all of them, except where privacy is truly necessary: in the HR director's office and—understandably—in the bathrooms. These gestures might seem purely symbolic. And if they are not accompanied by genuine changes in how a company operates, they would be, and employees would quickly see through them. Thus, when a leader says he will listen to his employees but routes all correspondence through a dedicated mailbox separate from his main, "work" email, people understand the fakery quickly. Likewise, a CEO who has several layers of "open door" guards will get little credit when her door, if you can reach it, is actually open. In neither case is this interpreted as "I listen to your ideas." Bob Davids, when he built Radica Games' Chinese facility, installed his desk—"the oldest, crappiest one at the company,"[8] in his words—smack-dab in the center of the office. "Once our employees could see I was dedicated to fairness and supporting them," he told us, "I had gained their respect and allegiance."

But even the most concrete proof of intrinsic equality may not convince some people. And they shouldn't be blamed. We're willing to wager that you might have been skeptical at first that a company could afford not to *control* its people, not to tell them how to do their jobs, and that all these "dressed-down," "egalitarian" CEOs were not hiding something up their rolled-up sleeves. Naturally, many employees don't believe it either, at least at the beginning. We mentioned earlier that for a whole year after Zobrist removed the time clock at FAVI, employees would look nostalgically at the place on the wall where it used to be. No doubt some of them were suspicious that, without the clock, they were being underpaid. And Ricardo Semler—who transformed Semco, a small "how" company he inherited, into a world-famous freedom-based poster child of Brazilian industry—recounted that, in the early liberation days, after he ordered security to stop searching people on their way out of the plant to check if they'd stolen something, people asked him to restore the searches.[9] They explained that they *wanted* to be searched because that way they had proof of their innocence if something did go missing. Clearly, they suspected that somewhere, controls—and punishments—were still intact. Indeed, people don't believe and interpret what leaders *say* but what they see them *do*—day after day, month after month. If everything a leader does satisfies people's *need to be treated as intrinsically equal*, the leader will earn their respect.

DON'T SHOOT THE MANAGERS!

At Harley, the process of building trust was sometimes halting and often fraught with difficulty. At the outset, its centerpiece was what Teerlink called "the Joint Vision Process." This was the process he exhorted the unions to join him in during the 1988 contract negotiations to define a "vision of the ideal future" through input from all levels. It was essential, because it would ensure that everyone would row toward the same, jointly agreed upon destination—that people would use their freedom to implement the *jointly* defined vision. It was a *process* because it was important not to foreordain the answer. If taken seriously, the process uncovers valuable information dispersed throughout the company about what it should be doing. A so-called vision that is simply imposed from on high—sometimes accompanied by a "buy-in" plan—won't become "theirs" without "their" input. In that case, the vision won't be emotionally embraced and owned by the people, who won't, in turn, be committed to implementing it.

But even if the liberating leader succeeds in involving frontline people, the task of enlisting everyone is not yet accomplished. Companies are composed of more than just top management and frontline people. Managers and executives—with whom people interact much more often than with their CEOs—have to join the effort of building genuine relationships for the company to succeed. Whether they will depends largely on the relationship the liberating CEO succeeds in building with *them*.

For Rich Teerlink, developing genuine relationships with managers didn't come naturally. In fact, deeply involved in building relationships with the unions, he simply forgot about them. The first warning sign that some managers were feeling neglected came from the unions themselves. On May 20, 1988, unions and top management met for the culmination of the year-long process of hammering out Harley's twelve-page "Joint Vision" document. All went well until one union official said he had a question for Tom Gelb, the vice president for manufacturing.

"What would happen if managers under your supervision failed to behave according to the terms of the agreement?" he asked.

"Easy," Gelb deadpanned. "We'll just shoot them!"[10]

But before any firing squads could be organized, the next step in the Joint Vision Process demanded sharing the vision with employees, including frontline managers. A top executive and a union representative were to make the presentations as a pair.

The first session, to a couple hundred workers at a town hall-type event, went "magnificently"—Teerlink thought. One could barely distinguish between an executive and a union representative—until he opened the floor to questions. The first hand to go up belonged to Tom, the head of accounts payable.

"Rich, that is really great," Tom began. Teerlink braced himself—every time Tom said that something was "great," trouble came next. And it did: "But who represented people like *me* in this process?"

Teerlink was stunned. They had been so focused on the relationship with the unions that it hadn't occurred to the executives that middle management needed representation to provide its input. In fact, Teerlink had assumed that the interests of the top management team and middle management were the same: "We didn't include the salaried [managers and the administrative personnel]; we had the answer for them." And in normal circumstances, the middle managers know this, limiting their need for consideration to being elevated, as one large corporation middle manager expressed it, from "cc: status" to "to: status," in the emails sent by executives. Leaving middle management out of the equation—that is, in cc: status—is a common mistake among would-be liberating leaders. But without their cooperation, changing a company's culture is next to impossible.

Thanks to Tom's question, the natural disregard of managers by top executives turned into consideration, opening the way for the former to join the campaign. More actions toward them would be taken in the following decade, but the basis for their involvement had been laid down.

Another group of key actors without whom no transformation would be possible were executives. So Teerlink began to involve them early on.

From the moment Teerlink was appointed president and CEO of Harley's Motorcycle Division in 1986, he began sharing with two other executives—Tom "Shoot the Managers" Gelb, and John Campbell, vice president of human resources—his vision that Harley could "survive and prosper only if every employee took responsibility for leading the company."[11] After abandoning a gain-sharing plan for a full-blown transformation of Harley, they all agreed that the traditional "how" structures in Harley led people to avoid personal responsibility. The "not-my-job" syndrome caused employees to limit their ideas and initiatives, and to comply—even with nonsensical rules about "how" to do their jobs—instead of committing to act in the best interests of the company. As Jim Paterson—the fourth executive to join the group—summarized it, in a "how" company you "would end up with a lot of Indians who don't know what to do without the chief."[12]

Paterson himself offered one example of how Teerlink gradually pulled top executives into the transformation process. "In March of '88, Rich took me aside and said, 'I want to name you president of the company,'" he recalled. "And a couple of weeks after that, he said, 'Oh, by the way—we're starting this Joint Vision Process, and you've gotta help make it work.'"[13] Together, they revived Harley's former practice of town hall-style meetings for all employees and conducted many of them, discussing and providing everyone with the information on operational and strategic issues. Then, after Paterson realized that a group of executives of the newly formed Operations Committee he presided over did not behave as role models for the unfolding transformation, he decided to involve them in the Joint Vision Process as well. Teerlink didn't have to do it alone—he had executives who started to share the transformation leadership with him.

With the help of consultants, the executives were trained to change their bad habits, such as attributing intentions to people who aren't present without first talking to them: "I believe Jane is against this proposal," someone might say, having never spoken to Jane about it. In this way, an executive could use one absent manager's imaginary objection to kill a proposal *he* didn't like. They were also taught to avoid the common tactic of keeping silent about something during a meeting, only to raise objections later: "Hey, I said nothing in the meeting, but this whole thing won't work in my place." This is frequently used to avoid conflict, but in effect it sweeps real disagreements under the proverbial rug.

As executives and managers worked to change their own habits and lead the transformation, more and more people noticed that Harley's existing "how" organizational structure got in its way by inhibiting people from having open relations and working well with one another. In 1991 things came to a head with a two-week strike at Harley's plant in York, Pennsylvania—the same plant that, three years earlier, had refused to engage in the Joint Vision Process.

Managers at the York plant had planned to impose a team-based work system along the lines of those used at Toyota and some other top manufacturers. But as the unions at the York plant were aware, there is a long list of companies at which this approach has been poorly implemented. Self-managed teams can succeed only if employees—along with their unions where they exist—and frontline managers have been involved from day one in implementing the work system instead of just being told to use it, as often happens in "how" companies.

Unsurprisingly, the union leaders weren't happy.

Teerlink and his team listened. What's more, they did their own review of the history of the practice, which revealed a paradox that other leadership teams might have overlooked: Executives in team-based companies almost never applied the approach to themselves, despite its supposed advantages. If "leaders by their actions are known,"[14] as Teerlink likes to say, they weren't exactly leading by example on the team-based approach.

WORKING IN CIRCLES

After their investigation, Teerlink and his team agreed with the union and sought to involve it and employees in building a team-based system. The group decided that fixed teams could become a handicap, with each team pursuing its own interests instead of the company's. What Teerlink and his colleagues arrived at instead was what they called a "natural work group": "Getting the right people to come together, to do the right work, and do it right."[15] Every word of that description was important. A natural work group would not be bound by lines of authority on an org chart or by divisional fiefs within the company. The right people were the people needed to get something done that needed doing, regardless of their place in the former hierarchy. And groups were not to be formed for their own sake, but because they were the natural way to do "the right work" in light of company's joint vision.

Logically, they decided to use this structure throughout the company, from the shop floor to the executive room. This concept of *natural*, or self-organizing, work groups is similar to one used at Gore, where two varieties of natural groups and their leaders exist: business—operating the business processes, such as manufacturing, sales, and so on; and functional—operating the support processes, such as training, development, and so on. Without knowing this, Teerlink and his group came to a similar composition of what they called a "circle structure" consisting of "create demand," "produce product," and "provide support" circles.

Each circle was a cross-functional, large, natural work group with a common purpose, all intersecting in a Venn diagram. It was not clear how the circles would be organized, and the group decided that it would need wise and competent counsel. From this, the most dramatic and symbolically significant executives' decision emerged: Totally voluntarily, Tom Gelb, the executive vice president of manufacturing, and Jim Paterson, who had earlier asked, for personal reasons, to move from the motorcycle division presidency to be executive vice president of marketing, agreed to resign and become coaches of their respective circles with no hierarchical "Indian chief" power whatsoever. Teerlink, the acting president of the division, became the coach of the "provide support" circle. To demonstrate that this reorganization wasn't just another management fad that the people could wait out, two of Harley's top three executives effectively gave up their jobs and the power that came with them to put the structure into practice. And within a few months, Teerlink would follow them.

Between mid-1991 and the end of 1992, Teerlink and his group started to discuss the new structure with others in the company. After the presentations, he'd ask, "What are the questions?"

"Who's in charge of the circles?" was often the first.

The ambiguity, he explained, was deliberate. Teerlink wanted a structure that was a little nebulous, so it would evolve organically to meet the company's real needs as they developed, rather than force the company to work around a structure arbitrarily imposed from on high. Teerlink would later describe the evolving, exploratory character of the concept: "Here's a way of organizing. Let's try and see what happens. No, we wouldn't have a full-blown natural work group concept within weeks or months, or maybe even years. But we'd be aiming toward that."[16] Leadership would be shared, both within the circles and among them, and would, hopefully, emerge where it was needed rather than flow from the center. This experimental, provisional way of proceeding—sometimes called "prototyping"—is typical of the liberating leaders we met. They decide to act not because they think they have all the answers, but because they know they don't. Only by putting out different ideas and by soliciting help and feedback from others will they discover what's working and what isn't.

When we asked Teerlink about the dramatic transition of the top executives to the coaches' roles, he got up and pointed at a statuette of three interconnected circles on the shelf of his home office.

"See that up there? Released in February 1999 by the Functional Leadership Group at Harley-Davidson? It simply says: 'Rich Teerlink, Leadership is your legacy.' I retired in February 1999," he said. Tears clouded his eyes.

We tried to continue but Teerlink couldn't; he was so touched by these memories that he had to take a little break. Once back, we asked why this was so emotional for him.

"Because here was the group that was living with this process that we had all constructed together. . . . [One day] Lee Ozley and I were sitting in the room saying basically that operating all this boxes and lines stuff [on organizational charts] is really inhibiting any kind of progress. And then, Lee says, 'What should a business do? Well, it should create some services and it should help.' And we put these three circles there. And looking at it we thought, 'We have to get people working more in concert with one another.' And damn! Making a Venn diagram and when you look at that, automatically, it says interdependence . . . it says we as a group are responsible. And let's get rid of the senior vice presidents."

Harley-Davidson was a large, heavily unionized industrial company. Launching liberation there, building an environment that treats people as intrinsically equal, required, first of all, treating the *unions* as equal partners. But not all incumbent companies are heavily unionized. FAVI, for one, wasn't. This allowed Jean-François Zobrist to build genuine relations directly with frontline people. The next chapter describes how he did it.

7

LIBERATING AN
ESTABLISHED COMPANY

How to Reach Out Directly to Your People

L ISTENING TO JEAN-FRANÇOIS Zobrist's fervor and irreverence puts one in mind of French revolutionaries, perhaps even *hussards de la mort*. The *hussards* were a couple hundred of voluntary cavalrymen who, in the early 1790s, sported the impetuous motto "*Vivre libre ou mourir*"—"Live free or die."

Zobrist, as it happens, did have a military—and rebellious—past.[1] At seventeen, after reading an article on paratroopers, he decided to enroll for training with a paratrooper unit. The army's age limit was eighteen, but Zobrist thought he'd be a good jumper and could contribute, so he modified his date of birth by one year on his identity card and got accepted. Later, after having been admitted to the artillery officer candidate school, Zobrist came to know the power of the hierarchy above him when he learned that his transfer was being blocked. "Your rank is a simple paratrooper, you aren't an officer candidate," his superior informed him.

So Zobrist did his *hussard* "ready, fire, aim" thing again. In the village in which he was stationed, during the night, he broke into the town hall to get the *Journal Officiel*—the French government's periodic publication of all new laws and decrees, which included the lists of all those admitted to governmental institutions of higher education, including officer candidate school. He tore out the page with his name and brought it to the colonel the next day to show the colonel that he'd be breaking the law by refusing Zobrist's reassignment—justice achieved. Of course, when the colonel learned that someone broke into the town hall, he understood who the *hussard* was.

"Was it you?" he asked Zobrist.

"Yes, it was. For fifteen days you took me for a fool. So I wanted to prove to you that I'm not," replied Zobrist.

We don't know whether the colonel thought Zobrist was wise. But Zobrist did get his transfer (he would eventually achieve the rank of second lieutenant in the ballistic missiles unit). Zobrist told us this story to try to explain what he called his flaw of acting first and thinking later. The subject came up after he told us how, at the age of twenty-two, he met the owner of the company he had gone to work for after leaving the army. The proprietor was a forceful but open-minded personality, and from time to time he would tour his property, asking, "How's everything? Fine?" Most of the time, he received—and in truth expected—only formulaic replies. When it was Zobrist's turn, he replied frankly, "Not at all, sir!" And then he explained all the ridiculous and badly functioning things that he saw happening in the company. The owner listened to the maverick and took steps to address the issues Zobrist identified. Sixteen years later, on April 15, 1983, this owner—as we described in chapter 1—flew him by helicopter over the FAVI plant and announced, to everyone's surprise, that Zobrist would be the new CEO. Zobrist accepted the offer, although what he saw at FAVI was not to his liking. But this time, he decided not to act first and think later.

Instead, for the first four months he was at the plant, Zobrist behaved, as he put it, as a kind of "tourist." He used this interim period to observe and listen to what was going on in the company. Zobrist asked the incumbent CEO, who had to leave in July, not to change anything during this transition. As a tourist he spent a lot of time on the shop floor talking with and listening to people about their families, where they lived, their hobbies—actions he assumed would not threaten local "how" managers. That assumption was only partly correct. Each time he walked into a manager's area, Zobrist's every step was shadowed until he reached the "frontier," where another manager was already waiting to receive the "baton." This provoked Zobrist to action; he saw in the surveillance a kind of primordial instinct to guard one's turf. And this, he felt, was incompatible not only with his own freedom, but that of everyone else at the company. Those managers viewed Zobrist as a visitor, and moreover as one whose intentions they did not trust. He called a meeting of the managers and said, "I understood well that every one of you made a pee-pee around his station. But what you haven't seen is that, from the first day, when I stepped down from the helicopter, I made a pee-pee around the whole plant. So, I'm at home all over this place."[2] It was Zobrist's first warning to the managers that their turf was no longer secure.

The incumbent CEO made him meet all the company's external stakeholders—from the mayor to the local heads of social security and administration—and Zobrist saw that everyone held his predecessor in high esteem. Zobrist also respected him highly. As a man of strong ethical principles, he never allowed himself to influence Zobrist's opinion of FAVI's people or practices in any way. At first glance, FAVI looked to Zobrist like a well-managed company according to the norms dominant in the 1970s. The CEO's office had a window overlooking the whole shop floor from above, and there were time clocks and penalties that would dock people's pay when they were more than five minutes late, which escalated for repeat offenders. There were two locked supply closets, a drink dispenser—free only in the summer—and adjustable wrenches to save money on maintenance tools. Then there was the bureaucracy. Every morning the CEO, in the presence of some key managers, would preside over the opening—and browsing—of all the mail that arrived at the company, no matter to whom it was addressed. There were departments of purchasing, of personnel, of planning; there were machine setters, foremen, workshop heads, team heads, and department heads.

And there were the meetings: of the executive committee, of managers, for planning, for reviewing the past month's quality problems. There was an annual lunch with managers, monthly bonuses to everyone—for quality, for tons produced, for perfect attendance, for when the temperature in the foundry got too high. And lastly, there were routine end-of-the-month furloughs—workshop by workshop—to keep pressure on the workers. Zobrist commented that if he hadn't started with this four-month observation period, he'd simply have continued to manage the company in the same old way, as it followed common practices used by industrial companies at the time. But he had observed and listened to people. And during these four months a different reality revealed itself to him.

One of his first epiphanies came with his encounter with Alfred and his gloves outside FAVI's storeroom, as we described in chapter 1. Armed with the accounting discovery he made as a result, Zobrist applied it next to the coffee machine. He calculated that having only one machine for the whole plant made an average refueling trip last three to five minutes. This made the *real* cost to the company of a cup of coffee *one hundred times more* than FAVI's cost of supplying the coffee itself. What's more, the "free" coffee offered in the summer was even more expensive. Even when free, the machine required special tokens, which had to be procured from the receptionist for each cup, making the journey even longer.

Zobrist found similar false economies throughout the plant. The adjustable wrenches, for example, which were used to save money on tools, rounded off the corners of the nuts and bolts on the machinery over time. This, in turn, required the use of pliers on the damaged equipment, wasting still more time, worsening the condition of the nuts and bolts, and accelerating wear and tear on all the equipment.

Most of the weekly "planning" meetings were spent making excuses about not following last week's plan and assigning blame elsewhere for these failures, leaving little time for the ostensible purpose of the meetings, which was to plan for the coming week's production.

The CEO devoted one full day a month to calculating monthly performance bonuses with managers. These bonuses, moreover, were arbitrary. The bonus for tons produced was unfair because a machine operator had no control over the size of a client's orders in any given month. As for the bonus given when temperatures in the foundry were too high, he noticed that some workers responded to this incentive by closing the windows in the summer to overheat the plant. Talk about unintended consequences.

Then there were the monthly furloughs when business was slow. In the first place, this punished the workers on the foundry floor for the performance of the salesman, which seemed wrong. It also created a disincentive to work faster and more productively—work expands to fill the time allotted to it, a law unknown to Newton and Boyle but familiar to any office worker.

Zobrist then reflected that, though the salesman did a good job, having a single person for that role for the entire plant was not sufficient—saving money on sales staff was another false economy. So Zobrist employed one of his bawdy metaphors: "I recalled in my youth while dating that the most difficult thing was not making love to the girls, but bringing them to bed. So I told myself that we'll need more people to bring clients to our company's bed."[3]

Finally, he noticed that, at the end of the day, many of the employees raced for the time clock. Some even gathered around it before the whistle blew to be the first out the door when their shift was over.

At first, all these observations were just that—observations. He knew that they pointed to something wrong, but like a lot of new executives facing a dysfunctional culture, he was at a loss as to how to deal with it. His first reaction was typical—he sought expert advice, traveling two hours to Paris to attend seminars on all the management tools that promised to help. He learned about statistical process control, Kanban, Toyota's "total productive maintenance," and even an esoteric theory of self-organization taught by the consultant and business philosopher Jean-Christian Fauvet. None of them seemed to be the answer. At the end of July, FAVI's owner flew into town to see off the outgoing CEO, and after the obligatory speeches and toasts, everyone went off for the requisite month-long French vacation in August.

By the last week of August 1983, Zobrist's stomach was in knots—he still did not know how he was going to confront the challenges facing FAVI, which by now had totally exasperated him. Then, while mowing his lawn one day near the end of the month, he had another epiphany.

OF LAWN MOWERS AND PROSTITUTES

The mower was misfiring. Zobrist, a tinkerer who does his own mechanical work on the ultralight airplanes he likes to fly, took apart the mower, cleaned the spark plug, and got it running again. As he returned to mowing the lawn, he mused over what he would have needed to do to make a similar repair at FAVI, taking into account the rules, procedures, and regulations the company imposed. The imaginary operation looked like this in his mind:

> *The worker, having no right to touch the broken equipment, calls the machine setter, who, after tinkering a bit, says that it's not a setting issue but a maintenance problem. He then goes to see the workshop head, who in turn calls the department head, who in turn calls the maintenance service. The maintenance head sends in the mechanic, who starts by cleaning up the carburetor. Finding no improvement, he calls in the electrician, who finally finds the bad spark plug. The electrician, like Alfred with his gloves, goes off to the supply closet to exchange the old plug for a new one. He comes back, puts in the new plug, and calls the setter. The setter starts the machine and calls in the controller, who verifies that the mower does in fact now*

work. He then informs the workshop head that the mower has been repaired. Finally, the shop head goes to find the worker—who has been assigned to another mower in the meantime—to instruct him to return to work on his original mower.

"Once I comprehended this sequence of events," recounted Zobrist, "anxiety, and then panic, overwhelmed me. My heart was racing. I stopped mowing, sat on the lawn, and lit a cigarette, saying to myself that I will never succeed. I will never find a way to give the worker the freedom to fix his equipment by himself, to have *his own* tools, and have a spare spark plug handy in advance. And if I even was to succeed, what would I do with all the setters, controllers, workshop heads, and department heads?!"

But his common sense forbade Zobrist from giving up: "What is right in the garden should also be right in the plant."

This common sense suddenly led him to his breakthrough conclusions of what to do in FAVI:

- For the company to be nimble, the decisions have to be made by the workers, in real time, on the ground.
- A good worker is one who takes initiatives.
- At home, all workers take initiatives.
- The current production structure had no justification other than blocking initiative.
- It is necessary, therefore, to dismantle this structure—or at least to orient it to other missions.

This exasperation with the "how" structure triggered his liberation campaign. So the morning of the first day back to work in September, Zobrist gathered his managers and said:

First, I'll never leave! We'll either hit the wall together or we'll evolve together. . . . Second, I'll offer you my resignation every five years, because I know that power makes one crazy—especially given the latitude our owner gives his CEOs—and I want to give you an opportunity to save the company if this happens to me. In addition, my strengths and weaknesses, which may be needed at one point of the company's life, may become incompatible with its interests at another moment. Third, I want to have nothing to do three years from now. Meanwhile, the plant works fine and I don't see any need to change anything right now.

This last remark was deliberately disarming. Although his training in Paris and readings had not provided him with a road map for dismantling the existing managerial structure, he became aware of the threat such a process would pose to many managers. Familiar with the work of management theorist Douglas McGregor, Zobrist adopted his advice on how to transform managerial structures: "It is necessary, of course, to build as many safeguards into the process as possible so that individuals can reject ideas and implications that are threatening (i.e., to keep the freedom of genuine choice in the open)."[4] Zobrist's safeguards indeed reassured a quarter of the managers, mostly from production, though they disappointed another group that *wanted* changes. The rest of the managers seemed to remain neutral. At the same time, Zobrist proceeded with some changes calculated to be unthreatening to "how" managers—but meaningful for the rest of the people.

This time, he was inspired by Jean-Christian Fauvet and, through him, by the Chinese Taoist military strategist Sun Tzu. Sun Tzu advised military leaders, over two thousand years ago, to avoid confronting the enemy and instead go around it or under it, as a stream would do with a rock, with the goal of occupying more and more of the terrain. He gave the former CEO's big office to the accounting department and had its big window overlooking—that is, constantly monitoring—the shop floor walled up. He then made the temporary office he had been using during the transition into his permanent one. The door to his new office, which was opposite the men's bathroom, was always open, which gave him the opportunity to have a quick exchange with almost any male employee at some point during the day. He also eliminated the daily ritual of opening all the company's mail—an intrusion into everyone's privacy under the pretext that the mail is professional—and the weekly "planning"—that is, score-settling and finger-pointing—meetings.

In addition to these little "nothings," there were some "little things" that he did change, being careful to leave the managers' prerogatives in place. He noticed that an order that would take one day to fill spent several weeks languishing in the office of the sales assistant, so Zobrist had orders routed to the production department first, and only then sent to sales to be recorded. At that time, pricing decisions were in the hands of an accountant, who could take two weeks to get a price to the salesman, so he gave the salesman authority to set prices himself.

One other little thing he did concerned a manager who stomped around the shop floor with a sour look on his face, terrorizing his subordinates and blowing up at least once every day. So one day in front of a crowd, Zobrist gave the sourpuss a dressing down of his own. "Are you cuckolded?" Zobrist asked. "Or ill? Is your child ill? No? So, what is wrong? Nothing? Then stop being huffy. It's cowardice." Zobrist knew even then what the studies cited in chapter 2 have shown: that being badly treated by one's superiors is a key cause of stress—and hence, underperformance—for subordinates. He also knew that the opposite—treating people as intrinsically equal—was needed in the company.

In recalling this story, Zobrist simply remarked that no employee can do a good job if his manager is always glowering. "Being in a good mood" would later become one of the company's four values.

After this confrontation, Zobrist went back to Sun Tzu's strategy of occupying the terrain by small, unthreatening steps. Now on his list was trying to get people to do what they wanted to do, instead of simply what they were assigned to do. So he'd move around the company of several hundred people asking them questions such as, "How long have you worked at this job? Aren't you tired of doing it for so long?" And a couple of weeks later: "If you had to start over, what kind of job would you like to do?" He'd then move people around according to their inclinations.

"Otherwise, I changed nothing," Zobrist recounted.

Faithful to his approach of not confronting the "how" managers, the "rocks" in the stream, he left in place many of the managerial practices and decisions he had found there—the monthly bonuses, the quality meetings, the locked supply closets, the coffee machine, the time clocks, even the adjustable wrenches. But he knew that these things were bad for the company.

FAVI's organizational chart looked like any other company's—it showed you who tells whom how to do their job, which way the lines of authority ran, and so on. While looking at it one day, Zobrist realized that it contained a second, very different kind of information. Written into the very structure of the company was the message *Man is not intelligent*. Otherwise, why employ supervisors and industrial engineers to tell others how best to do a job that they perform hundreds of times a day?

The chart also said *Man is irresponsible*. Otherwise, he would not need controllers, who were, in turn, controlled by others, and so on.

Man is lazy, the chart said. That's why he needs someone above him to dictate the pace at which he works.

It even suggested that *men are thieves*, and so everything needs to be kept under lock and key, with guardians employed to protect company equipment and supervisors to review requests for new items.

In short, Zobrist concluded, "the organizational chart was built on the assumption that *man is bad*." He decided the time had come for the stream to flow under the "how" managers' practices, and he called a meeting. The force of the stream, Zobrist explained, was the force of his convictions, which he hoped would erode the managers'.

"And what if we consider that man is good?" he asked the group.

An uproar ensued. One manager summed up the group reaction: "A good foundry worker is an idiot with muscles!" Perhaps he was inspired by Frederick W. Taylor, one of the world's first management theorists and consultants, who once qualified a steel-mill worker as "sufficiently phlegmatic and stupid to choose this for his occupation."[5]

Zobrist concluded then that the rocks would not easily be washed away. He would, instead, go around them and appeal directly to the frontline people. At 11 a.m. on December 24, 1983, Zobrist convened a company-wide meeting to present his Christmas wishes. Standing on the shop floor on a little podium made of a couple of palettes, he addressed his employees. His Christmas speech is worth quoting at length.

"It has been nine months that I have been among you. . . . During these nine months, I have observed you and seen people of courage, great professionals who love their job but who are prevented from working efficiently. I have arrived at the conclusion that people of your qualities need neither carrots, nor sticks," Zobrist began. He noticed a couple of production managers immediately turning pale. "Carrots and sticks are unworthy of professionals, which you are. That's why, once you come back from Christmas, the time clocks will be dismantled. . . . There will be no time clocks because you're not paid to make hours but products, and good products. That's why the bell will also be gone. There won't be bonuses anymore either. . . . [Instead,] we'll take the average bonus everyone received over the past two years and will add it to your salaries. There are no thieves among you, so the doors of the supply closets will be removed. . . . We'll put up a board and a pen, and everyone will mark what he took—no names—so we can reorder supplies at the appropriate time. . . . There won't be any paid drink dispensers, but for each workshop we'll provide two free cold water dispensers with syrups and two coffee dispensers. The adjustable wrenches are out. Each machine will have its own complete set of maintenance tools. And to allow everyone to equip himself as he desires, every employee will have a budget of up to [$100] to buy whatever he wants—on the condition that it is related to his work."

Zobrist paused to observe the stupefaction. The room was silent.

"There will be no more furloughs. If we are pushed to such measures, I'll apply them first to managers, myself included. There won't be any managers' lunches. We'll either eat all together or we won't eat!" Then Zobrist turned to the managers, who had huddled together, as if to protect one another against the clear threat to their professional ways, and continued. "How will we function in the future? I do not know. I'm sure that we will function differently but I don't have a replacement model. We'll learn by doing,[6] being people of good faith, of common sense, and of good will." With this last nonthreatening gesture toward the managerial rocks, Zobrist pushed ahead.

"If there is something we could inspire ourselves by it's the functioning principles of the world's oldest profession: prostitution! If this profession has survived thousands of years, its principles can inspire us too."

Here Zobrist was being deliberately provocative, even by French standards. Many of the liberating leaders we met were fond of precisely this tactic—putting their listeners off guard in order to convey to them something that they otherwise would not be willing to learn. That said, his chosen provocation in this case had a very French flair. In 1983, the erotic film *Emmanuelle* had been showing in France continuously for a decade and had been seen by millions. Having delivered the desired shock to his audience, Zobrist continued.

"The prostitute's first operating principle is to display herself. If she stays in her room, she won't get new clients. So, we will display ourselves too: to our clients of course, [but also] to our prospective customers, to our families, our friends, to the mayor, to the governor, to everyone who may be useful to us." Later, this principle would produce not only a sales leader for every twenty-something-member production team but would encourage everyone to be in touch with clients and other stakeholders, including going to see them without anybody's permission—even abroad—if an operator deemed this necessary.

"The prostitute's second functioning principle," Zobrist continued, "is to use makeup excessively to draw the eye to her. We'll do the same. We'll

clean up our equipment and paint it in red, green, yellow . . ." This principle led FAVI to wash and paint its equipment—something not done in
the early 1980s—as well as to become the first in France to introduce the
Japanese "5S" method, which creates a self-sustaining culture of a neat,
clean, safe, and efficient workplace.

"Her third functioning principle," continued Zobrist, beginning to
sound like *The Office*'s Michael Scott, "is that she specializes. If she doesn't
offer anything better than what one gets at home, nobody will visit her.
We'll do the same. We're currently only casting brass. We'll also machine
it, assemble it, and deliver it as well as design, optimize, and test it. In
sum, we'll make more and better [products] for our clients." According
to Zobrist, this third principle served as FAVI's corporate strategy for
years. As a result, specialized products rose to 97 percent of sales, from 4
percent when he took over.

"Finally, her fourth principle is not to transmit diseases to her clients. . . . We have three illnesses we must heal. One is being late on delivery. If we promise delivery Monday, we have to honor it. Otherwise,
customers won't believe that other, less visible things we have promised,
like quality or price, will be also honored." FAVI would go on to sport a
perfect on-time delivery record for the next thirty years.

"The second illness is our pricing. How can we prove to our clients
that our price is right? There is only one solution: never raise it again."
FAVI and Zobrist would keep this commitment, too, even refusing to
raise prices to account for inflation. As a result, FAVI's prices actually fell
in real terms every year, year after year, for nearly three decades, right
up to the present. Its prices are consistently the lowest in Europe, which
has allowed the company to weather challenges—whether from the rise
of China or global recession—that have devastated its Continental competition. In fact, today FAVI is so efficient that it actually exports some
of its products *to* China. And as the global downturn rocked the auto
industry and its free cash-flow suppliers in 2008–09, Zobrist was looking
forward to seizing market share during the turmoil. What's more, FAVI

has consistently kept its cash-flow margins comfortably in the double digits in a business—automotive parts supply—that is notorious for being squeezed by its customers, big car manufacturers.

"The third and last illness is poor product quality. And I have no cure for it. But it's you workers who can do everything. We in the offices, what we can do is to listen to you and try to help you. But note: It's you and only you with your equipment who can do everything." Zobrist concluded, "I've been watching you working for almost one year. Your mastery has convinced me that you hold in your hands the solutions to our problems." Zobrist then left as abruptly as he had arrived.

He was addressing FAVI's frontline people and using a powerful metaphor to convey a vision of the company he wanted to build, but he knew that much of what he said was a direct threat to his "how" managers. Although his ideas would likely occupy the minds of frontline people, the time had come to deal with the managerial rocks. Later he recounted that he felt as if he had just jumped with a parachute—a sensation he knew well—because of the irreversibility of the measures he took and the tension of nine months of "flowing around and under" the company's managerial practices.

DELEGATING IN REVERSE

Zobrist called his first-ever official managers' meeting and used it to announce that the traditional managerial role of telling people how to work, controlling, rewarding, and sanctioning was over. From now on, managers would facilitate, guide, and help others to measure their own results. He also announced that his first managers' meeting would be his last.

In place of the middle-management layer, he broke up the plant into some twenty self-directed, single-product, client-focused "mini-plants," each of which was responsible for every aspect of its own business, from hiring and training to purchasing, budgeting, and, of course, production. Having done that, he abolished the human resources and legal departments, too. He left one person in place in IT. That done, he ditched

FAVI's traditional budget process and controls. In their place, he instituted a single annual meeting between the leaders of all the mini-plants. There, they would agree to a business plan for the coming year. As in Gore's 150-person plants, the duplication of support activities—since each unit had its own—was wasteful only on the surface. In reality, once the hidden costs of the centralized bureaucratic processes are taken into account, moving the support activities to the frontline led to dramatic increases in efficiency and, therefore, to cost savings.

By making each mini-plant responsible for its own costs, Zobrist reversed the traditional bureaucratic incentives. In a traditional firm, all departments—especially "support" departments that are cost centers, not profit makers—strive, first, to maximize their share of the budgetary pie. Then they make sure they spend it all before the year is out—so they don't see their budgets cut the following year. Under Zobrist's new organization, each mini-plant was judged by its results, as if it were a stand-alone business. And because most of the support functions had been pared back or integrated into the mini-plants themselves, the plant leaders' incentive was not to maximize resource extraction from the company, but to show the best results for their unit at the end of the year.

Three further principles guided Zobrist as he liberated this traditional, bureaucratic "how" manufacturer. The first was "backward delegation," inspired by Jean-Christian Fauvet, one of Zobrist's intellectual mentors. His book, *Understanding Social Conflicts*,[7] written in 1973, analyzed why top-down company organization inherently leads to conflicts and underperformance. Like Townsend, who was writing at the same time, and McGregor, writing a decade earlier, he believed in management "by the people" and not "by the procedures." He recognized that some rules are necessary but insisted that they have to be invented by the people on the ground, and he proposed ways for companies to self-organize. Zobrist first came across his theory while attending Fauvet's seminar in Paris, but now these self-organization ideas connected to what he was trying to do at FAVI.

In fact, "backward delegation" was new only to the corporate world. Saint Thomas Aquinas, the thirteenth-century theologian—who, among other things, was interested in the methods of government—had espoused the same principle seven hundred years earlier under the name of "subsidiarity." Translated to companies, it means that all authority starts with the frontline people, not those at the top. The frontline people then pass authority for certain decisions or actions they deem non-critical to their work up the chain. This leaves the CEO with the decisions and tasks that no one below him was willing or able to do. Note that this is essentially the same as Robert Townsend's idea of the CEO as a blocking back or water boy, for whom no job is too menial if it helps other players to advance toward their objectives. It also dovetails with Zobrist's initial intention of not having to make decisions after three years.

The mini-plants assumed authority for all the roles they deemed essential for getting their job done right. This meant not merely the manufacturing itself, which had traditionally been their only sphere of authority, but also purchasing, finance, recruitment, training, and more. Existing and newly hired engineers in FAVI were simply asked, as at W. L. Gore & Associates, to find the areas where they'd like to contribute. This, naturally, ended up being the areas left out of the production teams, such as R&D or initiating continuous improvement methods.

This is radically different from a traditional delegation model, in which the *you-know-what* rolls downhill, and each layer of management takes whatever piece of authority is available and attractive to grab, leaving what remains for those at the bottom. It is also quite different from some periodically popular forms of "decentralization." Most of these begin with the assumption that all power resides in the center, to be doled out strategically *by the center.* But under this approach, people may be given authority or responsibilities that interfere with their jobs, while being denied freedom of action in areas vital to their work. Most important, "delegation" and "decentralization" don't question the "how" managerial practices, but, perhaps, legitimize them by making their impact less harmful. "Backward delegation," by contrast, lets the frontline workers decide for themselves which pieces of authority they need to do their jobs before the higher-ups can do it. In that, it's a radical departure from traditional managerial practices, so radical that it may not *need* traditional managers at all.

The second principle concerned not so much the transformation of managerial practices as the role of the CEO in them. Zobrist—an avid student of ancient China and history in general—opens his book, *La belle histoire de FAVI*, with the following mantra, inspired by China scholar François Julien: "The good prince is one who, by eliminating the constraints and the exclusions, allows everyone to blossom as he wishes." Zobrist dramatically eliminated everything in the old structure that he felt treated people as if they were "bad" and prevented them from "being good," from "doing a good job" by making the customer happy, and from achieving personal happiness and high performance for the company. As Zobrist said in his "prostitute" speech, he can't do the work, so the ultimate quality of the product, and the success of the company, is in the hands of the workers. He sees his job as eliminating barriers to their doing their jobs as well as they can. This almost always means destroying constraints—not tightening them.

The last principle was that transforming a command-and-control company is a radical undertaking—a break, as Zobrist calls it. He compares some would-be reformers to Louis XVI, the last French king. Like him, they are very intelligent, cultivated people, but they fold every time their reforms face opposition from the ruling class. Zobrist did try many nonthreatening ways to involve—and evolve—his "ruling class" of managers by "flowing around them" with his ideas. But unlike Louis XVI, he never folded to this class when they resisted and openly challenged the transformation. Instead, Zobrist charged, because frontline people needed to be treated well so that they would act freely for their own betterment and for FAVI's.

It will not do to be a cautious radical, and Zobrist's "ready, fire, aim" character was well-suited to swift action and decision making. Indeed, his first nine months at FAVI had been perhaps the longest period of inactivity that he had experienced in his life. His quick trigger finger was so well-known there that some of them would enter his office and place their hand over the receiver of his phone before they started speaking. "Please," they would say, "hear me out to the end before you call anybody." But Zobrist also saw his inclination to act in haste as a virtue of sorts. "It's the risk-taking issue," he told us. "Many people want to control it completely, so they analyze scenarios: 'If I do this, then the other may do that, then I can do this. . . .' They have too much respect for intelligence . . . [so] they never actually act. I respect common sense and intuition. I act first and then deal with the consequences. If my action was ill-suited, I then simply change my course."

To put this another way, Zobrist no more expected perfect decision making from himself than he did from his people. Many leaders, when they think about letting go of the "how" structures, can only picture the things that might go wrong. *What if some employee does X? Or calls some client and costs us an account? Or crashes a company car while on a personal errand?* One can come up with an infinite number of these imaginary disasters if one is determined to think about them. And mistakes happen—in fact, they happen all the time, even in the most tightly controlled companies. Top managers are not immune from making them. Zobrist's willingness to accept mistakes and missteps by himself was reflected in his ability to let others take risks, too. Just as Bill Gore, on a different continent, was fond of saying, "If you haven't made any mistakes, you're not taking enough risks," Zobrist accepted his own mistakes as the price of action. And he had the wisdom to expect no more—or less—from his people.

"Life is risk," he used to say. "Once you wake up every day you're at risk. There is only one state with zero risk—and it happens when you're dead." Talk about "live free"—with risk—"or die."

TREATING PEOPLE WITH GRACE
SO THEY ACT BOLDLY

Changing the CEO's behavior from talking to listening, removing bureaucratic symbols and practices that treat people as intrinsically inferior,
and radically transforming managers' "how" habits into "why" questions,
is a hard, often risky, and always lengthy process. A *hussard* "ready, fire,
aim" style may help to break a couple of hard rocks, but trying to transform people's behavior takes a long time. Zobrist spent nine months trying to transform the incumbent managers' practices before giving up and
eliminating that layer of management altogether.

In some companies this transformation took months—as at FAVI. At
others, such as USAA, Vertex, and Harley, it took much longer. But in all
of them the change in the way people were *treated* by the company and
its managers—now leaders—led to a change in how people *acted*. Instead
of complacency in executing bosses' orders of how to do their jobs—
which frequently led to ill will if not outright conflict—people erupted in
free action, brought about by the satisfaction of their key universal need:
to be treated as intrinsically equal. With this mistrust overcome, people
felt the confidence to express their other—formerly suppressed—needs
of growth and of self-direction. So they set out to satisfy these needs in
the new environment, striving both for their personal well-being and the
company's success. That's why our liberating leaders started with satisfying people's need to be treated as equals and proceeded to transform
every aspect of the corporate environment—behavior, practices, and
symbols—that denied this need's satisfaction. Until this need was satisfied and people were no longer treated as "resources," other important
needs that people had could not manifest themselves, and all managers
would hear from the "resources" would be their desires to get "goodies."

We were looking for a word to best characterize the environment that
continuously satisfies people's need to be treated fairly and as intrinsically equal. Bob Koski, Sun Hydraulics' liberating leader, we think, had

the best word for it—*grace*. Grace, he said, was a guiding principle of everything he did in his company. We think that grace—defined as a disposition to kindness and compassion, benign good will—is a perfect characterization of all the aspects of environment we observed in liberated companies, from the behavior of people with larger responsibilities, to the various business practices, and to the physical working conditions, all aimed at treating people fairly and as intrinsically equal.

An environment that treats people with grace is not merely nice to have. It translates directly into the way employees relate to everyone around them: colleagues, partners, suppliers, and, of course, customers. One day, a FAVI operator at the mini-plant producing gear forks for Volkswagen noticed a defect on one piece—a rare case, since at the time of our visit the company had produced more than twenty million pieces without a defect. He stopped the production and checked to see that there were no other defective pieces in the assembly or in the delivery stock. Having found none—but not yet satisfied—he consulted the mini-plant's sales leader, and together they decided to drive for more than six hours to Volkswagen's Kassel, Germany, plant. Once there, the pair simply asked to check if, by any chance, a defective piece had slipped into the recently shipped inventory. They found none. The local Volkswagen managers were astounded by the visit, and made it known to their head of purchasing, who elevated FAVI to a preferred European supplier. The operator did it simply because, at FAVI, one treats customers with fairness.

Many companies ask their employees to treat customers "well." But they get neither this behavior nor the business performance they expect because they haven't done their homework. As Koski wrote in his business plan for Sun Hydraulics, treating people with dignity and courtesy within the company is a key to doing the same outside the firm, leading to repeat customers, growth, higher margins, and other factors of world-class performance.

There are even more ways of demonstrating how treating people as intrinsically equal, with respect, dignity, consideration, trust, fairness, equity, courtesy, grace—whatever words one prefers—contributes to their individual and company performance. Indeed, satisfying this need leads people to trust the company enough to express their other fundamental needs. Satisfaction of these other fundamental needs within the company then leads to an array of behaviors aimed at what psychologists call mastery and happiness—well-being and vitality—and, in its turn, translates even more directly into a company's outstanding performance. What these needs are, and how their satisfaction translates to exceptional behavior, is the topic of the next chapter. But before you turn to it, consider for a moment a more literary take on the importance of being treated as a human being.

Vasily Grossman (1905–64) is often called the Leo Tolstoy of twentieth-century Russian literature for his novel *Life and Fate*. The nearly one-thousand-page epic depicts life during and after World War II on the Eastern Front, under German occupation, in the Nazi concentration camps, in the Soviet Gulag, and in the Soviet era. Because of Grossman's denunciation of Soviet totalitarianism and of the anti-Semitism of the Soviet population that fell under the German occupation, the Communist regime banished his book's publication in the early 1960s and made Grossman an effective dissident. The book's manuscript was smuggled out of the USSR and first translated and published in French in 1980. The Russian version came to light only in Mikhail Gorbachev's era.

Grossman started his writing career before World War II, but it was his four years as a war correspondent and his consequent research on crimes against humanity that allowed him to witness and gather the material for the book. While Grossman was engaged as a volunteer for the Red Army, his mother was trapped in July 1941 by the advancing Nazi troops in their native Ukrainian town of Berdichev. Herded into the ghetto, she was shot, along with tens of thousands of other Jews, in the town several weeks later.

In *Life and Fate*, the main hero, Victor—nicknamed Vityenka—receives a letter from his mother, a physician trapped in the ghetto. She describes what she believes will be the last days of her life, because she's sure she'll be killed. Here is an excerpt describing her leaving her apartment for the ghetto and how she has been abandoned by almost everybody—with the exception of a stray dog and one man who continued to treat her as a human being.

An announcement was soon made about the resettlement of the Jews. We were each to be permitted to take 15 kilograms of belongings. Little yellow notices were hung up on the walls of houses: "All occupants are required to move to the area of the Old Town by not later than 6.00 p.m. on 15 July, 1941. Anyone remaining will be shot."

And so, Vityenka, I got ready. I took a pillow, some bedclothes, the cup you once gave me, a spoon, a knife and two forks. Do we really need so very much? I took a few medical instruments. I took your letters; the photographs of my late mother and Uncle David, and the one of you with your father; a volume of Pushkin; *Lettres de mon moulin*; the volume of Maupassant with *Une vie*; a small dictionary . . . I took some Chekhov—the volume with "A Boring Story" and "The Bishop"—and that was that, I'd filled my basket. How many letters I must have written to you under that roof, how many hours I must have cried at night—yes, now I can tell you just how lonely I've been.

I said goodbye to the house and garden. I sat for a few minutes under the tree. I said goodbye to the neighbors. Some people are very strange. Two women began arguing in front of me about which of them would have my chairs, and which my writing-desk. I said goodbye and they both began to cry. I asked the Basankos to tell you everything in more detail if you ever come and ask about me after the war. They promised. I was very moved by the mongrel, Tobik—she was particularly affectionate towards me that last evening.

If you do come, feed her in return for her kindness towards an old Yid.

When I'd got everything ready and was wondering how I'd be able to carry my basket to the Old Town, a patient of mine suddenly appeared, a gloomy and—so I had always thought—rather callous man called Shchukin. He picked up my belongings, gave me 300 rubles and said he'd come once a week to the fence and give me some bread. He works at the printing-house—they didn't want him at the front because of his eye trouble. He was a patient of mine before the war. If I'd been asked to list all the people I knew with pure, sensitive souls, I might have given dozens of names— but certainly not his. Do you know, Vityenka, after he came, I began to feel once more that I was a human being—it wasn't only the stray dog that still treated me as though I were.[8]

8

FROM MOTIVATION TO SELF-MOTIVATION, PART ONE

Beyond Grace and Intrinsic Equality

Whenever the people are well-informed, they can be trusted with their own government.

—THOMAS JEFFERSON[1]

THOMAS JEFFERSON WROTE these words to a Welsh political philosopher, articulating both the *possibility* of self-governance—and its conditions. While the sentence served as a defense of and a supplement to the Declaration of Independence Jefferson had penned thirteen years earlier, it was also a seed for Jefferson's vision, still decades in the future, of "a system of general education, which shall reach every description of our citizens from the richest to the poorest."[2] How important this project was to him is attested to by Jefferson's request that his three greatest achievements be mentioned on his tombstone: the Declaration of Independence, the Statute of Virginia for Religious Freedom—and the University of Virginia, the fruit of his educational ambitions. Creating a university should have been an easy project for a political genius and a former U.S. president when Jefferson started it in 1814. Let's see.[3]

It took five years, but Jefferson managed to get the Virginia General Assembly to pass the laws needed to charter the university. Funding the school would be a separate struggle. In the meantime, Jefferson, with his passion for architecture, helped to design the famous rotunda and Colonnade Club. He spent four hours a day for several months assembling a 6,860-volume library for the fledgling university, an impressive collection for the time. With the help of fellow Virginian and U.S. president James Madison, Jefferson defined a political curriculum for the school. Finally, he recruited the first eight professors, five of whom came all the way from England.

Perhaps the most distinctive of Jefferson's undertakings was the self-governing organization he designed. To begin with, all the rules and procedures that were in place at other American colleges were completely abandoned in Jefferson's plan. No courses or programs were required, leaving students totally free to choose what they wanted to study.[4] To reinforce this freedom of choice and the competition among professors to offer compelling courses, Jefferson designed an incentive scheme with a base $1,500 annual salary, plus $25 for every enrolled student. The distinctions between freshmen, sophomores, and upperclassmen—seniors—were abandoned. Moreover, the whole hierarchy of a traditional university—the president, provosts, and other positions of authority—was eliminated. The university was to be totally self-governed by the faculty with a rotating chairman, overseen by a board of visitors: Jefferson, Madison, Monroe, and a few more cool names. And regarding the students, "Jefferson had worked out a plan for student self-government for he believed that young men from the best families could be counted on to govern themselves and remain reasonably well-behaved."[5]

In March 1825, after many years of effort, he assisted at the opening of the University of Virginia's idyllic Charlottesville campus, welcoming the first 40 students, a number that grew to more than 116 during the year. Happy and at the age of eighty-one now, Jefferson retired to his mansion at Monticello. There, a mere five miles away, he would host small groups of students for dinner on Sunday, and at other times would observe his young university with his spyglass, taking advantage of a hole he had had cut through the trees. Until . . .

Less than one month into that first academic term, Jefferson received devastating news. A group of fourteen drunken, masked students had gathered on the lawn after dark with a cry of "Down with the European professors!" When two professors arrived to investigate the riot and tried to unmask one student, they were welcomed by profanities and worse. The first was attacked with a cane and the second had a brick thrown at him. To add insult to physical injury, sixty-five students signed a resolution the following day condemning the two professors for daring to unmask the student. The last straw: Jefferson's own great-grandnephew was one of the fourteen rioters.

Rising in the famous rotunda in the presence of the current and former U.S. presidents James Madison and James Monroe, and facing the "drunken fourteen," Jefferson began by declaring that what had happened was one of the most painful events of his life. But then, overcome with emotion and with tears in his eyes, he couldn't continue and had to sit down. The others took over, the meeting proceeded, and the "rioting fourteen" were expelled, including Jefferson's relative.

On Jefferson's recommendation, strict regulations were adopted: Every student must rise at dawn, stay in his room after 9 p.m., wear a uniform, and deposit his funds with the proctor, who would provide small sums. Gambling, smoking, and drinking were prohibited. So much for freedom and self-government.

This is the kind of story that haunts liberating leaders. Here are people finally treated as equals, but instead of assuming the freedom and responsibility that goes with it, they revolt.[6] The self-governed freedom the leader envisioned turns into anarchy, and he who wanted to make no more decisions is called back to assume the role of the authoritarian, which he loathes. If even Thomas Jefferson could not succeed in building a freedom-based organization, is it possible that the whole idea is utopian?

Yet Gore, Zobrist, Koski, Teerlink, Westphal, and Davids launched their liberation campaigns without plunging their organizations into anarchy. Their visions were dubbed as utopian by some, too—but they succeeded. All of them did more than simply build an environment that treated people as intrinsically equal. They went further and built an environment in which people became motivated to assume freedom and responsibility; in fact, they became self-motivated. We will return to UVA to find out what went wrong for Jefferson there. But first, let's look at what exactly our successful liberating leaders did to get people to take part in their liberation campaigns instead of revolting or resisting them.

IS IT *POSSIBLE* TO MOTIVATE PEOPLE?

Since at least 1943, when Abraham Maslow published a famous article on human needs and motivation, psychologists have been engaged in a passionate debate over this question. But in the business world, most companies have considered it settled for decades. Motivating people, they say, is not hard once a company finds the right mix of tangible rewards to align people's material interests with the company's goals. The problem is, the more closely psychologists look at the motivation—or engagement—levels of people in organizations, the less tangible rewards seem to matter. Instead, it's the things people do *themselves* that matter most.

Consider the following "natural experiment." A psychologist found himself disturbed by a group of kids that one day had come to play football under his window, making a lot of noise. So he went out and said, "You guys are really great. I enjoy watching you so much that every time you come to play here I will give you one dollar each." And he gave a dollar to each kid. The next day, when the kids were again enthusiastically playing football, he came out and said, "I really enjoy watching you but the thing is that I have no bills, just coins today. I can give you two quarters each." The kids were not delighted with this pay cut, but took the money and continued to play. The story continues until after two days, the psychologist offered them just a dime each, which one of them proudly refused and said, "We are not going to play here for a damn penny." And the kids never came back, much to the satisfaction of the psychologist.

Many psychologists think that this story is apocryphal, but it continues to circulate because it reflects what they know from hundreds of real experiments: If you take people who are deeply engaged in something because they enjoy it and you offer them tangible rewards for doing it, a shift happens. Mentally, people establish a causal link between these rewards and the activity—something psychologists call a perceived locus of causality—and this link will undermine the initial, intrinsic reason for doing the activity, such as considering it enjoyable or important.

Companies call these tangible rewards "bonuses" or "perks" and firmly believe they motivate people.

One famous Silicon Valley company that hires thousands of bright, enthusiastic young techies was known for providing great free food for all, including visitors. The young techies would wax lyrical in the blogosphere about how they enjoyed their work—and the great free food. Then business slowed down and a big boss wrote a memo to all that the free food was being abused by some and that measures of economy would now have to be taken. That—unsurprisingly to psychologists but surprisingly to the management—sent shivers of disappointment up and down the blogosphere. Paradoxically, as soon as a perk becomes established, it loses its motivating power and becomes a potential liability.

Besides the tangible rewards given independent of specific activity engagement—such as a salary—or unanticipated rewards—such as an unexpected bonus—all other forms of tangible rewards significantly undermine people's willingness to engage in an activity for its own sake. This, arguably, does not pose a challenge to "how" companies.[7] There, tangible rewards are one more system to make people do what they are told to do. But it posed a big difficulty to the liberating leaders. Bob Davids expressed this unequivocally: "It's absolutely impossible for one human being to motivate another."[8] Yet, they continued to seek ways to get people to join the liberation campaign instead of resist it. The breakthrough came when they adopted a *creative* approach of trying to solve a different—*redefined*—problem.

GETTING CREATIVE

Creativity research is a burgeoning multidisciplinary field, of which the major focus is how creative insight, the "Eureka!" phenomenon, occurs: the apple falling on Isaac Newton's head, Alexander Fleming spotting mold killing the bacteria in the petri dish, Spence Silver of 3M intrigued by a weak adhesive leading to the invention of Post-it notes. To untangle this puzzle, researchers view the phenomenon of creative insight as a pair: problem + solution. Ultimately, insight is an original and useful solution. But quite often, a lot of creativity goes into finding the right *problem* or in redefining the one at hand. As the early twentieth-century philosopher John Dewey said, "A problem well put is half-solved."[9] Thus, the "Eureka!" of creative insight often occurs by redefining the problem one is desperately trying to solve, in particular when one is under time pressure.[10] Consider the following case reported by two leading creativity scholars, Todd Lubart and Robert Sternberg. It is a true story of an executive working in one of Detroit's car makers and unhappy in his job. Actually, he liked the job and the salary but he couldn't stand his boss anymore. So he went to see a headhunter, who promised to find a new job for him quickly.

In the evening, he told his wife about the appointment. She, in turn, told him about her day. As a psychologist, she was teaching thinking skills to high school and college students. That particular day, she had been teaching a thinking technique called "problem redefinition." The technique consists in reversing the terms of the problem, enabling the person to look at the problem from a novel perspective. Such perspectives can sometimes be so different that *no one* had ever looked at the problem that way. While listening to his wife, the executive suddenly had a "Eureka!" moment. Here is how Lubart and Sternberg describe what happened next:

> The next day he returned to the head-hunter and gave him his boss's name. He asked the head-hunter to look for another job – not for himself this time but for his boss. The head-hunter agreed and, before long, found something. The boss received a phone call offering him another job, not realizing, of course, that the offer was the result of the teamwork of his subordinate and the head-hunter. As it happened, the boss was tiring of his current job and in short order accepted the new position.
>
> The icing on the cake was that, as a result of the boss's accepting the new job, his old job became vacant. Our high-level executive applied for it and ended up with his boss's job.[12]

We don't necessarily suggest that you try this gambit yourself. We've heard personally—so far—of two such successful attempts in companies, but we presume that at some point bosses will start to suspect something fishy about the unsolicited job offers, especially after it inspired an episode of *The Office*. Even so, the story shows how a creative insight, redefining an otherwise insoluble problem, can lead to a great solution.

Our liberating leaders had this type of creative insight while facing the motivation problem, which they initially believed had no solution. So they redefined it into a different one: *"How does one build an environment where people self-motivate?"*

This redefinition allowed them to immediately set aside all the traditional corporate solutions, which are not aimed at self-motivation but rather at controlling the motivation externally through tangible rewards, such as bonuses, promotions, perks, awards, distinctions, and "president's clubs," and through the threat of punishments. Our liberating leaders first dismantled many of these "carrots and sticks" incentive systems, then found a host of solutions through the newly redefined problem. Each solution was specific to their people, companies, and industries, but all helped to build *corporate environments* conducive to letting people motivate themselves to take part in the liberation campaign.

We don't know how all of our liberating leaders came to the creative insight of redefining the "how to motivate people" problem into "how to build an environment where people self-motivate." We do know, though, that some—such as Bill Gore, Robert Townsend, and Jean-François Zobrist—were familiar with the work of Douglas McGregor, whose one key focus was on motivating people—not only to join corporate transformation efforts but also, to act in the best interests of the company. McGregor wrote: "The answer to the question managers often ask . . .—How do you motivate people?—is: You don't. Man is by nature motivated. . . . His behavior is influenced by relationships between his characteristics as an organic system and the environment. . . . Creating these relationships is a matter of releasing energy in certain ways rather than others. We do not motivate him because he *is* motivated. When he is not, he is dead."[13]

McGregor also contrasted the traditional "manufacturing" approach with what he called an "agricultural" approach: "The individual will grow into what he is capable of becoming, provided we can create the proper conditions for that growth."[14] Robert Townsend translated these ideas into his own agricultural approach to encouraging self-motivation: "Provide the climate and proper nourishment and let the people grow themselves. They'll amaze you."[15] In other words, if the environment is properly nourishing, people will motivate themselves to take part in the transformation efforts or perform their regular activities. The question is, What is this properly nourishing environment?

THE RIGHT NUTRIMENTS

Man is but a reed, the most feeble thing in nature, but he is a thinking reed. The entire universe need not arm itself to crush him.

A vapor, a drop of water suffices to kill him. But, if the universe were to crush him, man would still be more noble than that which killed him, because he knows that he dies and the advantage which the universe has over him; the universe knows nothing of this. All our dignity consists then in thought. By it we must elevate ourselves, and not by space and time which we cannot fill. Let us endeavor then to think well; this is the principle of morality.

—BLAISE PASCAL[16]

The seventeenth-century French philosopher Pascal used this metaphor to contrast the fragility of our organism with the force of our mind. But there is another piece of Pascal's metaphor: the reed in its natural environment. Most reeds, of course, are not crushed by nature but get from it what they need to grow and develop to their programmed potential. If, on the other hand, a reed does not get from nature what it needs—water, light, minerals—it will not develop to its potential, and if its needs are severely denied by nature it may even perish.

This extension of Pascal's metaphor reflects the view of *human* needs developed by the University of Rochester psychologists Edward Deci, Richard Ryan, and their associates for the last three decades in, perhaps, the most ambitious contemporary theoretical and empirical research on motivation.[17] In the first half of the twentieth century, behaviorists and drive psychologists viewed man as naturally seeking *peace* (of body) and hence motivated to eliminate the tension of unsatisfied physical needs. To caricature, man is like a python who will move in search of prey, but his ideal is to lie under the sun immobile and simply digest the poor mouse. In 1943, Abraham Maslow extended this view to man's seeking not only peace of body but also of mind and thus being motivated to eliminate the tension of unsatisfied psychological needs—belonging, esteem, and self-actualization—too. To caricature again, our python, after eating, would seek out the company of other pythons, where he is likely to hear, "Good job, great catch!" Then, having found this company and received his approbation, he'll continue his quiet digestion under the sun. Unlike these earlier psychologists, Deci and Ryan—and our liberating leaders—view people not as aiming at peace of body and mind but programmed for *mastery*—of activities and areas of study, not people— and *happiness* (vitality and well-being).[18]

As child psychologists Jean Piaget and Lev Vygotsky have shown, we engage from a very early age in all kinds of play in order to master different aspects of our environment. We enjoy doing it to the point of ignoring hunger, fatigue, and the risk of being hurt—like those young football players outside the psychologist's window.[19] Similarly, as adults, we seek mastery and "fun" in many of our leisure activities. Given an *appropriate* corporate environment, we seek the same at work. But the appropriateness of the environment is not a minor point. As with Pascal's reed, naturally seeking to develop its potential, the ongoing natural human activities aiming at mastery and happiness demand what Deci and Ryan call *nutriments.* The reed's fundamental needs of light, minerals, and water have a counterpart in the human fundamental needs: "relatedness," "competence," and "autonomy."[20] If the nutriments are present, a person will reach mastery and well-being. But if they are lacking, she will not fully develop. For this reason, Deci and Ryan argue that these needs are as fundamental to human development as the reed's light, minerals, and water. According to this account, other candidates for fundamental needs, such as *power*, which have been postulated by earlier motivation scholars, are ruled out: Their nonsatisfaction does not prevent human mastery and well-being. (It's not because one lacks power over others that one cannot master a subject and become happy, as mountain climbers and other sportsmen prove.) And as with the reed, if one of the three nutriments is lacking, even if the other two are fully available, the person will still develop deficiently. As part of their research, Deci, Ryan, and their associates analyzed people's diaries. They found that the "good" days for people were those when they reported having experienced relatedness, competence, and autonomy—all three of them.

Deci and Ryan looked for these three needs/nutriments in people across a variety of cultures. They found them everywhere, even though they are interpreted differently in different places. In the West, for example, the need for autonomy is satisfied individually, in opposition to others, while in the East Asian tradition it is satisfied within harmonious relations with others. These findings led Deci and Ryan to argue that the three needs are innate and universal.

Overall, in their numerous laboratory and field studies, these researchers have discovered that the properly nourishing environment— with practices aimed at satisfying people's three universal needs—leads to self-motivation. When people are treated with consideration, when they are provided with support for growth and self-direction, they self-motivate and take initiatives, leading to increased performance and enhanced personal well-being.[21] When, on the contrary, the environment is controlling and deprives people of their universal needs, then motivation becomes externally controlled and people do only what they are rewarded or punished for. This does not lead to increases in people's well-being, and creates only short-term performance benefits, if any.

Deci and Ryan's extensive empirical work led them to a conclusion similar to McGregor's: Human motivation does not need to be controlled; people are self-motivated to act in search of mastery and well-being when provided the "nourishing" environment. McGregor redefined the "How does one motivate people?" problem into "How does one build an environment where people self-motivate?" Deci and Ryan advanced this redefinition further still: "*What is in the environment that prevents people from getting the right nutriments and what has to be rebuilt in it so they get them?*"

Liberating leaders make a similar redefinition. Methodically, they listen to employees to understand what in the work environment is depriving them from satisfying their needs of being treated as intrinsically equal, growing, and self-directing. Then, they start to transform this depriving environment into a nourishing one, which we'll explore in further detail in the next chapter. But now, back to Thomas Jefferson.

WHAT WENT WRONG—BEFORE IT WENT RIGHT

It's 1824. Jefferson is satisfied with how the university project—which, recall, he considers essential for the United States as a self-governed country—is advancing. He has compiled an outstanding library and devised the departments and courses, which include ancient and modern languages, philosophy, mathematics, law, and medicine—Jefferson hired the first full-time medical professor in the United States—but no theology, of course. The Jefferson-designed campus, which then Harvard professor George Ticknor called "a mass of buildings more beautiful than anything architectural in New England, and more appropriate to a university than are to be found, perhaps in the world,"[22] has been essentially finished, thanks to a $180,000 loan and a $50,000 appropriation Jefferson obtained from Virginia. And though the rotunda is still in the process of being completed, he entertains there a visiting revolutionary hero, the Marquis de Lafayette, at a lavish dinner. As the university was rushing toward its opening day, all the pieces seemed to be put in place except one—the professors.

To the dismay of John Adams, who teased him for his lack of patriotism, Jefferson wanted only European professors for his university. But the big European names refused to come to what at that time looked like an academic desert. Concerned that his envoy's "return without any professors will completely quash every hope of the institution,"[23] Jefferson had to settle for five younger professors. The bigger compromise, however, was these professors' lack of regard for the university's unique principles of self-government and respect for the students. The worst of them was George Blaetermann, a professor of modern languages, whose lectures involved heated altercations with students. He once knocked a student's hat off, upon which the student punched him.

Recall that Jefferson wanted not only an aesthetically beautiful and academically first-rate university. He also wanted a self-governed institution—an environment opposite to that of Yale, Harvard, and others, which he called "despotic seminaries."[24] Well, what he got by overlooking the European faculty's authoritarian tendencies was worse than the New England colleges' culture—he got the hierarchical culture of European colleges, of which the New England schools were only a copy. The heavy atmosphere maintained by professors, together with draconian restrictions imposed on students after the "drunken fourteen" riot, bred a resentment that soon started to show up in ways much more extreme than the routine soiling of their rooms.

In 1831, another riot broke out. In 1836, students smashed the windows of professors' residences with sticks and stones and fired numerous muskets, leading the faculty to arm itself and flee, along with their families, to the upper floors. In 1838, students attacked a professor's residence yet again, smashing windows and battering down the door. The following year saw more unrest, as two students assaulted the faculty chairman and horsewhipped him in the presence of more than one hundred other students, who did nothing to stop the brutal abuse.

Then came November 12, 1840. On that day two masked students were shooting and making a ruckus on the lawn. The faculty chairman, John A. G. Davis, came out to intervene. When he tried to remove the mask of one of the students, the student shot and fatally wounded Davis. The shock was tremendous—not only within the university but in Virginia and beyond—and the university descended into turmoil.

Jefferson wasn't around to do anything about it—he had died on July 4, 1826, about a year after the university's inauguration and exactly fifty years after the United States' birth. We can't know whether, faced with the evidence that self-government wasn't working, he would have judged his own choices for the university critically. But with hindsight and armed with recent psychological insights, we can say that the institutional environment Jefferson built did not provide nutriments for people's universal needs and thus, students were not self-motivated to take part in the freedom-based project.

Sure, this environment treated faculty as intrinsically equal. For the first time in America—and perhaps in the world—professors had no one above them. Until 1904, when its first president was finally named, the University of Virginia remained self-governed. To this day, UVA's president enjoys much less authority than his counterparts in other universities. The environment Jefferson built also provided all the nutriments for the young professors to grow and to self-direct. As a result, although this self-government was a very unusual way to run an academic institution, the professors supported it fully. Indeed, they even used their freedom of action against one institutional aspect installed by Jefferson they considered unjust—the incentive that tied their salary to how well they succeeded in attracting students into their classes. For reasons we now understand, they rightly perceived this tangible reward as a controlling scheme. They fought against it and, in 1850, got it abolished. But unlike the professors, the students did not find the institutional environment nourishing.

From day one, their professors—used to the authoritarian European universities' ways—did not treat them as equals. And after the "drunken fourteen" clampdown, students were practically infantilized. Throughout this period, students were forced to wear uniforms and to conform to a 6 a.m. wake-up and a 9 p.m. curfew. The pocket money they were allowed was too meager even to afford "a little chicken supper."[25] As we now know, when the need to be treated as intrinsically equal is denied, people can't be self-motivated even if their other two needs—growth and self-direction—are satisfied.

Regarding education and growth, in 1838, facing a lack of instruction in English composition, a group of students launched *The Collegian* magazine, which, under a variety of names, has survived until the present day. And regarding self-direction, although Jefferson founded the university on complete separation of church and state, in 1832 students initiated a movement to raise funds for the employment of a chaplain. The faculty and the board of visitors approved the initiative, and the faculty elected a chaplain each year, but he was paid by the funds collected by the students and had no official connection to the university. Overall, from what we understand today about the appropriate environment for nourishing people's universal needs, the University of Virginia did not succeed at inspiring self-motivation.

But this story is not only an illustration of how a project for a freedom-based organization may fail to get people to join it and make them revolt instead. It's also an illustration of how such a project can be turned around. Because it did eventually succeed—although Jefferson did not live to see it.

Soon after the 1840 killing of the faculty chairman, a distinguished judge, Henry St. George Tucker, was appointed to succeed the slain law professor. Gradually, Tucker became aware of the students' festering resentment toward all the restrictions of their personal freedoms and successfully led the effort, with the faculty, to abolish them. Then, after dismantling the hated rules, Tucker started to build a different basis for relationships between professors and students.

He noted that the faculty always presumed that students were cheating on examinations (and some indeed did). But instead of reinforcing the surveillance, Tucker proposed a revolutionary measure that was very much in the spirit of Jefferson's original vision of student self-government. This measure became known at UVA as the honor system.[26] On a symbolic July 4, 1842, Tucker offered to build trusting relationships with the students: "Resolved, that in all future examinations . . . each candidate shall attach to the written answers . . . a certificate of the following words: "I, A.B., do hereby certify on my honor that I have derived no assistance during the time of this examination from any source whatsoever." The students quickly embraced the principle and assumed total responsibility for the protection of this self-government freedom, and not only in the classroom. Following the Civil War, for example, the honor system expelled students caught cheating at cards, defaulting on payments of debts, and insulting ladies. More than one and a half centuries later, the honor system is still in place, self-governed by students, who, like their ancestors, continue to drink, play cards, and—of course—date, but who respect certain limits that *they*—not the university authorities—impose on themselves.

Tucker's actions offer us two lessons. First, he rebuilt an environment that nourished students' universal needs, and they responded in a way that would make Jefferson proud. Second, failing to build such an environment—something, alas, Jefferson did—leaves people unmotivated to take part in a liberation campaign. For a modern business parallel to the early years at UVA, consider the Danish hearing-aid maker Oticon.

A DANISH MIRACLE

A century and a half after Judge Tucker breathed new life into Jefferson's vision for the University of Virginia, Lars Kolind decided to launch a liberation campaign of his own. His target seemed ideally suited for the purpose—an old, quiet company of medium size, set in its ways yet with tremendous potential for expansion and growth, if only it could shake off the shackles of its past.[27]

Kolind was appointed CEO of Oticon in 1988. Oticon was a leading European maker of hearing aids, but it was threatened by competition and technological change and reluctant to do anything to shake up its comfortable existence. When Kolind arrived at the headquarters on September 1, the company's clubby culture quickly became apparent. He had no trouble finding a parking space: His assigned space, right next to the entrance, was prominently marked by a sign with his name and title already on it. The chairman and the outgoing CEO were waiting by the front door to lead him to the management dining room, where several dozen senior managers welcomed him with champagne, snacks, and speeches.

Kolind soon learned that since its founding in 1904, this family-owned company had had only two CEOs. In order to ensure that Kolind became fully immersed in the company's traditions, the board of directors wanted him to serve as CEO-in-waiting for six months. Kolind didn't think tradition and the old ways were exactly what Oticon needed, so he managed to talk the board down to a one-month transition. And on his way home, he took down the sign that marked his parking spot.

Oticon was in trouble when it brought Kolind in. In 1987, the company had lost $7 million on $52 million in revenue. It was the high-cost manufacturer in its market and yet was still churning out outdated products. Its competitors—Sony, 3M, Philips, Siemens, and others—were quickly moving to digital hearing-aid technology while Oticon was stuck in the analog age. According to Kolind, Oticon's people viewed themselves as the BMW of the industry, but their products looked more like old Volkswagen Beetles in the marketplace. This state of denial was a serious problem, but it wasn't the only one. Oticon's corporate culture was "steeply hierarchical, conservative, and almost aristocratic, with a strong resistance to change," as Kolind described it.

Yet Kolind had come to Oticon to change it. He'd become exasperated with the bureaucratic cultures of other places he'd worked and believed that a company could be rebuilt along radically free lines. He'd vowed to realize his vision if he ever got the opportunity, and this was that opportunity. But first, Oticon had to stop losing money. So, on October 1, 1988, his first day as full-fledged CEO, he announced that all future expenditures—expense reports or any financial commitment besides planned buying of necessary manufacturing supplies—would have to be personally approved by him. Not exactly a liberating first step, to be sure, but even while taking this draconian measure, he added a twist: If he didn't deny an expenditure request within twenty-four hours, it would automatically be approved. In this way, he tried to bring costs under control without creating a huge bureaucratic backlog—the onus would be on him to clamp down on unnecessary expenditures. Even with this liberalizing proviso, the order quickly had an effect. The requirement to apply to the CEO for new spending, together with a few denied requests, produced enough discipline on costs to turn the negative cash flow positive before the year was out.

Simultaneously, Kolind visited audiologists and hearing-aid dispensers to get insight about Oticon's bad image and misguided products. On November 18, 1988, he called a two-day management seminar to devise a new company vision. The old "Leader in hearing technology" turned into "Helping people (with impaired hearing) to live as they wish with the hearing they have." This new vision—admittedly not very inspirational—nevertheless helped refocus the company, leading to the closing of several departments and the laying off of 10 percent of the staff. Sales soon started to grow, the company returned to profitability, and both the board and employees seemed to be happy. But not Kolind.

He performed a thorough analysis of the company's operations, which confirmed his initial intuition: Oticon's "rule-based, departmentalized, hierarchical engineering culture" had to be changed. Kolind wanted a self-directing, innovative company that would stun the world with world-class products.

So, on Christmas Eve 1989, he sent out a four-page memo titled "Think the Unthinkable!" His managers thought it was a joke. But Kolind was serious. He got the board—which perhaps didn't read it too carefully—to approve his plan in principle, then he expanded it to a six-page manifesto and sent it out to all 150 employees in the head office. Its key part is worth quoting at length:

> We will change the concept of a job to better match the talents of each individual. Everyone will have to do more than one job, including something he is not formally qualified to do (multijob).
>
> We will discontinue the current hierarchical departmental

structure and replace it with projects. There will be project leaders to run projects, gurus to ensure a proper professional standard in everything we do, and mentors to help support every employee to do his best. All current job titles will have to go.

Ninety-five percent of all paper should go as well. We will install a state-of-the-art computer network that will allow every one of us to freely choose where to work every day. We will stimulate oral dialog and avoid writing e-memos to each other. Talking is more fun.

We will create an open and inspiring work place with no walls or partitions. There will be plants and trees on wheels, perhaps 500 or 1,000 of them, to move around when we move from one project to another. We will create the most exciting and creative work place in the country. It will be nothing like an ordinary office.

We will all need to understand not only what we do, but also how this fits into the overall picture. If everyone knows that, we will need less conventional management and control. This allows us to spend more time on tasks that benefit the customers.

To sum up: we will all do more of the things we like to do and we are good at. We will get rid of all barriers, and will work as one big team. That will make us more valuable and in turn justify a higher salary.[28]

Then, late in the afternoon on April 18, 1990, he convened a voluntary, unpaid meeting to discuss the note—and 143 out of the 150 employees showed up. After a brief explanation, Kolind asked for questions. A long silence ensued. Finally, one secretary stood up and suggested that they hold a vote on the transformation. Kolind, who probably held his breath at the time, would later write that close to eighty per cent of employees voted in favor of the change—but, the managers, who looked petrified, were opposed. Over the beer and the sandwiches, the ambiance was euphoric. People wanted to make the change happen. It wasn't easy.

Many in senior management were not happy. To mend the situation, Kolind advised those resisting the project to concentrate on running the current business. He added that other employees—those in favor of the change project—would take care of the transformation. Kolind notes that former middle managers hadn't altered their ways, persisting with their traditional activities of managing and controlling their former subordinates. These latter, however, didn't pay much attention and espoused their newfound freedom of action. Faced with all this resistance, Kolind decided to spend some time establishing a common set of company values and management norms. After several days of meetings, the senior management team agreed on eight values. By now, the first three will sound familiar to readers. They were:

- Employees want to be treated as independent individuals who are willing to take responsibility;
- Employees want to develop within their jobs and gain new experience within the company; exciting and challenging tasks are more important than formal status and titles; and
- Employees desire as much freedom as possible, yet accept the necessity of a clear and structured framework.[31]

Senior managers also agreed on specific practices through which they would live by these values. Even so, many did not adhere to them, still believing that the whole thing would just blow over and Oticon would return to being a "normal" company. So Kolind summoned them to his office one at a time and issued an ultimatum: "Choose whether you want to be part of the game or quit." Naturally, the senior managers all agreed—nominally—to play their boss's game.

The next challenge was finding a new head office in which Kolind's vision could be realized. His initial dream was to construct a world-class building right alongside the company's main plant, at the edge of a dramatic and picturesque fjord. The Danish government would even have helped fund the project to promote development on this remote land. It was the sort of idea of which Jefferson might have been proud—except Oticon's employees were less than enthusiastic about moving to the middle of nowhere, 250 miles from Copenhagen. Kolind's next architectural inspiration was a beautiful Renaissance castle already equipped with a modern conference center and, again, support from the regional government. It was, in addition, cheap, but it didn't fly with his staff either: At fifty miles from Copenhagen, it was still too remote from the capital for Oticon's urbanites. Pressed for time, Kolind turned to the classified ads, found an old Tuborg drink factory in a suburb of the capital, and leased it for ten years. The next challenge was information technology.

Every IT vendor said that building a totally paperless office—with all computers linked and all incoming and internal documents electronically stored—was impossible. But like USAA's Robert McDermott two decades before him, Kolind succeeded: Hewlett-Packard and Andersen Consulting (now Accenture) took up the challenge. And to make sure people would use all that technology—only 10 percent to 15 percent of the staff were familiar with PCs—the company bought a computer for each one of them for Christmas in 1990, complete with office software and games, to be used both for work and for leisure. From there, things really got rolling.

People were allowed to organize their own work schedules. The new office furniture consisted of identical drawerless desks that could be used by anyone and rolling caddies to hold a few files and personal items, which could easily be moved to any desk (and to a storage room if a person was traveling). To make the furniture changes easier, the company's old furniture—in particular, senior managers' desks, sofas, lamps, and antique clocks—were put up for auction internally. All were bought up cheaply by employees on one summer day in 1991. Other design features included conference rooms without chairs, and meeting spaces—such as around a coffee bar—also without chairs. A survey had shown that development engineers spent 75 percent of their time on administrative tasks—and meetings. So making people stand for meetings—or at least, not staring at the table but at their colleagues—promised to reduce the time spent in them.

Then, like Jefferson, Kolind decided to show off his project, unfinished though it was. He dubbed it "The Company of the Future" and invited in the media and fellow businessmen. In the week following Kolind's press conference, Danish newspapers and magazines all ran articles on Oticon's "spaghetti organization." Oticon was still several months away from even completing the construction on the office, but the stream of visitors was constant—eventually they would reach five thousand a year.

In the meantime, however, as at UVA, the unfinished project ran out of money. But unlike Jefferson, who successfully appealed to the government of Virginia, Kolind found his reception before Oticon's board unsympathetic—they had begun to question the wisdom of the whole enterprise. So Kolind proposed a different solution: He would raise the money to finish the construction from the employees. It worked: Even the union representatives, after consulting with their base, invested. Most of them, including Kolind, took out personal loans to do so.

Then came the grand opening. On August 8, 1991, to the surprise of Oticon employees, the event was covered not only by the Danish media, but by major international news outlets, too, including CNN. All of them filmed the new building's most spectacular feature: a big glass tube descending from the first floor mail room through the ground floor company restaurant and to the basement recycling container. In the mail room, all incoming mail was scanned and then shredded, "feeding" the glass tube. Through it, the bits of paper fell like snowflakes as a constant reminder that the paperless company of the future wasn't an impossible dream.

But Kolind's vision wasn't manifest only in the almost total absence of paper. In the coming years, Oticon employees would spontaneously launch dozens of new projects and potential new products—at one point, Oticon had seventy such projects under way simultaneously. And in an echo of W. L. Gore & Associates' fluid structure, people could often find themselves leading or participating in three or more of them at the same time. To manage this profusion of innovation and activity, Kolind put in place a Products and Projects Committee to review and monitor everything that everyone was suddenly doing.

The time to market for new products was reduced by 50 percent, and Oticon started to churn out one innovation after another. Just two years after the inauguration of Kolind's office of the future, Oticon was generating half of its total revenue from these innovations. In the summer of 1995, Oticon launched DigiFocus, the world's first all-digital in-ear hearing aid, despite having given its competitors an eight-year head start on digital technology. Sales, which had already doubled between 1990 and 1994, had doubled again by 1999-a 400 percent increase in revenue in one decade, accompanied by double-digit profit margins.

Kolind began to feel that he had succeeded. In 1995, Oticon took over a big Swiss-owned competitor and conducted a successful IPO. At the same time, he spearheaded an international expansion, expanding branch offices in half a dozen other European countries as well as in the United States, Australia, and New Zealand.

But all was not well back at home, despite the short-term successes. Unbeknownst to Kolind, the Products and Projects Committee had become a major source of discontent and frustration within the company. People felt that the committee was micro-managing projects, suspending them or holding them up arbitrarily, and in general not upholding the values propounded by Kolind and parroted by the management. Kolind had created the physical edifice he desired and he had gone some of the way toward freeing Oticon's people. But he absented himself too much from maintaining the new culture. And as a result, he didn't get the early warning signals about simmering employee discontent.

So one day in 1995, the pot finally boiled over. Oticon's employees called a spontaneous meeting to voice their anger. At the meeting, they loudly denounced the constant violation of Oticon's values by the top management. The Products and Projects Committee was singled out for its intrusiveness and seemingly arbitrary behavior. It was viewed by the rank and file as tyrannical and capricious. Employees who had been told they would be trusted believed that they were not being treated as equals, and they demanded changes. The former middle managers who had lost their managerial prerogatives saw their opportunity and joined the calls for change. And the senior managers to whom Kolind had issued his ultimatum—"You're with me or against me"—saw an opportunity to lash out as well. All of them got the changes they were looking for, but these only accelerated the erosion of the culture Kolind had wanted to build.

Following the confrontation, Oticon was divided into three parts according to market segment: mass-market, mid-market, and high performance. This stratification, Kolind would later comment, turned the spaghetti organization into lasagne. The Products and Projects Committee was replaced by the Orwellian-sounding Competence Center. This group of senior managers, far from addressing the complaints directed toward the old committee, doubled down on them, taking upon itself the authority to start new projects and so killing whatever initiative still lay with frontline people. It also started appointing project leaders and constrained their earlier ability to negotiate compensation for project members. The liberation campaign was effectively over.

During this period, according to the people who knew him, Kolind himself became disenchanted, even bored, with the company he had tried to transform. He lingered on for a few years, but shortly before the tenth anniversary of his arrival, he quit.

WHAT WENT ROTTEN IN THE KINGDOM OF DENMARK?

Oticon's case is widely studied in business schools around the world. Whether that's because traditional managers find comfort in the failure of Kolind's grandest ambitions is hard to say. But like Sun Hydraulics—another company popular in business schools—Oticon is more studied than understood. So let's take a closer look at what went wrong.

At the beginning, Kolind did a lot of things right. Indeed, Oticon's liberation campaign has striking similarities with many others in our book. For example, its organization around projects initiated by "natural leaders" is much like Gore's. Its elimination of the middle-management layer is similar to FAVI's approach. Its paperless office is reminiscent of USAA's, and its office layout and design resembles Richards Group and the Finnish company SOL, as we'll see later. Yet, its most fundamental similarity is not with all other liberation campaigns that succeeded but with one that initially did not—UVA.

Like Jefferson, Kolind tried to launch his liberation campaign with senior managers (or professors) who were not convinced of the project or of the need to change their ways. Kolind had seen from his first day that Oticon's senior management enjoyed a clubby, comfortable existence. Even in hard times, they had clung to their privileges. But he did not remove them from their positions of authority. Instead, he made them "an offer that they couldn't refuse," at least openly. Then, as members of the Products and Projects Committee, those same managers didn't behave like the sponsors they had supposedly committed to being, but as the same old "bosses" under a different name.

What's more, they made their decisions with ever-changing criteria and without bothering to explain them to the people affected—like too many "how" managers, they didn't feel that they owed their people those explanations. This was not only disheartening, but it led people to wonder what the company's vision was and what their "charge" was in pursuing it. Moreover, Kolind was officially a member of the Products and Projects Committee, and so some of the blame for its actions was directed at him personally.

In other words, the culture Kolind built had many—even most—of the characteristics of a liberated organization, but it was missing some features that are critical to maintaining freedom in the workplace. Oticon's vision was neither sufficiently clear nor owned by everyone. And critically, neither the CEO nor other key leaders in the company took it upon themselves to ensure that people both understood the company's vision and understood their role in it—their "charge," in other words. The result was both natural and expected: People started to pursue their *own* goals. This often led to pushing one's project at the expense of others for no better reason than it was one's own project, lobbying the Products and Projects Committee for resources and visibility, and the rest. Kolind had wanted projects to compete but what he got instead was the "rule of the jungle," as Vertex's Westphal called it. The Products and Projects Committee, which was supposed to help orient activity toward the company's goals, instead became the locus for lobbying and internal competition—the inevitable higher bureaucratic layer to resolve lower-level conflicts. And the more power it wielded, the more it attracted people's effort and attention, and so distracted from the work they were supposed to be doing. People began to measure their success by their ability to commandeer resources from the committee, rather than by their impact on the company's business or bottom line. As one employee put it, "You end up in situations where you act in some sort of anarchy and steal resources that others control."[32] Employees knew that something had gone wrong, but without a management that was ready to listen instead of tell, they lacked an outlet to express frustrations that could have resulted in a mid-course correction.

It is possible, by the way, that some senior managers *were* listening. However, remembering Kolind's rough treatment early on, they were more likely to hide problems from him than to bring them to his attention—nobody would want to be branded as a "problem" manager. And Kolind himself had been taken up with other things too often to listen to his people and to act as an effective culture keeper. So tensions and frustrations built until the people rose up in open revolt. The culture was discredited. Kolind understood this danger perfectly, in theory. He even wrote, "The more freedom . . . we as a company want to give to staff, the more clarity we must create about mission, vision, strategy, and values."[33] And yet he still failed to maintain this clarity.

The backlash was predictable. Oticon's employees had been promised freedom, but the hierarchy that was shown the door sneaked back in through the window—of the Products and Projects Committee. This loss of control naturally produced a counterstrike against the perceived source of stress—the top management.

People at Oticon had certain trappings of freedom—they could set their own work schedules and move their desks—that is, caddies—anywhere in the company's open space. But when it came to the most important aspects of their work, managers had continued to exercise the power of life-and-death authority over the projects that, in theory, frontline people were supposed to organize their work around.

It is curious, but true, that people who are promised freedom but then denied it—whether they worked at Oticon or were enrolled at UVA in its earliest days—perceive the lack of freedom much more strongly and so behave unpredictably when confronted by it. A person who has no expectation of freedom may, in fact, see their situation as normal and prove more docile than one who has had it offered with one hand and taken away with another. Kolind had, in a sense, released his own monster by promising more than he, as leader, delivered in the end.

Kolind's story is important because a liberation campaign isn't easy to pull off, and Oticon's case shows how even subtle mistakes can grow into serious problems down the road. Of the three universal needs discussed earlier, Oticon fell short most clearly when it came to self-direction, and as with Jefferson's faculty, it was the layer of management between the visionary and the frontlines that short-circuited the nourishing environment. It was Kolind's responsibility, as it was Jefferson's, to listen for the signs of this before they blew up. He failed to act as Oticon's "culture keeper"—a concept we'll explore in chapter 13—and so he left his employees feeling betrayed.

But now let's turn to building an environment that does nourish those needs. Done right, this will lead people to act both on their own initiative and in ways that serve the company's vision. The leaders in the following chapters show that it can be done.

9

FROM MOTIVATION TO
SELF-MOTIVATION, PART TWO

Work and Management Practices That Nourish

ROBERT TOWNSEND MAY have been the first liberating leader to transform a needs-depriving corporate environment into a nourishing one. In 1962, when he became a CEO of Avis, he already had one liberation campaign under his belt from his time as an executive at American Express. There, he had put into practice his radical approach to removing everything that stifles employee initiative. But that was on a smaller scale in American Express's investment and banking division, where essentially everyone worked in the same building in New York. At Avis, he faced a different reality, with about one thousand rental offices— each with several branches—scattered all over the continent. He also faced a sleepy company that had struggled to make a profit for thirteen years without success. Making Avis profitable thus became Townsend's first priority. To make it the top priority of Avis's thousand or so offices as well, he turned each one of them into its own profit and loss center. In itself, this is not an unusual measure. It put the ultimate responsibility for profit making in the hands of the frontline managers and led Avis out of the red—which was Townsend's initial goal and condition to start the company's full liberation. This devolution of responsibility was the first step in making clear who owned which monkeys. But it did not immediately resolve the question of who should get credit for success.

"When Avis finally broke into the black for the first time," Townsend recounted, "our management developed a severe case of 'us' versus 'them'—'us' being the geniuses at headquarters and 'them' being the people in the field in the red jackets who were renting cars and paying our salaries and doing an enormous amount of hard work."[1] That didn't sit well with Townsend's "agricultural" approach—which, to begin with, treats people as intrinsically equal. So he made his first move to build a liberated environment.

At one Monday meeting, he casually made the following announcement: "By the way, we're all going through the Avis school for rental agents at O'Hare Field."

"There were great screams of rage from these busy executive geniuses," Townsend recalled, to which he said, "Listen, it's not necessary. I'm not ordering you to do it. All I'm telling you is, until you go through it with a passing grade, you're not in the incentive compensation plan."[2] And to prove how important he felt this was, he added, "I'm going through it next week."

It wasn't easy. The executives lived in a motel, studied in the afternoon, were tested every evening, did their homework at night, and rented cars to real customers, wearing their "I'm a trainee" buttons all morning. Townsend recalls:

> One morning, I was renting a car at O'Hare and this customer came to the counter. I was taking a long time getting the keys right, processing the car control card, checking the credit card, smiling at the other people in line so they wouldn't drift over to our competitor. And he said, "Will you please hurry up? I'm in a hurry."

And I said, "Give me a break, I'm a trainee."

"Would you tell me how on earth a training program could pass somebody as clumsy and as ignorant as you seem to be?" he said.

And I said, "Well if you want to hear something really sick, I'm the president of the company."

Whereupon he forgave me completely, and said, "Hey, at least you're out here figuring out what's going on. My president never leaves his office."[3]

This—not entirely voluntary—training program for executives transformed the corporate environment. "When we got through that course," explained Townsend, "we were wearing red jackets at headquarters. The 'us' and 'them' thing was history."[4] Forcing his executives a bit to go through the course—with the threat of withholding tangible rewards—was necessary for Townsend. If he wanted to build a free environment, he *had* to transform the executives' arrogant attitude toward Avis's frontline people: It wasn't optional.

You might doubt that simply training executives to do others' jobs would transform their attitudes and, with it, the corporate environment. And you'd be right to be skeptical. Building an environment of equality requires the elimination of *all* of the symbols and practices of "us" versus "them"—reserved parking spaces included. But at the same time, treating people as intrinsically equal is not enough to get them to self-motivate and embrace their freedom and responsibility. Other parts of the environment—its many *work practices*—have to be transformed, too, so that they nourish people's needs for growth and self-direction. At Avis, this work-practice transformation was jump-started by the training program.

While in training, Townsend and the other executives realized that they were asking rental agents "to do an impossible job." Filling in rental agreements by hand was cumbersome and stressful—especially with long lines of clients waiting for their cars (this was in the 1960s). The agreements could not be eliminated—they were an essential component of the car-rental business. But, just as rowing gave way to sails and motors, handwriting gave way to computers. And Avis became one of the first in the car-rental business to install them—in order to reduce the stress on their rental agents. This, in turn, allowed the agents to focus more on their customers' needs and do their most important job, which was to keep the customers coming back.

This was followed by a systematic effort by Townsend and his thousand managers to identify every other work practice that prevented people from doing their best. They created a comprehensive list of questions that left no stone unturned: "What made you mad today?" "What took too long?" "What was the cause of any complaints today?" "What was misunderstood today?" "What costs too much?" "What was wasted?" "What was too complicated?" "What's just plain silly?" "What job took too many people, and what job involved too many actions?"[5] Townsend explained that you don't ask all people all those questions. You try one on one person, then move to another area and try another question on another person. Then, Townsend and his managers got busy removing the ropes and barnacles that prevented people from showing how fast and how far they could go in their boat. This freed them, too, to adjust their sails on the fly when the wind changed.

It is easy to ask for these improvements. It is not easy, but it is necessary, to be rigorous about implementing them. If your company can't remove *all* the work practices that deprive people of growth and self-direction, if it knowingly leaves in place even one—say, mandatory buying from a single, centrally chosen supplier—employers will point to this work practice as an excuse for underachievement. Instead of being *self-motivated* they will be resistant. That way lies the game of dangling extravagant tangible rewards to motivate—bribe—people to do what they are not willing to do or don't believe is possible because of obstacles put in their way.

The good news is that leaders don't have to take care of removing obstacles and solving problems by themselves all the time. They have to cut the ropes and clean the barnacles to get the boat going. Once people see the change, see the boat *really* moving with no one at the helm telling them how to do their jobs, the *natural leaders* will emerge to overcome the new and inevitable obstacles and challenges. Later in this chapter we'll meet a few of these natural leaders.

But what about the boat's helmsman, or company management? It may be objected that, however annoying the helmsman can be, he cannot be simply removed, because the management fulfills the vital role of co-ordinating business activities, of keeping the trains and boats running on time. This line of thinking would seem perfectly reasonable if we hadn't already seen—at Gore, FAVI, and Harley—that the commanding helms-men, the "how" managers, are not the only way to fulfill this role. Beyond the alternative *work practices*—how one accomplishes a task and in what conditions—there also exist alternative *management practices*—how one leads. In order for people to join a liberation campaign, management practices must be rebuilt. And Jacques Raiman, the chairman of GSI, the European leader in outsourcing payroll services, was more aware of that than anyone in France.

FROM HELMSMEN TO NOURISHING LEADERS

Or maybe he wasn't. In 1979, Raiman was not yet thinking of how to transform his managers' practices. Inspired by Townsend's book *Up the Organization*, he dismantled and rebuilt dozens of GSI's work prac-tices—including the filing of financial reports and expense bills. But changing *managers'* behavior was not on his mind back then. Instead, he was busy with a big issue: the conflict-ridden labor relations he had inherited in two newly acquired midsize companies. Jean-François Cot-tin, GSI's human resources director—who was opposed to "managing human resources" and kept his "HR department" to one person, him-self—introduced Jacques Raiman to Yves Tillard, a consultant whose approach appealed to Raiman. Tillard analyzed the labor situation and identified a common cause for tense union-management relations: the "how" management practices. In March 1980, he shared his findings with Raiman and together they developed a plan to change GSI's managers' habits through a series of two-day seminars.

That's right. A seminar. Yes, we've all been to some pointless seminar or "off-site" at which we had to catch one another falling backward to build trust and talk about feelings while secretly thinking a thought that we'd previously believed impossible: "I wish I was back at my desk." Or, as they say in France: "If seminars changed something in everyday practices, it would have been known loooong ago." You'd be fully justified to think the same about the GSI seminars, too—if it was not for all the little ways that they were different.

For starters, Raiman hadn't simply agreed to let Tillard facilitate the seminars at GSI: Raiman, the chairman, also agreed to do his best to help out at each one of them himself. He didn't assist at all of them—just about half, but people expected and were bracing for his presence every time. And the number of those he assisted in—in France, Italy, Spain, Switzerland, the Netherlands, Belgium, Germany, the United Kingdom, and two U.S. states—amounted to 150. That, multiplied by two days, is equal to more than a full year of the company chairman's work time—travel excluded. So there was not much talk in GSI about the chairman who doesn't care about the "pointless" seminars. And when Raiman could not assist at a seminar, either the CEO, Jacques Bentz, or the head of a relevant division went in his place. Plus, there was always a head of the local business unit present. This was the second important difference in GSI's seminars: They were never imposed from on high. Seminars were only organized when the head of the business unit asked for it *and* committed to participate himself. The third special feature is even more impressive. Altogether, during a fifteen-year period, GSI put on three hundred seminars dedicated to changing managers' practices in its different business units and departments.

That last feature shows that Raiman and Tillard did not expect that they could change management practices instantly or even quickly.

People's habits don't change overnight, and they never change if people don't want them to. As Rich Teerlink put it, "People don't resist change; they resist *being* changed."[6] GSI's two-day seminars always ended with the participating managers choosing for themselves what practices they would commit to change. They were not forced to commit to any, but if they did it was made public and followed up on later at another seminar—again with the presence of the head of the business unit and, usually, Raiman or his CEO—to assess the progress. Though some managers chose not to change their ways—and some heads of the business units declined as well—most transformed their "how" habits that were depriving people's needs into leadership practices that nourished them. It wasn't simply the seminars that accomplished this; it was also the extraordinary dedication of the chairman and the CEO—in actions, not in words. It was also the choice given to the heads of the business units to initiate them, the choice given to managers to decide whether to change their practices, and the outstanding scale—in quantity, time, and geography—of these seminars in the company. Raiman retired in 1995 when the company was acquired by ADP, the leading American payroll and human-resources outsourcing firm. But the seminars are still running at ADP-GSI for new managers and employees.

Harley-Davidson used different sorts of seminars to modify its "how" culture, ones facilitated by consultants who taught top managers to stop pretending to listen, stop being manipulative in debates, and so on. In both companies, the format was dictated by their size and their preexisting organizational structure. At smaller companies, managers can be educated directly by their superiors—even over dinner—to adopt nourishing habits. That's what Bill Gore did in the early days of his company.

DEVELOPING NOURISHING
LEADERS RIGHT AWAY

Although Bill Gore's inspiration for his start-up's freedom environment came from DuPont's R&D Skunk Works, he wasn't looking simply to create great working conditions for researchers and engineers.[7] W. L. Gore & Associates was a small industrial company facing the typical challenges of production, sales, recruitment, growth, and profitability. But Gore knew that success would come from self-motivated people taking daily initiatives to meet these challenges—not from supervisors. Management's role—as he envisaged it—was to act in the service of the rest of the people and to nourish their needs. It wasn't easy, though. Some Gore supervisors didn't care about the universal needs of people but rather about drafting policies or skimping on work conditions and equipment. But unlike most companies—including DuPont—Gore did not translate these challenges into a problem such as, "What is the optimal *managerial structure* to run and coordinate all these business activities?" Instead, he stuck to its creative redefinition: *"What kind of leaders should we have to get people to self-motivate to run and coordinate these business activities by themselves?"*

Bill Gore knew that "how" managers' and supervisors' practices do not make people self-motivated to build a freedom-based environment and do their best, day in and day out. After Gore stumbled upon manager Les Lewis's "formula for failure" of *not* caring about people's needs, he started monthly Socratic dialogue dinners with his supervisors. Once it appeared that supervisors were changing their habits, Gore abandoned both managerial titles and the authority attached to them. Supervisors became nourishing leaders. But that was not enough.

In 1961, as the company's sales of their only product at the time—Teflon-coated wires and cables—was picking up, Gore looked for ways to expand their sales network. This was not long after the company had moved from Gore's basement into a small plant up the road, where it still operates. That same year, Burt Chase joined the fifty employees at Gore. Right out of college, he didn't know what he wanted to do and started as a product inspector checking that the cables' and wires' insulation was sound. He hadn't been at that long when Bill Gore approached him and said, "We're interested in trying our own salesperson. Would you be interested in going to California?"

"I don't have any experience in California. I don't know the customers. I don't have any sales experience," Chase started to reply.

"Well, you know, you can learn, you can figure it out. The question is, Are you interested in this kind of an opportunity?" Gore said.

"OK. That sounds really great to me," said Chase. "When do you want me to go?"

"That's kind of up to you. Why don't you figure out when you should go," replied Gore in his typical, never-telling-what-one-should-do style.

"What else do I need?" Chase continued to probe.

"You've got to figure out what else you need and how you're going to go about this," was all Gore provided as an answer or, rather, nonanswer.[8]

And Burt Chase—because he liked sales and was supported by the company's nourishing environment—indeed went to California "to figure out" his own answers to his own questions.

"That's a formula for failure," you may think. Sending out a rookie—in sales and in management, a couple of years out of college, to a big region, remote from headquarters, to "figure out" his answers sounds like an irresponsible decision on the part of Bill Gore. But there's more. Bill Gore knew that Chase had an interest in sales, but his credentials in the field were something short of stellar. When he'd joined Gore, he'd let it be known that he'd previously applied for a salesman position at several insurance companies—and failed the sales tests.

With all that in mind, "formula for failure" may not do justice to Gore's assignment for Chase. "Recipe for disaster" might seem more like it. But Gore was not, primarily, concerned with building a managerial sales structure in California, and so he wasn't seeking an expert manager to put on top of it. No, whether it was sales in California or production in Delaware, Bill Gore was looking for nourishing leaders, not managers who would tell people "how" to do their jobs. As he didn't have many such leaders in his small start-up, he had to cultivate some himself. He was ready to accept the risk and demonstrate the patience needed to develop them. Burt Chase soon tested both.

After he succeeded in getting the sales business off the ground for the western half of the United States, Chase realized he needed more people to keep it growing. So one day, he phoned Bill Gore.

"I have no experience at all [in finding people]. What should I do? Help! Send me somebody," Chase said.

"Well, you know, I don't have anybody to send you. Why don't you just hire somebody," Gore replied.

"How do you do that?" Chase wondered.

"Why don't you figure it out? You know how people get jobs and such things. Figure out how to hire." As you may have noticed, "figure it out" was a favorite refrain of Gore's.

There's no question that Gore was taking a risk on Chase, especially given his discouraging results on the insurance sales tests. He could have botched the whole project (he didn't). The alternative—taking Chase's "monkey," telling him how to hire and how to run operations—would have traded the risk of Chase's making mistakes for the certainty that he would neither grow into his new role nor take ownership of it. What's more, if Bill Gore practiced "how" management with Chase, that would show Burt Chase how to treat the team he was to assemble out west. According to Chase, in a future leader, Bill Gore was expecting "the capability but not experience." Gore did not offer leadership roles to people he did not think capable of assuming them. Yes, Chase had failed those insurance company tests, but Gore no doubt felt that they were measuring the wrong things. The fact that Chase had taken them showed that building a sales team was something he *wanted* to do, which Gore likely saw as more important than Chase's thinking he knew how to do it (especially since he didn't). Gore, according to Chase, was "giving you confidence, and saying 'You're going to get a new experience, it will help you grow, help you be stronger and if you have to hire somebody else, you will learn how to do it more effectively, more efficiently. . . . Figure out how to train them and get them some experience.'

"And," Chase clarified, "there was an expectation, 'Please communicate with us, tell us what you're doing, tell us what's happening out there. We need to know, because if there is help [required] . . . we need to know about it. We need to know when we should come out and visit, and when one of our technical people should come out and visit the customer with you. . . . Use us to help gather the information you need, but then you make your decision; don't turn it over to us.'" In other words, Gore didn't want to feed Chase answers, but he didn't want him "out of sight, out of mind" either. The headquarters was there to provide help—but not to take his monkeys off his back.

As Chase developed into a leader within Gore, the business that he'd been sent west to build grew. At a certain point, Chase got the idea that many of his prospects and clients expected to see the magical word "manager" on his business cards instead of the simple "associate" that was on everyone's cards at Gore, in accordance with Bill Gore's prohibition on titles in the company. On his next trip to headquarters, he explained the situation to Bill Gore, outlining why he believed his lack of a title hurt sales, and asked for help: He wanted Gore to allow him to put the title "regional manager" on his cards. That request exhausted Bill Gore's patience. Chase received a rare lecture from Gore—which lasted half an hour, according to Chase—about titles and how most of the time they exaggerate one's capability.

"The word 'manager' just doesn't tell you anything," Chase recalled Gore telling him. "What do you manage, where are your strengths? Is it leadership, administration, organization, planning, analysis?" Bill Gore continued to grill Chase. "You're telling me you're good at all of those if that is my expectation of you as a manager?" Receiving no argument from Chase, he concluded, "I have other people that I need that are good at some of these things," and he named people that he had to rely on to do certain aspects of "management."

In the end, despite the clear demonstration that he "didn't like the word 'manager,'" Gore said to Chase: "You can do what you want, just . . . don't . . . bring that card around here. If you decide to put that stuff on your card, I don't want to see the card. I don't want anyone else to see the card. It's for the marketplace only."

"And so," Burt concluded, "I put 'regional manager' . . . on the damn cards."

Help received and case closed? Not so fast.

What about that "damn"? It hinted that Bill Gore's lecture had had an effect. Chase still thought he needed the cards, but now he wasn't any happier about it than Gore was.

"'Regional manager' seemed kind of harmless," explained Chase. "But then . . . as an experienced person now, I was helping to articulate the culture. . . . As a role model . . . I wanted to practice the culture. I wanted other people to practice what we want to do and I've got a title on my card [that got] in the way."

That was the solution Gore hoped Chase would find by himself, the type of nourishing leader he hoped Chase would develop into. And though Gore took a risk and needed plenty of patience, Burt Chase proved he was worth it. "We were a no-titles organization by Bill Gore's definition and it took this example to really prove it to me," Chase explained. But then Chase delivered the real punch line: "I realized that it wasn't just as an associate [for my colleagues] that I shouldn't have this title; it really didn't serve me well in the marketplace anyway." A "manager" title, Chase explained, didn't just make others feel inferior. It also prevented him from nourishing their growth "because the way you develop relationships, truthful, honest, open, frank relationships," Chase continued, "is to get to know somebody, get to know them for what they know, so that they can take advantage of your strengths and what they know about you; you've got to talk to each other, so it's not the title on the card that gives them that information, it's the conversation that gives them that information."

Bill Gore's nourishing leadership had won Chase over and made him enthusiastic not only about taking part in building a freedom-based environment in the company, but also about developing into a nourishing leader himself. From a "simple associate" Chase became a *nourishing leader* who practiced in his new job the management practices that fully satisfied his own people's needs to be treated as equals, to grow, and to self-direct. But this was also an illustration of something else: Chase's story is also one of a "simple associate" who became a *natural leader*, who took responsibility for solving problems that business situations demanded.

Bill Gore's approach for growing natural leaders was "to take a chance and give somebody an opportunity" to lead, said Chase. If you took that opportunity out of a person's hands, he wouldn't be self-motivated to take part in building a freedom-based environment—or for leading the business.

It worked out fine for Burt Chase. He spent all forty years of his professional career at Gore, assumed more and more leadership responsibilities, became a self-appointed theorist of Gore's culture, and eventually wrote a book on it. It was Chase—though he has been retired for some time already—whom Gore's PR person appealed to in order to explain to us the company's culture and its emergence. Not a bad career for a person who failed sales tests before joining Gore.

Here, by the way, is one test Chase failed to pass in an insurance company, as he recounted:

"If you walked into a potential client's office and the receptionist said he's busy right now, but you could see through the door that he was in there, sitting at his desk, would you find a way to skip the receptionist and talk to this person?" he was asked.

"No way," answered Chase. So his interviewers concluded that he was not aggressive enough.

Bill Gore saw something in Chase that the insurance salesmen didn't. Chase would prove him right in spades.

All organizations, from start-ups to *Fortune* 100 companies, have business issues that require attention. Most formulate a response by asking, "Which manager should we assign to take care of the situation?"

Not liberated companies. Wary of managers who—perhaps—will grab the helm, "take care of the situation," but forget to satisfy the needs of the people who are part and parcel of a sustainable solution, liberated companies creatively redefine the problem as: *"How can we help a person concerned with a business situation to take the lead in it naturally?"*

THE COMING OF THE NATURAL LEADERS

Harry Quadracci, Quad/Graphics' CEO, and his brother Tom—a co-founder and Harry's eventual successor—also understood how to nourish natural leadership. Quad/Graphics was started in 1971 as a small, Pewaukee, Wisconsin-based magazine printer. After a slow first decade, the company began to grow quickly. To ensure high-quality printing, it invented sophisticated equipment of its own over the years. Rather than keep its innovations to itself, Quad set up its QuadTech division to sell this equipment, even to its competitors. Harry Quadracci believed in the benefits of feeling your competition breathing down your neck.

Tom Quadracci served as QuadTech's first CEO. In the early 1990s, Karl Fritchen was Tom's young manager of Asia-Pacific sales operations. Fritchen's leadership opportunity came in Japan, where QuadTech had always worked with local distributors to sell their products. One day, on the eve of a trade show, Fritchen discovered in a local English-language newspaper that their distributor had gone bankrupt. The show's organizers promptly closed the QuadTech booth with yellow tape, fearing non-payment. The first thing Fritchen did was wire money from the United States to the show organizers so he could gain access to the booth. Then, during the weeklong show, Fritchen met with different companies willing to represent QuadTech printing equipment in Japan. But he was not convinced. So Fritchen picked up the phone and called Tom Quadracci, his boss, in Pewaukee, Wisconsin.[9]

"Tom, I think we should put our own office in here," he said. "What happened with our distributor happened to a lot of people caught financing projects when the bubble burst and they were unable to pay. I think that others may be in the same situation." Fritchen then added one more argument against local distributors: "Here, if they sell one of our products to Mitsubishi, they can't sell it to Toshiba. So if you link up with one, you're missing a whole other part of the market."

"OK," replied Tom. "Speak to a couple of business consultants, and find out what's involved."

Fritchen did, and every single consultant he talked to advised him against establishing an independent distribution network in Japan. Fritchen put together a report, sent it back to Pewaukee, and called his CEO again to debrief.

"What do you think?" asked Tom Quadracci.

"I still think we should start up our own office," replied Fritchen. "I know that all the data says the opposite of speaking directly to our customers. But I'm convinced that they'll support us. We should do this. We've got a great reputation of Quad/Graphics knowing the print market."

"Hang on a minute," said Tom Quadracci, and put Fritchen on hold. A minute later, he said, "Karl, I've got Harry on the phone. I want you to outline to Harry what you just told me."

Being in sales for the past four years and therefore constantly on the road, Fritchen had never met Harry Quadracci. Yet he repeated his arguments in exactly the same way.

"OK, sounds like a good idea," said Harry Quadracci. "I want you to stay in Japan, find office space, hire staff, and then when you're all done, come back to the board and explain why we did this."

"He didn't say, 'Put together a plan, present it to the board, get approval, then go back and do this,'" Fritchen later told us. That was the reaction he would have expected at another company. "My previous employer was so radically different that I just fell in love with this place immediately when I walked in."

Unlike the quiet Bill Gore, whose discontent seldom translated into lecturing, Harry Quadracci was extremely—and frequently—temperamental. One of the things that would set him off was when, instead of helping leaders to emerge naturally, an outside person would be called in. Steve DeBoth, a relatively new plant manager, found this out the hard way.[10] Soon after he had hired an outside candidate for a customer-service-representative job, he got a call from Harry Quadracci.

"I heard you think you hired someone," his boss said.

DeBoth explained that he needed an experienced person and found a woman who had already resigned from her previous company.

"How could you?" Harry Quadracci asked angrily. "Do you know that that job is one of the most coveted in the company by all the folks who are working on the manufacturing floor? How could you take that opportunity away from them?" Then, after he calmed down a bit, Quadracci explained, "Do you know how many tens of millions of dollars I have spent in lost productivity because I didn't hire an experienced pressman and let a second pressman learn how to run the press? Don't you think I know what it costs me? Here, you go ahead and take an opportunity away from them. Don't do it again."

DeBoth never repeated the mistake, and later said, "He was so angry because what drove him was providing opportunity for people. He really got his joy from seeing someone do something they couldn't do years or months before, watching them grow."

Bill Gore and Harry Quadracci had different—even opposite—temperaments. But they both created environments that helped people closest to a business situation develop into natural leaders. These environments also helped natural leaders develop into nourishing leaders who enhanced others' self-motivation. We saw this with Burt Chase as well as Karl Fritchen: Since the Quadracci brothers helped Fritchen become a leader, he was willing to do the same for others: "I've lived those experiences [of being trusted to take the lead]. The feeling you get as an employee to have that happen to you, you want all your employees to have that same type of feeling and commitment to your organization." Today Fritchen is the CEO of QuadTech himself.

Of course, what liberating CEOs like Gore and the Quadracci brothers do is only one way to facilitate the natural emergence of leaders. At Gore, experienced associates—called sponsors—direct younger colleagues to areas whose needs are a good fit with their skills and inclinations; it is then up to the individuals to prove to the people working in that field that they can be useful. "When I sponsored them," Burt Chase recalled, "I gave them a list of names, and I said, 'Why don't you go meet these people and talk to them about your experience, where you've been, and find out what they're doing, what their business is. Take a couple months to do this. And I'll hear from them, and I'll hear from you. And maybe we can then decide where you might make a commitment, where you might start.'"[11]

At FAVI, work team members simply decide among themselves whom they deem best to become their next leader. Back at Gore, anyone who's interested in initiating and leading a project can start doing so while continuing in his current role. If he succeeds—as a leader—in attracting enough followers, he can gradually migrate to that new role, as we saw Dave Myers do in developing Elixir guitar strings in chapter 1. At FAVI again, it goes even further. If nobody emerges to lead an opportunity, the company will not convene a meeting to search for an interested person. Instead, because no leader has naturally emerged, the opportunity will be deemed not worth pursuing. Here is how Rich Teerlink summarized a similar approach at Harley-Davidson: "I have a very simple philosophy: If a decision has to get made, it will get made. [I often heard] 'We've got to get this thing done.' Why?. . . If we [the leaders] just let things go, it might solve itself. We don't have to intercede. Whose problem is it? Is it my problem or is it someone else's problem?"[12]

You may say that this laissez-faire attitude is all well and good in flush times, but can this approach possibly be maintained in a crisis? If there is no person concerned with the situation and emerging as a natural leader to take care of it, shouldn't the people ultimately responsible for the company grab the helm and tell others what to do? A crisis presents a sore temptation to reassert control and "do something."

But recall one of the reasons you gave up control in the first place: Those who have the best information to judge the severity of the situation and the best available solutions are the men and women *on the spot*. In "how" companies, their knowledge is ignored because the upper echelon believes it knows better. But in a freedom-based company these people and their knowledge are trusted. If they think their efforts and company resources are better spent elsewhere, their opinion is highly regarded and most often followed. Recall Vertex. Jeff Westphal first grabbed the helm and wanted everyone to redouble their efforts to salvage a failing project. But then he changed his management style and listened to people who had superior knowledge about the field. One of them emerged as a natural leader and helped to reorient the company's resources toward a new, ERP-based software project. This saved Vertex and formed the basis of its continuous sales growth for years to come. Top managers in a crisis do not suddenly become omniscient. Indeed, grabbing the helm and trying to right the ship may well exacerbate the problem by cutting the leadership off from vital information.

AN OPPORTUNITY NO ONE SAW

Perhaps the most dramatic illustration we've heard of a person who saw a business opportunity—to win a huge client—and took a natural leadership role in it happened at GSI, whose liberating leader, Jacques Raiman, you've already met. In this situation, nobody in the company thought to grab the helm simply because nobody—except one employee—ever saw this opportunity.

One day in the early 1990s, Jacques Szulevicz,[13] a salesman for GSI, learned by chance—through friends at other companies—that Disney, which was building their European theme park and resort just outside Paris, was organizing a bidding contest to outsource their information systems. Szulevicz immediately thought that this could be a huge opportunity to win a client with a worldwide reputation—a first for GSI. He told Jacques Raiman about it and got strong encouragement. However, while trying to obtain the bidding details, Szulevicz received disappointing news: The deadline for submission was over. Annoyed at having just painted the great prospects for the deal to Raiman, he decided not to give up.

Szulevicz learned that Price Waterhouse was organizing the bidding for Disney. After several calls, he tracked down Robert N. in London, who was in charge of organizing the bidding, and gave him a call to explain.

"You sound very nice, Jacques," Robert replied. "But the deadline has passed."

"Look, you have nothing to lose," Szulevicz continued. He turned the conversation to London and the life there. Quickly learning that Robert loved great food, Szulevicz offered a proposition: "I'm coming. I'm coming to see you and to invite you for lunch. You have nothing to lose and you'll have at a minimum a good lunch." Robert agreed, perhaps forgetting the famous adage most often attributed to Milton Friedman: "There is no such thing as a free lunch."[14]

So, without asking for anybody's permission or authorization, Szulevicz arrived in London and hosted Robert for lunch. Szulevicz was pleasantly surprised that Robert spoke very good French and was married to a French woman. The small talk was going nicely as they enjoyed good appetizers and wine. And then came the main course.

"Look, Robert," Szulevicz said. "I'm doing this not only for me but also for you."

"How's that?" asked Robert, surprised.

"You organized an international bidding, right?" began Jacques. "You invited all the biggest companies, including the French leaders, right? There are three leaders in France: EDS, IBM, but"—Jacques paused—"you forgot the third: GSI."

"Yes, but we took the biggest European companies," Robert replied, in an attempt to justify his choice.

"You are right," Szulevicz continued. "But may I add that we are number one in Europe in payroll outsourcing?" After allowing this information to sink in, he concluded: "So you see, Robert, we are in the same boat now. Disney is a major client for you. You can't do this to them." Szulevicz's call for help didn't go unnoticed by Robert, who by now had realized Milton Friedman's wisdom.

"Look, Jacques," Robert started. "I'd like to help you, but you know how rigorous the Americans are. I will give you the name of the head of the Euro Disney Project. Only he can reopen the bidding."

Szulevicz thanked him, of course, but asked Robert to phone the Disney executive in advance and prepare him for his call. Back in Paris, Jacques called the man responsible and explained his case.

"Look, I'd like to help you," the executive, briefed by Robert, began. "But this type of decision is very serious at Disney. Only the Euro Disney president here in Burbank can do that. You should get hold of him." And he gave Szulevicz the name.

Reaching the top guy wasn't easy, of course, but after several calls Szulevicz got him on the line.

"Sorry for my French accent," Szulevicz said, and proceeded to explain his case.

"I appreciate your perseverance," replied the president, perhaps forewarned about Szulevicz's determination. "But I don't think I can help."

"You know, I know Disney very well," Szulevicz continued, not giving up. "It would really be a dream for us." And to prove his knowledge of Disney, he added: "Make a dream a reality! I implement your slogan."

"I can't see how," said the president.

"Mr. President, I propose a deal to you. If I teach you things you don't know about Disney, will I earn credit in your eyes?" Szulevicz asked, only to hear hearty laughter from the man, who had a twenty-five-year career at Disney.

"OK, you got it," said the president.

"Great. Mickey was not called Mickey at the beginning," Szulevicz offered.

"How was he not called Mickey?" replied the surprised president.

"No. He was not called Mickey," Szulevicz started to explain. "You know that Walt Disney was working in advertising?"

"I know that," said the president.

"And I will tell you even more. It was then, in the 1920s, when he did this mouse drawing. It had no ears, no shorts. And the first mouse was named Mortimer; it was called Mickey much later," said Szulevicz.

"You're sure?" asked the president, increasingly excited.

"It's our deal, Mr. President," Szulevicz replied.

"Jacques, I'll verify this point, and if you're right, you'll hear from me," said the president, ending the conversation. Soon, Szulevicz's telephone rang.

"Jump on the plane. We'll figure out how to meet," Szulevicz heard from the other end of the line. From this, he understood that the president envisaged reopening the bidding.

Szulevicz booked the next flight to Los Angeles, then ran to announce the good news to his chairman, Raiman, who was in a meeting. Raiman listened, erupted in applause, and then turned to the others and said, "He's a great salesman!"

Szulevicz left for Disney's Burbank, California, headquarters and came back with an opportunity to bid for Euro Disney's information systems business. For GSI, this meant a huge investment simply to compile the RFI (request for information) and show how great GSI was in a preliminary "beauty contest" before it would even be officially invited to bid. This demanded significant resources and at that moment, the company's executives split into two groups. One faction declared it a folly; GSI had absolutely zero chance of winning against EDS or IBM. The others said, "Why not?" Chairman Raiman sided with the second group and gave Szulevicz his support once again: "We'll do it. It's worth a try."

Thus, Szulevicz was back on the field, though this time he needed a team. He gathered twenty IS specialists from the toughest project he had won for GSI: operating IS for a steel giant in the French smokestack industrial north. "They would start every day at 6 a.m. and lived in a region where there was nothing to do but work and work," Szulevicz said later. "I couldn't help with this situation, and when visiting them would take them for a good meal, to have a good time, to provide moral support for them. So I decided that all these guys who had sweated there would now go to Florida for three weeks. As a salesman, I had no formal authority to pick them but I just did it. And they became strongly dedicated, with a real will to fight for this contract."

Despite having no formal authority, Szulevicz became not only a natural leader of a business opportunity to win a big contract but also a nourishing leader of the people he enlisted into the effort.

After the U.S. beauty contest, Szulevicz rolled out the decisive—though unofficial—contest in France. He soon learned that Euro Disney had a lot of difficulties, unsurprisingly, with the Kafkaesque French local political authorities and government regulating bodies. So Szulevicz organized a cocktail party in a fancy hotel and, using his personal network, invited all the concerned mayors, administrators, and Euro Disney executives. "Imagine," he commented, "the surprise of the Disney executives, who for months had tried to get in touch with this or that French official, and here I am introducing these guys to them? Don't ask the cost of the event!" Why would he do that? "I wanted to show them that if we worked together I could help with the most intricate challenges of running their company here in France." The sideshow can sometimes be more important than the main show, particularly if the sideshow is French.

Running against EDS, the uncontested number one provider of IS outsourcing, GSI was like a 180-pound French NBA rookie (say, Tony Parker, drafted in 2001) defending against the 330-pound Shaquille O'Neal, the most dominating center of his time in the NBA. Szulevicz had to find something other than a frontal challenge. A huge fan of cartoons—recall his knowledge of Disney history—he had his "Eureka!" moment: Instead of writing a formal document, he would make a cartoon in which the viewer discovers GSI and its proposal like a visitor to a

Disney theme park. When he announced his plan to the executive board, the head of finance, who until now had put up with all of Szulevicz's extravagant expenses, exploded. He was now convinced that all this fuss would never lead to a contract with Disney. But Szulevicz persevered and found a great creative cartoonist—whom he paid only his costs, with a promise of a share of future revenues if GSI won the contract, in order to appease the head of finance. He got what he believed was a really great film, sent it to Disney, and waited.

Soon, the verdict came: As expected, Texas-based EDS won, getting 75 percent of the $300 million a year contract; but second place went to . . . GSI, which got 25 percent. Szulevicz later learned that his assistance in France and the creativity of the cartoon proposal convinced Disney that GSI could be both a valuable and resourceful partner.

So, exhilarated and extremely proud of himself, Szulevicz ran to announce the great news to Raiman. The chairman listened calmly, lighting—as he often did—a cigar.

And then Raiman said, "*I want it all.*" Not in French—"*Je le veux entier*"—but in English, so that the symbolic impact wouldn't be missed. Szulevicz couldn't believe his ears. Here he is, announcing the biggest contract ever for GSI with the biggest client the firm had ever landed, and his chairman was not happy. But there was an even unhappier player in this story than GSI's chairman: EDS. And the giant showed its frustration. Imagine if the slam-dunking Shaquille O'Neal was blocked by rookie Tony Parker and fell on the floor in front of his hometown crowd.

"EDS was extremely pretentious," Szulevicz said later. "Great technicians, huge resources, but very bad salesmen. In fact, they never won a bidding contest against GSI." But that was later. In the meantime Szulevicz was back in the game looking for a way to "win it all." Being a Frenchman, he continued to offer Euro Disney executives his vast connections to help with any problems they experienced running their activities in France, something EDS was not able to do. Moreover, having built a strong relationship with Euro Disney's key executive assistant, he'd learn about the problems and offer help even before the executives asked for it. He then expanded his assistance to "concierge" services. A big follower of the theater and music scene in Paris, he helped the Americans get tickets to the best shows and tried to spend time with them so that "they didn't feel lonely in Paris." Through his exchanges with these executives he also learned that there was some discomfort between Euro Disney and EDS, because EDS insisted on imposing its preferred technical solutions on its client. Then, big news broke: Euro Disney's chief operating officer in charge of IS outsourcing, Larry Sullens, had been short-circuited by EDS, which had been unhappy with Sullens's choices and had complained to his superiors. Moreover, knowing that Sullens was under pressure to finish everything before opening day, EDS was pushing him to drop GSI in order to accelerate and simplify certain clauses of the contract, which was still in negotiation. The COO was both furious—"cuckolded," according to Szulevicz—and pushed to the wall, which made Szulevicz's day.

Szulevicz quickly invited Sullens to lunch. Somewhere between the main course and dessert Jacques touched upon the sensitive issue.

"I'll be honest with you: EDS is our competitor so I'm talking as an interested party. But you won't be able to work with them," he said.

"Why?" asked Larry, intrigued.

"Because, one, they behave badly with their French suppliers," Szulevicz said, planting the first doubt. "For example, they had a serious row with all the hotels in the [Euro Disney] resort. I don't know if you realize what it takes to work well with French suppliers. Two, EDS will have to hire and manage French people here. It's not simple to deal with French labor."

"You're right, but what can I do?" asked Sullens, giving Jacques an opening to detail his suggestion.

Lunch ended. Sullens called his Burbank headquarters and explained to his superiors that he was experiencing serious difficulties and delays with the main contractor, EDS. On the other hand, the second contractor, GSI, was doing a great job, always helpful and resourceful. It could be useful to reopen the bid and allow GSI to run for the whole project. The American boss asked to see GSI. Sullens swiftly passed this news to Szulevicz, prompting him and another colleague to jump on yet another Paris-L.A. flight.

Once there, Szulevicz met a group of executives and explained, "You asked us to come, but I want to say that you have nothing to lose." Szulevicz began with his favorite opening: "The fact that you show EDS that you're meeting another supplier proves that you are not stuck, that you have leverage over them. So it will make them more flexible. But, as far as GSI is concerned, we'll fight with all the energy you know we have. You'll receive a great proposal. At a minimum, you'll get better prices and better conditions, but most important, you won't have your hands and feet tied."

"This is fine, but it's impossible that in one month you could catch up with the contract clauses already negotiated with EDS during an entire year," the U.S. boss countered.

"Well, you don't know me. I'll make it work," Szulevicz replied. He picked up the phone and called Chairman Raiman, putting the loud-speaker on.

"Hello," Szulevicz said. "I'm here with our Disney colleagues who have a question: Do you think we'll be able to make up the backlog in the negotiation process we have with regard to EDS? Can GSI dedicate the resources so that in one month we catch up?"

"Sure. We can do that," Raiman replied, and wished everyone good luck.

The Disney executives were clearly impressed that Szulevicz could call his chairman at home late in the evening Paris time and get a response like that. Seeing their reactions, he added, "We'll book a suite in Prince de Galles in Paris for one month and will iron out everything there."

"This would really surprise me," the U.S. boss replied. He liked this posh Parisian hotel on the Champs Elysées very much but was always frustrated when trying to book there; the hotel was full months in advance—a frustration Szulevicz was aware of from his Euro Disney sources.

"Yes, we'll start with booking you at Prince de Galles and move from there. We'll work day and night and get it done," Szulevicz repeated confidently.

Back in Paris, Szulevicz dropped by his chairman's office.

"We have a chance if we do this and that and that," as he detailed all the things he envisaged to nail down the contract with Euro Disney, Prince de Galles included.

"You've got some nerve, haven't you?" reacted Raiman.

"We have to go for it," Szulevicz said, and got his chairman's nod.

"He'd always accept my initiatives," Szulevicz later told us. "He trusted me. And it was damn important. It redoubled my energy when he'd say 'I trust you' with committing the company, so much of its money and all. You fight then with such energy."

So after booking the Prince de Galles through a connection, Szulevicz and his two colleagues arrived every morning at 7 a.m. and worked with their Disney counterparts in a suite till 2 a.m. They even decided to eat only sandwiches when hungry, a revolutionary initiative for French businesspeople, though easily accepted by their American counterparts. Szulevicz made a point of calling Raiman every time there was any doubt in the eyes of the Americans so they could hear the full support he had from his chairman and the authority he enjoyed.

In reality, Szulevicz did not have full authority on every detail and would coordinate some contract elements behind the scenes with Raiman and a special task force at GSI. And Szulevicz, like any other GSI employee, had to behave according to the company's "rules of the game," which had been in effect since Tillard's seminars in the early 1980s. One of these rules was *the duty to consult* for any decision with serious impact on the company (recall Gore's similar *waterline decision* principle). However, after the consultation, it was up to Szulevicz to make a decision, to inform the consulted persons about it, and to assume responsibility for the outcome—good or bad. But the fact that Szulevicz could decide many things by himself and get an OK by a simple call to his chairman not only moved things along quickly but also made a big difference in the eyes of the Euro Disney negotiators. Compared with the slowness of EDS, which had to refer every single point up through their hierarchy and wait days for an answer, GSI's nimbleness was impressive.

The month ended and the contract was ready, with the stamps and signatures on all the clauses validated by both parties. GSI became eligible to bid for the whole Euro Disney IS business. In the end GSI "won it all," just like Chairman Raiman had asked Szulevicz to do—all $300 million a year. The contract continued years after both men had left the company.

Could Szulevicz have failed? Of course he could have. But this story would still be valuable because it illustrates the kind of initiative and risk taking that is possible for a natural leader in freedom-based companies but unthinkable in "how" companies. It is an example of a business situation in which an opportunity was felt by only one person in the company, the salesman Jacques Szulevicz. And it was felt at the gut level, not through calculations. As he remarked to us later: "From the management control point it was a fundamental error and if a controller had said to me, 'Jacques, you're completely crazy' he would have been right; I would never be able to rationally convince him. All I had was just a feeling." Yet at freedom-based GSI he could act on his intuition and give it a chance in the sales game where—as the saying goes—"One has to fail often in order to succeed fast." And the fact that he was operating essentially outside of the company, as a salesman, didn't change much. EDS's sales staff was doing the same, but they still had to call and get approval through their hierarchy for every single move they wanted to make. That stifling environment made them ultimately lose not only this but every future bidding contest they had against GSI.

Szulevicz knew all that. When EDS fired their sales staff for losing to him, the company called Szulevicz and offered him a "treasure"—as he put it—to come to EDS as a salesman. He refused. "I love money. I love it very very much," explained Szulevicz. "I collect beautiful objects. But here, I didn't hesitate a second. Morally, when I shave in the morning, I like to be able to look myself in the mirror." He added, "I never had any trust in EDS," reminding us of his earlier observations about the company's stifling hierarchy, which he used against them. "You accept a double or a triple salary—and others besides EDS offered them, too—but then you leave after one year because culturally you're different and it can never work. It's like, you know, me willing to spend a night with Miss World. But from that to marry her?"

In fact, Szulevicz's decision to decline the offer, as well as his overall natural leadership, fit into the "rules of the game" followed by everyone at GSI. GSI's CEO at the time, Jacques Bentz, once commented that at GSI "There are as many bosses as there are employees."[15] Jacques Szulevicz's company provided him with an environment where he motivated himself to become such a "boss," a natural leader in an objectively hopeless business opportunity. Indeed, GSI's environment constantly satisfied his universal needs: full respect and trust by the company's leaders, for example, to engage big GSI resources if he believed in an opportunity; the possibility to grow, such as allowing him to work on the company's biggest deal ever; and self-direction, such as allowing him to make essentially all the project decisions—including the decisions to spur others to self-motivate, as he did with the team that was working in the north of France and followed him to Florida to fight for the Euro Disney contract.

"I couldn't justify rationally why this opportunity was worth pursuing, but I had the full trust of [Raiman] and a few other top executives," Szulevicz said. He also added that when he felt disrespected, he let his chairman know.

Raiman had a habit—when thinking deeply about something—to puff his cigar, stop talking, and look at the ceiling—instead of at his interlocutor. "You'd feel despised," Szulevicz said. "So, one day I told him about his habit, and he was really sorry. He never thought that it might cause others to feel disrespected. He excused himself and changed it."

Despite that—or perhaps, thanks to that and all the other experiences they had together—the two remained friends many years after both their careers ended at GSI. Szulevicz had a real admiration for his former chairman: "I venerate him totally because he's somebody whom I love like my father, even if we sometimes disagreed," he told us. "If he called me right now and asked me to do something for him I'd do it immediately. First, I owe him a lot and then it's a duty, because everything he did was not for his personal interest. He could have become a [government] minister, he could have done anything he wanted. But simply when he learned of something that seemed right to him, enriching for others in almost a biblical sense, well, he just did it, that's it. He didn't ask himself many questions."

Raiman, in fact, does call Szulevicz from time to time to ask for help, for example, in gathering donations or sponsors for his foundation. And every time Raiman finishes explaining his request to Szulevicz, he adds, "I want it all!"

10

IN SEARCH OF LOST BOOTS

The Big Payoff from Letting People Self-Direct and Grow

I F DANTE WERE alive today, a customer-service call center might have been one of his circles of hell. To this underworld he would have consigned CEOs who had condemned their employees to long hours of answering calls, deflecting customers' requests, and being measured not by the problems they solved but the volume of calls processed each hour. It is unenviable, thankless, high-turnover work—at many companies. USAA's Robert McDermott called it "the most boring of all work." And yet, in many ways, the insurance giant is one big call center.

A call center is also one of the unlikeliest places, you would think, to find a liberated workforce. It's one thing to think of talented salesmen such as Burt Chase, Karl Fritchen, and Jacques Szulevicz, when freed to act on their own initiative, seizing the opportunity and becoming natural leaders. But what about the majority of "ordinary" people, who are less prepared to do so by training, disposition, or current occupation? Whether these people can also become natural leaders is a critical question for a liberated company. In these companies, there are no bosses to grab the helm, so it falls on whoever is closest to a problem or opportunity to deal with it. And call-center operators are as "ordinary" as it gets. But at USAA, McDermott was convinced that if he provided employees with the right conditions for growth and self-direction, they would reveal their talents for natural leadership no less than the "extraordinary" people do.

Most of us cringe at the thought of calling "customer service"—even the most helpful operator at the other end of the line is usually powerless to address our problems. Savvy veterans of call-center battles know that they have little hope of more than a perfunctory "I'm not authorized to do that" unless they can get their call bumped up at least one, and possibly two, levels above the frontline employee who first took their call.

USAA is different. The San Antonio, Texas-based insurer has the kind of call center that customers actually like to get on the phone with. Not only are the customer service reps happy to help, but they are *able* to. Many claims are settled and problems resolved on the spot, on the first call, with the first person a customer talks to. This, by the way, is their key performance measure—not the number of calls answered.

There's no arguing with the results. In McDermott's twenty-five years as CEO, USAA grew its owned and managed assets four hundredfold, with only a sevenfold increase in the number of employees. In 1995, after getting into banking, it was named the Best Bank in America by *Money* magazine for its outstanding financial services. And in 2007, it topped *Business Week*'s first-ever customer-service rankings as number one in the country, a feat it repeated again in 2008. Today it is the fifth-largest home- and car-insurance company in America, despite voluntarily limiting its core insurance business to current and former military personnel and their families.

But it wasn't always like that.

When Robert McDermott took over as CEO of USAA in 1968, the insurer was bloated, inefficient, and underperforming. The hapless employees, many of them wives of servicemen, were tightly controlled—it took no fewer than fifty-five separate steps to do even routine tasks, such as add a child to a policy. McDermott explained the routine: "The first person would open the envelope and pass it onto the second person, who would take it out, and so on—like the assembly lines in Detroit for the automobiles." Employees were controlled down to the length of their pencils—literally. Much of the work was done in pencil in those days, and you couldn't get a new one until your old one was shorter than an inch and a quarter—and yes, they measured them. Alfred's latitude in exchanging his old gloves at FAVI looks like freedom in comparison to this.

It's little wonder, then, that employees were leaving in droves. "Attrition was high at USAA," the retired general told us when we interviewed him one warm late-winter Texas night.[1] That was putting it mildly. Employee turnover "was 41 percent, while in the insurance industry as a whole it was about 8 percent." McDermott saw at once that all these things—the bureaucracy, the stifling rules, the high attrition, and the poor business performance—were linked. USAA was founded in a San Antonio hotel by a group of military officers. Their idea was to create a mutual insurance company aimed at serving officers like themselves who had trouble finding insurance elsewhere. It would later expand to all servicemen and -women and their families, but when McDermott arrived, it could only convince three-quarters of America's troops to join. The solution, for McDermott, began with the employees.

Nobody dreams of working in a call center. But USAA has always depended on it. It has to, because its customers—many of them active servicemen and -women—are scattered all over the world. So McDermott couldn't dispense with this thankless job, but he could make it more satisfying and—who knows?—maybe even enjoyable. "I had to make the jobs more meaningful," he said. That meant ditching the bureaucracy and giving his people the authority to do what their job title implied— serve their customers. In place of a multilayered, slow, and bureaucratic claims-approval process, he authorized the people answering the phones to settle claims up to a certain amount on the spot.

"I would approve anything that made the job easier," he said. That meant automating the most tedious, repetitive tasks. It also meant training—as much as sixteen weeks before a representative would get online. Training his people to do more than read a script to a customer with a problem would help them do their jobs and take advantage of their newfound freedom.

But McDermott had a deeper motive for empowering his people with tools and skills. "If you enrich the jobs," he said, "you enrich the people." McDermott talked a lot about people's "God-given talents." His view was that everyone was good at something—was good *for* something. And if their job allowed them to pursue that talent and that interest, it would be fulfilling. It would make them happy. Answering phones doesn't need to be dreary if your job is not just answering the call, but helping the person on the other end of the line—sometimes with life-size issues. For some USAA employees, helping people in this way might be just what they were after. Others would find satisfaction in something else, and so McDermott's campaign to remake USAA into the best customer-service organization in the country had another element—freeing his employees to move around within the company. If their interests and talents ran toward information technology, he'd train them in that. If they had a mind for the law but no legal education, he'd train them in that and send them off to claims processing. Like Bill Gore at W. L. Gore & Associates and Jean-François Zobrist at FAVI, he actively encouraged people to break out of what they were doing if they felt stuck or inclined to try something else. Instead of pinning people down, he gave them the tools to grow and, with that growth, the freedom to choose what they *wanted* to do inside the company—or in some cases, anywhere else.

In many traditional companies, this kind of mobility is discouraged. After all, it takes time and money to train someone to do a job, and the last thing an employer wants is to waste those resources when an employee wants to move on, unless, of course, her unit is trimmed down—which is unfortunately how "mobility" is often practiced in companies.

Well, it turns out there is something worse than that—keeping people in jobs they don't want to do. We mentioned in chapter 4 that Jeff Westphal of Vertex likes to tell new hires, "Welcome to Vertex; you're free to leave." Westphal's point is that he doesn't want anyone to feel trapped into working there if she's no longer happy. Zappos's Tony Hsieh, recall, takes it a step further and offers new hires a quitting bonus of $2,000 if they quit during their paid training.

The freedom to leave is the ultimate form of mobility—especially when it's subsidized. But if you've got nowhere to go, this freedom is worth no more than the freedom to sleep under the bridges of Paris. McDermott didn't exactly pay people to leave, the way Hsieh would forty years later. But he did train his employees in whatever fields they chose—giving them real opportunities to grow and to self-direct their career choices—even if those opportunities eventually took them away from USAA.

And so, the training programs McDermott implemented became an employee-education project. Most of his employees had never been to college, so he partnered with local universities to teach classes at night—at the company's expense and in whatever subjects captured his people's imaginations, provided it was related in some way to work. It all came back to this one thing: Satisfying people's needs of fairness, growth, and self-direction made them happy and they, in turn, made customers happy. And if you kept the customers happy, the business would take care of itself.

It's not every new CEO who would come into an underperforming, sluggish company and begin by rewarding its employees with fairness—including equal pay for men and women—education, and greater freedom of action. Many, in fact, would do exactly the opposite—embark on a program of cost cutting, including benefits, and a more rigorous set of controls over employee performance: the proverbial tightening of the thumb screws.

But when McDermott came to USAA, the company had an implicit employment-for-life guarantee. USAA was run mostly by former military men, for the military, and many of its frontline people were themselves military spouses in the garrison town of San Antonio. It was not the sort of company, in McDermott's view, that would respond well to mass lay-offs or draconian measures. Tony Hsieh's pay-not-to-play program works for Zappos because it is a young, fast-growing company based in Las Vegas. A CEO like McDermott, with thousands of employees already, did not have the luxury of trying to influence the culture through hiring. He would need another way.

Moreover, he was convinced that his people knew a lot more about the business he was now running than he did—and could quickly acquire more knowledge when necessary. They just needed an opportunity to act on what they knew. "I couldn't sit on top and make all those [customer service] decisions," he told us. "I didn't know how to handle them—even the typewriter, you know? But that wasn't the point. [The point] was to give [the employees] the opportunities to get into the frontline [where] all services [are] delivered. . . . Top-down isn't going to get the right thing [done]." In other words, McDermott saw his people as part of the solution, not as the problem. At the same time, he didn't see himself as a solution or as somebody who could deliver the solution. All he needed to do was give his people the tools—and the skills, if they needed them—and then set them loose.

For McDermott, education would start his employees on a journey of self-discovery that would, in the end, redound to USAA's benefit. "In the service," McDermott recounted, "I learned what a great thing for America [the] GI Bill of Rights was. That's what made America great after World War II. The Germans had the highest level of education going into it," the former P-38 Lightning pilot recalled. "Ten years after the war, we had the highest level of education in the world. Choice and assistance was the key to that. And we put that into our . . . system here at USAA." A former dean of the Air Force Academy who transformed it into a first-class academic institution, he explained how it worked at USAA: "We had six colleges and universities . . . come into our building at night and use seventy-five training classrooms. . . . And we picked up the tuition if [employees] made C grades or better for a baccalaureate, as long as they passed their courses. And then B grades or better for a master's degree. So we wound up with the most highly educated workforce in the whole financial services industry in the United States." On any given day, about 30 percent of USAA's workforce was in some kind of training or educational program.

And with that education—and mindful of his own ignorance—McDermott turned them loose on their own firm. People would "come up with ideas to do it better, to serve better and cheaper," he said. Here, too, education helped. If an employee identified a need within USAA, McDermott would train them to fill that need, instead of hiring an outside expert who might know everything about computers but nothing about USAA. He summed it up this way: "We enriched the jobs . . . and we enriched the people that do the jobs by giving them more information and education."

Underlying it all was the Golden Rule, which McDermott referred to repeatedly when we met him, and which became a powerful competitive advantage for USAA that persists to this day. "Serve others as you'd like to be served. Service is what we're all about. If we serve people they'll come back to us." And they have, and still do, which is why USAA not only dominates its market segment almost totally—97 percent of servicemen and -women are members—but why its customer satisfaction ratings are sky-high.

McDermott spoke about "service" in religious terms, and that is how he thought of it personally. When we asked him to explain his approach to running USAA, he thought all the way back to his childhood in Readville, a tiny hamlet in what was then rural Massachusetts. Today, Readville has been absorbed into the greater Boston metropolitan sprawl. But back then, it was "a little crossroads, with maybe two or three hundred people," he said. It was near there, in Canton, that a young Bobby McDermott would first watch planes take off and land and decide he wanted to become a pilot. And it was in the hamlet of Readville that McDermott was taught the lessons that would guide his governance of USAA half a century later. "Like Robert Fulghum, who says, 'All I really need to know I learned in kindergarten,' I say, 'All I need to know I learned in Sunday school,'" McDermott explained. Even so, he was careful to say, "I'm not trying to preach to the world." While it has a religious dimension for him, the message is a worldly one, whether you are of a different faith or no faith. And that message is similar to Gore's principle of "fairness" and Sun Hydraulics' "courtesy": Treating people as the unique, equally valuable human beings that they are, whether they are subordinates, colleagues, customers, or suppliers, is good for business. McDermott's Golden Rule is his own personal gloss on the same principle.

It should come as no surprise that this basic concept comes up again and again at these liberated companies. Each of the leaders we met and studied came back to the notion that he was just one man, and that excellence could be achieved only by fully utilizing the knowledge and capabilities of everyone in the organization.

But if you are Robert McDermott and you are coming into an organization of thousands of people, many of whom have been treated with suspicion—recall the measurement of pencils—and sometimes contempt for years, the challenge lies in getting those people to believe you when you say you think of them as equals and expect them to act that way. The leaders at Harley, GSI, FAVI, and USAA each took a different approach, one that was tailored to the particular organization he was liberating and its history and challenges. Rich Teerlink involved Harley's unions in corporate decision making in a way that they had never experienced, while taking down the barriers that separated management from the blue-collar workforce. Jean-François Zobrist first tried unthreatening methods with controlling managers but in the end stripped them of their authority, though he maintained their salaries and let them find other useful, or at least nondamaging, roles in the company.

McDermott set his people free to do their jobs, but he recognized that in a large, bureaucratic organization, there were likely to be a lot of people who didn't want to be in their jobs at all but were unable to leave. Zobrist had something of the same problem, although on a smaller scale. In McDermott's case, then, his education program was two-pronged: It served to improve the knowledge and education of USAA's workforce, but it was also a signal to employees that USAA thought of them as more than Henry Ford's "pair of hands." Thus it operated alongside the automation programs, the preauthorization to approve claims, and the bureaucracy busting to show people that USAA was a different kind of company. In the process, he redefined their jobs, too: They were now to serve the *customers*—in fact as well as in name. All of this together—the bureaucracy-busting, the devolution of decision-making authority, and the educational benefits—constituted McDermott's campaign to move from "how" to "why." In the process, he changed the way USAA's employees thought of their relationship to their customers—transforming Dante's call-answering robots into natural service leaders. In fact, USAA service is so legendary that our acquaintance and a USAA member told us: "When I have a bad day, I just call them."

This is not just happy PR talk. In 2005, a member called USAA to conduct some business about her home insurance. But the sales rep, trained like everyone else at USAA to be conversational and helpful, not just transactional, picked up on the worry in the woman's voice and asked: "You sound distraught. Is there something wrong?" The woman explained that her husband had Alzheimer's and had been missing for four days. The police couldn't find him.

After a short pause, the rep said, "You have a credit card with us. Why don't I call over to our bank and see if we can get your husband's credit-card transactions over the last few days. It might tell us where he is." The information was found and the sales rep happily shared it with the woman, suggesting that she call the police right away to pass along the information. Using the credit card data, the police found him in a hotel many miles away from his home. Not a bad display of customer-service leadership for a call-center operator.

Although such service is considered par for the course at USAA, this case—perhaps due to its emotional impact—merited not only a story in the company's internal newsletter but was also slated for publication in the company's annual report. And the message was clear to both employees and customers, who are known as members in USAA parlance: "We do whatever we can to help our members." And at USAA, "whatever you can" means *whatever*—including breaking the rules, as shown by the story of another remarkable USAA employee.

A member who had recently been diagnosed with breast cancer called to see about getting her life-insurance coverage increased. The USAA rep, June Walbert, walked her through it, including the cost, and got the policy written. But a couple of months went by, and the member called back. "You know," she told the customer-service representative, "I just can't afford this. What did I get myself into?" Contractually, she was stuck. At most companies, continuing the conversation from there would have been akin to beating one's head against the wall. But the rep looked at the file and said, "You know what, this is wrong. We should not have done it."

Walbert continued the story: "I felt like we, as a company, didn't hold up our end of the bargain. We should have really talked to her more to make sure that she didn't take that policy. So I just broke the rules. I said, 'We're going to undo this policy, give you back what you had before. You had a good policy before. Let's leave it alone.' I sent this to our underwriters and they didn't give me a hard time. . . . They just said, 'You're right. We shouldn't have done that.' That was what was best for the member."[2]

We asked what helped her take such an action. "I think that our robust training program is really what I would call the 'secret of the ninja' to USAA's success as a liberated employer," she offered, spontaneously homing in on the key role of education. "Because whenever you have sufficient training, it increases your technical skills, which in turn, increases your confidence to serve the member well." In this case, natural leadership meant bending, or breaking, the rules to do the right thing. Walbert didn't *look* like a corporate maverick, ready to break the rules at any opportunity. She's middle-aged, petite, blond, and unassuming—nothing heroic about her on the surface. But looks can be deceiving.

It turns out Walbert is a reserve lieutenant colonel in an Army paratrooper unit. This is how she describes her other job: "It's where you take a helicopter into a combat zone, and you're inserted expeditiously via rope from it. That's why I consider things in terms of, How do ninjas think about this?" Indeed, ninjas are free not to worry too much about corporate rules. At this point, we thought she could have been a character in a James Bond movie, a thought a colleague confirmed by adding, "And she likes champagne, too."

But our USAA sales-rep-lieutenant-colonel-ninja deadpanned, "I don't think I look that good in a swimsuit."

That, too, was a vital part of USAA's freedom culture: the freedom of a frontline employee to crack jokes with visitors just out of a private meeting with the company's CEO and in the presence of the head of public relations. "Know our customer, understand their current issues, and then provide solutions that may or may not involve USAA products."

"Do whatever you can" indeed.

IT'S ALL ABOUT DOING A GREAT JOB

Now, to some, this talk of treating people well, helping them grow, and letting them self-direct may sound hopelessly touchy-feely in the face of the imperative to "run the trains on time"—especially in tough economic times. Stéphane Magnan tells his own story about the importance to the workforce of a nourishing environment. In 1982, at the age of thirty-one, Magnan was given charge of the five-plant aluminum foundry Montupet, owned by Pechiney, then Europe's leading aluminum producer. But

Montupet was no FAVI. In fact, the executives at Pechiney had recalled Magnan from his executive job in their U.S. division into Montupet not to improve its performance but to shut it down for good at the minimum cost to Pechiney and with as little labor unrest as possible. France's first-ever Socialist president, François Mitterrand, had nationalized large chunks of the economy, and Pechiney's leadership thought that it would be easier to use the supposedly ruthless Magnan, "*l'américain*," to shut down the plants.

But that wasn't at all his state of mind. Magnan quickly realized what an appalling, festering relationship the former management team had built with the plant employees: "People would look down at their feet when I would walk by them!"[3]Magnan was dismayed, but he also saw opportunity: The company had real potential—if the relationship with the workforce could be fixed. So after a month of observation, he offered Pechiney a different plan—to turn the plant around. Montupet wasn't worth much in its present state anyway, so Pechiney agreed to let him try—as long as it wouldn't cost anything—and Magnan started his liberation campaign, adopting many of the devices we've seen at Harley, FAVI, USAA, GSI, and elsewhere. In fact, Yves Tillard, the same consultant who helped Jacques Raiman liberate GSI, helped Magnan. In this case it was a foreman who, once he understood Magnan's vision for the company, suggested that his CEO contact Tillard. In two months all the managers—this foreman included—went through quick Tillard-led seminars to learn the kind of change the company was looking for. Then, to improve their own managerial practices, managers and their teams attended two-day team seminars, similar to those Tillard conducted at GSI. Again, they weren't just some "pointless" seminars—Magnan, like Jacques Raiman, assisted in each one of them. And as in other liberated companies, people started to perform miracles.

When asked how he recognized that the liberation campaign had turned the corner and overcame people's distrust, Magnan didn't have to think long: "The people began looking me straight in the eyes, saying hello, smiling." Then he quickly added, "Also, I had the numbers. The scrap went down dramatically. And the strike days, too. . . . When I came to the company, the relations with unions were so conflict-ridden that the former management was working on manufacturing schedules with an expected thirty days of shutdown per year due to strikes." It's not every CEO who, after explaining his vision, gets advice from a foreman on how to implement it—and takes that advice right away.

The "miracles" continue today. Just a year before our interview, the company experienced some technical problems in delivering cylinder heads—the company's key product—to Renault and Nissan. Worse, the two clients suddenly faced a surge in demand and put enormous pressure on Montupet to ship the parts. Nobody could find a solution until a team of operators—very much like FAVI's operators do regularly—hit the road on their own and went to see the client plant's operators and supervisors to explain to them the technical difficulties. This established both trust and cooperation between the two companies' teams and the problems were soon resolved.

In other words, this talk of "treating people as equals," "personal growth," and "self-direction" is, in the end, all about allowing people to do a great job. The turnarounds accomplished by Zobrist, Teerlink, Westphal, Raiman, McDermott, and Magnan, and the start-ups founded by Gore, Davids, Forward, Quadracci, and others we'll see, attest to that. Still, the question is worth looking at more closely. In "how" companies, most decisions, policies, and rules are made at the top, or near it. In this arrangement, the need for a "relationship" between company and employee is limited: Workers are given orders and told what to do and how to do it. They are measured—and controlled—according to whether they follow them. People, in turn, measure their employer according to how much they get for their complaisance in the form of compensation and perks—"goodies." These goodies are then often used to satisfy the universal needs—to be treated as equal, to grow, and to self-direct—that are unfulfilled at work. When an employee restores a colonial house through hard work on weekends and over holidays, for example, he gets admiring reinforcement from family and neighbors, learns new skills, and runs his project as he deems best.

Nevertheless, many of these forms of control—those policies, procedures, and bureaucracy—are there for a reason. Some of them are, as Gordon Forward of Chaparral Steel put it, relics of some rare or singular mishap in the past that gave rise to a rule—his so-called managing for the 3 percent. But many rules serve another function as well: They are an institutionalized way of "communicating" with one's workforce, even if the messages are often demoralizing, if not demeaning, frustrating, and likely to produce inefficiency.

The alternative communication means we have described—from CEOs' listening instead of talking, removing the signs of executive privilege, of executives and managers being nourishing leaders to their teams, not raising their voices, removing bureaucratic symbols and practices, radically transforming or eliminating the HR and financial control departments—all these measures appear extremely diverse. For liberating leaders, though, they were undertaken for one common reason: to create a corporate environment that satisfies people's universal need to be treated as intrinsically equal, with fairness and respect, so they can do a great job.

THE CASE *FOR* BUREAUCRACY

In 1922, the sociologist Max Weber could not know of liberated companies. The emerging corporate world was composed of "how" companies, and in an attempt to understand their success, Weber wrote an article on the necessity of bureaucracy. Following G. W. F. Hegel, he explained that unlike feudal organizations, in which relations were based on personal favoritism bestowed by authority holders to their vassals, bureaucracy treats everyone in an impersonal and absolutely fair manner by applying the same set of right regulations. Put aside the fact that many corporate regulations may be not only wrong but downright stupid and unfair to most. Weber seemed not to envisage a third way between personal favoritism and "fair" regulations: that relations between people of different levels of responsibility can be both personal *and* fair. In fact, liberating the workplace begins by de-bureaucratizing and re-humanizing relations, by making them based on human fairness and equal treatment, so people feel like *human beings* instead of *human resources*.

But belief in bureaucracy's absolute fairness through regulation is utopian, too. Contrary to Weber's idealistic view, most real bureaucracies evolve into a type of monstrous "feudal bureaucracy,"[4] a government of *nomenklatura*—etymologically, of people called by names. The *nomenklatura* are personable and considerate to those who are "one of them" but treat others in a dehumanizing manner, often referring to them as "numbers," "files," "full-time equivalents," or even "fluids," as one European corporation designates the temps, to be managed along with the water and electricity.

But even if bureaucracy is replaced by an environment that satisfies people's universal needs, the imperative of coordination remains real. For people to act both freely *and* effectively, they must first understand and "own" the answer to Zobrist's "Why?" question, so that they can aim at the correct goal. In other words, they must understand the company's vision as well as how their own actions comport with that vision. Think of Bob Davids, going over the list of supplies that his winemaker, Kris, had requested. Davids reviewed the list not in order to find places to cut costs or corners, but to ensure that Kris had made each choice with Sea Smoke's vision in mind of making the best wine humanly possible from that vineyard. Those were very early days at what is still a small and young company, and Davids felt that going over the list was important for reinforcing Sea Smoke's vision in the mind of a key employee. Even so, course corrections and reminders became necessary over time to keep people focused on that vision, as when Kris tried to save a buck by using old oak barrels for the white wine instead of making it world-class.

Rich Teerlink, likewise, spent more than a year trying to establish and put on paper a "joint vision" for Harley-Davidson—one produced and shared by management and union members alike. Establishing a vision for the company that is widely accepted is critical to the liberation campaign because you cannot replace something with nothing. Of course, a vision by itself can be hard to apply to particular circumstances, even when it is well understood. That's why liberated companies generally have a set of guardrails, as it were, to guide employees' choices.

W. L. Gore & Associates' principles of fairness, commitment, and the waterline are an example of these guardrails. At GSI, they called their version of these guiding principles the "rules of the game." These guardrails often share similarities across companies, but they are never the same in any two companies. That's because in each company, they emerge organically as a way of bolstering people's self-discipline within the firm. The moment they start to ossify into formal policies—"No one is allowed to wear a tie!"—they lose that virtue and become arbitrary constraints. That's why, at their most effective, they are simple, unwritten, and self-enforced. A leader in a traditional company who finds himself thinking, "What we need around here is a little discipline!" ought to consider looking around for the causes of the lack of discipline. He might be surprised by what he finds.

But for the vision and these principles to inform employees' daily work, they, too, must change work habits they might have developed while at "how" companies. Some will be willing to do so, while some will not. Others may be willing but skeptical. After all, if "how" control works to some degree, however imperfectly, and with less hassle and risk, why not stick with it? Many successful companies existed for years with "how" cultures and decision-making policies. And just as they used to say that you'd never get fired for buying an IBM, we doubt there are many top executives who have lost their jobs for tightening the controls over employees. They may call it "cost control" or "reorganization," or some such. But whatever name it goes by, it's a fact of life when a company hits a rough patch: Tighten the screws, take away perks—such as free food—scrub all the expense reports a third time. And quite often it works—or at least it seems to. Recall Alfred with his gloves, a form of financial control no doubt thought up by an accountant looking to save a few francs a year in the budget by preventing Gordon Forward's "3 percent" from taking an extra pair home. On the face of it, the policy was a success: Spending on gloves went down. But of course all the ancillary costs in lost productivity, bureaucracy, and paperwork—not to mention the salary of the supply closet "doorman"—are never accounted for on that budget line. And that's to say nothing of the order that might go out late or the products not made, on the margins, because of these various "operating efficiencies" that, like barnacles on a boat, make the whole company a little less—our liberating leaders would say, much less—swift.

THE ILLUSION OF CONTROL

Jacques Raiman of GSI understood this phenomenon all too well. In fact, Raiman eventually came around to the radical view that all financial controls were little more than creative fictions. Two stories illustrate the point.

The first takes place in the early days of GSI, in 1979. GSI is growing quickly while, at the same time, Raiman is trying to instill a new, freer culture in the company. They had grown to one thousand people, and Raiman had started to hold regular seminars with employees in small groups so that he could explain GSI's new, informal "rules of the game"—and give people a chance to voice what sorts of problems they might be having.

"[Earlier] I had implemented a financial reporting system," Raiman recalled. "And the finance department was, in fact, the police, the internal KGB." It was, in other words, management's tool for keeping an eye on all corners of the company and enforcing budgets and spending policies. Or so they thought. During one of these seminars, the head of operations in Grenoble, France, spoke up.

"Well, Raiman, I'll tell you how it really works," he said, according to Jacques. "We establish our budget, fine. If one month we are above budget we're congratulated, but if another we are under the budget the sky falls: investigations, inquiries, discussions. So, it's not complicated: When we are above budget we cheat and instead of reporting the sales, we keep them for the next month. That's for me and the executive team, but the salesmen cheat the same way. You believe, Raiman, that you know [thanks to all the reporting] the reality, but you know nothing."[5] After the corporate scandals in the United States in 2002 and 2003, there was a huge and expensive attempt to crack down on precisely this kind of manipulation of financial reports. One result of this was a requirement that a company's top executives sign a sworn statement attesting to the truth and accuracy of their financial reports. Anyone who signs such a document should be aware that Raiman's story is not unique, and neither the passage of time nor of voluminous new laws has changed the fact that the real experts on your company's various budgets are the ones near the frontlines who manipulate them to make their numbers and beat the system whenever possible.

Even so, this is one of those truths not often spoken in polite company, never mind in the presence of the company chairman. Raiman said that the executive's candor was the result of his efforts, up to that point, to foster openness and frank communication. Raiman continued, "So, while on the train on our way back to Paris, we decided that we would not function like that anymore. Management [financial] control is here to help managers understand the numbers, not to be 'Moscow's eye.' If a business unit head has some performance problems he'll talk directly with the division head." In other words, business units would still report numbers to the center, but the "KGB" would be dismantled. Missing a number would not be treated as a crime because it is, instead, a symptom of a problem. And treating it as a crime encourages a cover-up, which may actually delay getting to the root of the problem. Integrity would be restored to the reported numbers by *removing* the fear of the secret financial police.

The financial controllers were not pleased. "They made a big fuss," Raiman said. "The finance director said that I wanted to destroy the financial controls, that I didn't like them [the controllers] anymore, and that I wanted to destroy the company." Raiman assured him that he wasn't out to fire the finance department, but that he did want them to play a different role. As for the director himself, Raiman left him in place but limited his duties. "I wasn't sure I had convinced him," Raiman remarked. "So he remained the head of accounting, and as a finance director dealt with relations with the banks, investors, et cetera."

Once they decided to scrap this strict financial policing, they embarked on another series of meetings with executives to explain the new approach. "I remember one [meeting] in Paris," Raiman recalled. "Together with [human resources director] Jean-François Cottin, we tried to explain to a dozen of our executives a [new] company model based on respect for people. We told them that this new system was realistic, while the old one wasn't because all the [reported] numbers were false."

This did not produce the result that Raiman had been aiming for, however. "They said that we needed *more* control," Jacques noted with a rueful smile. "Then, others said, '[This new system] is fine for us; we must be respected and be autonomous. But you won't do that for the data-entry shop floor, with the ignorant girls there, right? For them it's a drubbing,'" not freedom, that is needed.

When we asked Raiman how he dealt with this resistance, he characteristically responded not with exasperation, but affection. "I'll tell you: I liked them very much,"[6] he said, suggesting that, even if some of them didn't share his convictions about how to run the company, he had a strong personal bond with them. To this, Cottin, whom we interviewed together with Raiman, chimed in. Besides, he said, "The first rule is that when somebody does something stupid, the most important thing is that he admits it rather than be condemned." Since they were, in effect, asking that this principle be applied to the financial reporting, they ought to try to apply it in their own dealings with the executive team.

"So, I asked myself: How can I convince them?" Raiman continued. He sent these executives to America for training and brought in outsiders to hold conferences in the company "to show how important it is to ask frontline people's opinion, make them participate in the decisions." Raiman described the process of pushing this new freedom- and respect-based culture down through the company as a series of incremental, nonthreatening steps, not some big bang. "We didn't make any big speeches," Cottin added. "We just acted, a lot of little acts, steps." For a CEO who wants to change executives' and managers' practices, this nonthreatening, patient way is the only effective way to do it. One of their techniques was to show the difficulty, if not the futility, of effective controls in an atmosphere of distrust and disrespect. "Here is a beautiful story," Raiman began by way of illustration. His eyes twinkled.

"It's a story that I heard from a CEO of a French subsidiary of a U.S. company. A young engineer who worked in the south of France was sent on a mission to a paper plant in the extreme north of Norway. So he said good-bye to his wife and left for four days wearing loafers. But, once there, in freezing temperatures, he had to buy fur-lined boots. Back in France, he filled in his expense report, including fifty dollars for the boots."

But before long, "he got the report back with a finance control note: 'REREAD THE PROCEDURES: CLOTHING CANNOT BE INCLUDED IN THE EXPENSES.' So the engineer deleted the 'boots,' and added three dollars here and there on other lines to keep the same total. And he sent the bill back with a sentence at the bottom: 'FIND THE BOOTS.' The CEO who told the story gave me a copy of this expense report and we circulated it all over GSI." The moral of the story, for Raiman, was that strict financial controls are often illusory. And when they defy common sense, their chief result is that you end up knowing *less* about your business and its expenses than you would if you trusted people more to use their best judgment. But not everyone at GSI was convinced of this.

"We were losing money in Spain," Raiman explained. "And one day a

Canadian—who was a controller and had worked before in a command-and-control American company—came to see me and said, 'Do you want to stop losing money? I will identify all the gaps in the expense reports, I will verify all of them, and you'll see how the money will appear.'"

Raiman replied, "It won't work; this way won't work." The man said, if Raiman wouldn't support him, he would quit. So, Raiman told us, "I let him leave." Raiman did not believe that GSI's Spanish business could be fixed by minutely examining every expense report. On the contrary, he believed it would alienate and anger GSI's people there, who would feel besieged and persecuted by the financial secret police and start making up the numbers "to beat the system."

Raiman was not alone in disdaining KGB-style financial controls. Nor does this attitude necessarily imply leniency toward abusers when they are exposed. Quite the reverse, in fact. Most of our liberating leaders, including Zobrist and Harry Quadracci, knew how to pull the trigger on the freedom abusers because they knew that everyone else in the company was aware of the abuse and was waiting to see what the CEO would do about it. Most—except Raiman. A person who worked with him in GSI recounted that Raiman loved and trusted employees so much and was so saddened by the news that some abused their freedom—such as cheating on expense accounts—that nobody wanted to bring him such news. So, unwillingly, Raiman made himself incapable of acting against these abusers. This, understandably, demoralized the majority in many places who played according to the company's "rules of the game."

But Raiman aside, you might ask whether such a trusting approach is even possible in a post-Sarbanes-Oxley world, with new layers of federal bureaucracy demanding more and more precision on the part of internal company controllers. Richard Arter, the head of investor relations at Sun Hydraulics, put it this way: "Our position on that is that we need to pass the test. We don't necessarily need to get an A."[7] In other words, it is possible to comply even with onerous financial reporting laws and still treat your people with trust.

Indeed, it may well be easier that way—as Jacques Raiman suggests, a punitive financial reporting system is more likely to lead to "smoothing" and other fudges than one that is less oppressive. "As an economist," Raiman told us, "I learned in my youth that there is a trade-off between effectiveness and fairness."[8] He continued: "But what one learns in a company is that fairness is the *basis* of performance and not vice versa. For me, a fair manager is one who values you for what you do. From the moment that running a company is compatible with moral principles one learned in childhood, it becomes *un bonheur*."[9]

Raiman's last statement echoed one of Zobrist's remarks, that his daily tours of the shop floor to listen and converse with operators were his quest for *bonheur*, for happiness or joy. But it was his reflection on the relationship between fairness and performance that intrigued us. Indeed, Raiman used two different meanings of fairness: economic and moral. While talking about the trade-off, he refers to the economic *un*fairness of the competition that—since Adam Smith—has been viewed as the basis of a country's economic performance. But when he talks about fairness as a basis for the company's performance, he refers to moral fairness, to the way a company and managers treat people. In the first case, he mentions the simple notion that underlies Smith's market economics: Material self-interest drives economic action and performance. In the second case, Raiman formulates a more complex precept: *The satisfaction of people's need to be treated with moral fairness leads to their enhanced effectiveness and to enhanced company performance.* This enhanced economic performance—gains in productivity, profits, and so forth—then, in turn, paves the way for providing *economic fairness* to people through profit sharing, bonus, or ownership schemes.

It may seem hard to believe that fairness and respect can be appreciated by people even more than a bigger paycheck. Needless to say, in a perfect world you would want all three—fairness, respect, and maximum remuneration. But we do not live in that world, and so we have to make choices. On at least two occasions that we know of, unions at liberated companies, when given the choice, did, in fact, choose fairness and re-spect over their pocketbooks.

THE "THEORY Y" UNIONS

The first comes from GSI. A large chain of stores had solicited bids for outsourcing its payroll services. In an arrangement typical to this type of outsourcing, the chain's whole payroll department, complete with its union, would be integrated into GSI. But the chain had outsourced sev-eral other back-office functions in the past, and in one case the inte-gration of the chain's employees with the new company had gone very badly. As a result, the chain's trade unions were on their guard. They insisted on conducting their own investigation of the candidates, includ-ing meeting ADP-GSI's union representatives. When the contract was awarded, ADP-GSI got a pleasant surprise: Not only had it won the bid, but ADP-GSI learned that it was the only candidate that had passed the union's vetting. Given the sour outsourcing history, the chain's manage-ment was definitely not ready to go against the unions and risk a strike, so the union's favorable opinion of GSI had played an important role in winning the contract.

Most people assume that unions are focused single-mindedly on ex-tracting material "goodies" for their workers from their employers. And yet this French union put GSI's ability to satisfy their higher needs—for fairness and respect—above those material considerations. Perhaps many other trade unions would do the same—if only they were offered a similar choice and not simply "goodies." At any rate, Jean-Luc Barbier, chief of ADP-GSI's corporate clients division, was certain about the eco-nomic benefits of treating people well in the company: "It surely provides us a competitive advantage in getting clients."[10] That's more than you can say about denying a traveling salesman pocket money for snow boots in Norway.

The second story comes from Harley, in the midst of Rich Teerlink's liberation campaign. In early 1994, the news at Harley-Davidson seemed so good that management started to worry about the bike maker's future. Demand had driven up the waiting list for a new bike to a whopping eighteen months, and Wall Street—grown quickly accustomed to Harley's fat margins—had started to hold the company to ever-higher standards of performance. Pressure was mounting, and without new capacity, Harley seemed in danger of overheating. This meant a new plant. But Teerlink didn't want just any new plant. He envisioned one that was radically different from the existing ones, built from the ground up to encourage work flexibility, more employee involvement, and more freedom of action.

For most American companies, all this would point in one direction—south—to build a union-free facility in a right-to-work state. Most of Harley's executives and managers liked the idea of going to a southern state, too. But for Rich and some of his colleagues, such a move seemed likely to disrupt the relationships with the unions that they had been building over the years. They convinced their colleagues and—even harder—the board of directors not to write off the unions, and presented the idea for the radically different new plant to the presidents of the two unions' parent organizations. The unions agreed to support a new plant that would profoundly change existing work rules and practices.

What's more, the union locals said that they were ready to change the work rules in the existing plants to match those envisioned in the new plant, but—using the famous "yes, but" negotiation strategy—asked management to agree not to build the new plant after all. Instead, the efficiency gains from the changed work structure would be used to expand capacity at the existing facilities. After giving this proposal a hearing, management agreed to scale back, but not eliminate, the plans for the new plant. A team of three people—one manager and two union representatives—set out to search for a new site. And in every place they visited, city officials were ready to roll out their sales pitch to woo corporations. Harley's team was bemused to see how, upon learning that two out of the three visitors were from the unions, the city fathers would skip

hurriedly over the slides intended to show how good the local environment was *for management.*

After all these trips, the team came back with a ranking of the top three
locations, with Kansas City, Missouri, where the plant was finally built,
topping the list. But it was the number two choice that flabbergasted Rich
Teerlink when he saw it. This three-member group, two of whom were
union representatives, listed as their runner-up a city in a right-to-work
state in which the unions could never hope to organize the workforce.

This collaborative spirit remains intact today. Steven Sleigh, the director of strategic resources for the International Association of Machinists—one of Harley's two main unions—recently said:

> [Douglas] McGregor's seminal work spurred managers and
> union leaders alike to rethink the command and control work
> environment. Now, a full generation and a half later, my own union
> has dedicated substantial resources to fostering high-performance
> work systems rooted in McGregor's view that workers can think,
> plan, and be creative. In this information age, this view should be
> dominant, rather than unusual, as it remains today.[11]

11

THE ANTI-MAD MEN

One Man's Quest for Peace and Liberty in Advertising

I F MAKING CALL-CENTER operators' jobs fun seems tough, Stan Richards may have had it even tougher—he wanted to build an ad agency that was free from the dysfunction so common in his business. Richards, in other words, was an ad man who hated the advertising business. And that drove him to exasperation that, eventually, brought liberation to his business. He quit his firm after one year to set up the freelance shop that eventually became the Richards Group. His goal was to show that "the way it's always been done" wasn't a good enough reason to keep doing it that way.[1]

When his agency grew close to 150 people—a danger zone, he says, echoing Bill Gore's concerns about that number—Richards became particularly fearful of the emergence of the rivalry between the different departments typical of any ad agency: the accounts people disrespecting the "creatives," and the creatives scorning accounts as empty suits. What he wanted was, in his phrase, to create "The Peaceable Kingdom," the title of the book he'd later write about his journey.[2] Even if lions weren't going to lie down with lambs in his Dallas office, accounts and creatives were going to get along and work together.

This was personally important to Richards, but there was a business rationale for it, too—employees who didn't spend their time suspecting or undercutting their fellow workers would be able to direct more of their energy and attention to keeping the clients happy. Consequently, they would contribute to the company's healthy growth instead of creating a toxic and ultimately unsuccessful business environment.

Still, you can't just sit down with your accounts people and your creatives and implore them, "Can't we all just get along?" Well, you could. But it would do about as much good as Rodney King's plea did during the L.A. riots. Everyone would smile and nod, and agree to redouble their efforts. Then they'd go back to their respective lairs and start trying to figure out who in the other department had accused them of sabotage, prompting this little get-together, and how to teach the culprit a lesson.

So Richards got creative. In a traditional ad agency, accounts and creatives have their own turf—and their own floors wherever possible. This keeps them well insulated from each other. And so this is where Richards struck first. From the earliest days, he decided that people would be assigned seats more or less randomly—accounts would sit next to creatives and vice versa—but with one constraint. Richards didn't want a creative and an account executive who were working for the same client to sit side by side. In fact, he wanted them separated whenever possible. So a creative and an accounts person might be cheek by jowl, but they wouldn't be working on the same things at all. If you needed to talk to your accounts guy, you were going to have to walk.

The way Richards saw it, this arrangement had a number of advantages. By mixing everyone up, he was emphasizing that they were all in the same boat; it would minimize the us versus them dynamic found at many agencies. Familiarity, in Richards's view, would breed respect.

But Richards's plan was even more devious than that. By using desk assignments to encourage people to wander the halls, he was nudging his people to mingle. He wanted them to bump into one another, see other people, and maybe learn a little about what others did at the agency.

Richards was so serious about the virtues of people walking around that when he needed to rent a second floor to house his growing firm, he knocked a huge hole in the ceiling and built an open atrium with a staircase to connect the two. He didn't want to lose the unity of space that his jumbling of different departments had accomplished, or create a new, separate floor that could develop into somebody's little fief. Later, he did it again, and then again, creating a dramatic four-story atrium in the heart of his office space. He wanted to do it a fourth time, but the fire code prohibited it. So he grudgingly ran his fourth staircase up to a fire door instead of to a balcony, like on the lower floors.

And while people are not forbidden to take the elevator between floors, when they do somebody might well inquire jokingly whether they broke their leg over the weekend. Because the stairwell is a light, airy, open, and pleasant space, it's not hard to get people moving through there— and naturally bouncing ideas and information along the way. None of this bumping would occur, of course, if people simply took the elevators. Office etiquette everywhere dictates that impromptu meetings are never held in elevators. "Well, that was a true danger," Richards recognized. He compares stepping into the elevator to visit another department at most agencies to passing through "Checkpoint Charlie," the spot in Berlin during the Cold War through which visitors between East and West Berlin had to pass.[3] Richards's stairwell is, by contrast, an open border.

Richards played with traditional uses of office space in other ways, too. The workrooms in most offices are dark, windowless "dungeons," in Richards's words, where the unfortunate are sent to "copy and collate and put things together." The Richards Group's workrooms—the ones with the copiers and the staplers and the rest—are on the outside, with large windows, plenty of natural light, and a nice view. As Richards put it, any one of them "could be a CEO's office."

He explained: "The whole idea is to send a clear signal to anyone who comes in here to do the routine work that we need to do, that there are no unimportant people, there are no unimportant functions, and that everybody in this organization will be treated with the highest level of respect in everything that we do. Now, it's not a big investment to take a nice piece of space and turn it into a working place. And it comes back to benefit us a hundredfold, because what happens is, everybody recognizes that what he or she is doing is significant. And consequently the work just gets better as a result of it." Richards went on to explain that, at an ad agency, a typographical error in a piece of copy is one of the worst things that can happen. That is, unless the misspelling is done by one of the cows in the Chick-fil-A ads that the Richards Group designed. In that long-running ad campaign, cows are depicted engaging in a guerrilla marketing campaign to discourage the consumption of hamburgers. "Eat Mor Chikin," their suspiciously misspelled billboards often read. Everyone knows cows can't spell.

But otherwise, getting the details right is important, and so the person who double-checks those little things, who collates the presentations for the big account pitch, that person is performing an equally vital role for the firm. And Richards wanted to signal that the agency sees the importance of this work by giving those who do it an attractive place to work.

As you will by now appreciate, changing the geometry and the geography of an office, by itself, is not enough. It may even seem manipulative—shouldn't truly free people also be free to move about the office in the manner that suits them, and to arrange their seating according to their own preferences? We concede that there are liberating leaders who would look askance at Stan Richards' seating policy. On the other hand, those leaders do not run advertising agencies, which come with a particular set of internecine rivalries that can be very hard to counter—particularly when each group clusters on its own floor—and which can in their own right be an obstacle to each person's acting in the best interests of the business.

The point of liberating a workplace is *not* to return to some

Rousseauian state of nature in which man, unchained by society, lives a radically free and individualistic existence. If such a state were either possible or desirable, we would not need firms at all. But it is not possible. And so, in the real world, we work together to the extent that it is cheaper and more efficient to do so than to work apart, as the Nobel Prize-winning economist Ronald Coase has convincingly demonstrated.[4] And so, when an advertising agency squanders resources or misses opportunities because of some turf war between account managers and creative directors, that is not freedom in action. It is, rather, the result of the construction of institutional barriers to freedom: in particular, the notion peculiar to the ad world that certain questions may only be raised by creatives while others are the sole province of the account managers. No wonder Richards wrote, "Abolishing office doors and, later, walls . . . was probably the most profound act of cultural liberation we've ever undertaken."[5]

Note that while this *specific* problem is peculiar to the ad business, it is a species of one that we have seen repeatedly faced by leaders in the companies they liberated. At FAVI, a machinist could not make repairs on his equipment—only maintenance was allowed to do that. At Harley, work rules strictly defined what workers with various job descriptions could and couldn't do. And at USAA, they literally had one person to open the envelopes, another to remove the forms from the envelopes, a third to unfold and sort them, and so on.

Just like Zobrist, Teerlink, McDermott, and others, Richards wanted to blur those lines. And he knew enough about the existing dynamics of his industry to know that it would take more than an office party or an exhortation to work together to get that done. He needed to break up the fiefs physically in order to break down the barriers mentally.

All but the most dogmatic creative directors will admit, at least in private, that even account managers sometimes have a good creative suggestion, and vice versa. The problem that Richards faced was putting those good ideas from the "wrong" sources into action. And his solution was to force people to bump into one another—by separating them and shoving them together by turns.

At the same time, he liberated Richards Group employees in other ways—although choosing when to get to the office was not one of them. Stan Richards has a thing about people getting to work on time—before 8:30 a.m. in Dallas. That's 9:30 a.m. in New York, and as Stan puts it, he wants people in the office in case clients on the East Coast need to talk to someone. In fact, Stan Richards is so serious about it that everyone in the company has a personal identification number, and they are supposed to "clock in" by typing that PIN into one of the keypads found at the entrances to each floor of the office before 8:30 a.m. each day. It's a time clock of sorts, albeit one that you never clock out of.

This bit of regimentation is a source of both angst and humor at the Richards Group. A number of people have T-shirts with "8:29:59" emblazoned on them. And when we visited the Richards Group, we were introduced to the employees at what they call a "stairwell"—a short, sometimes raucous meeting held in the four-story stairwell in the center of the office. The employees held a poetry slam in which they attempted to describe the company for their visitors in verse, and more than one of the poems mentioned the mad dash that some people take through the parking lot and the lobby to key in their PINs before the clock strikes 8:30. We take this public ribbing of Richards over the policy as a sign that Richards Groupers see the clocking-in regimen as a quirk rather than a source of serious resentment.

At the same time, Richards shares the belief of Zobrist and others that people don't need to be clocked to get their jobs done. "Some bosses worry they won't get an honest day's work from people. They *must* worry about it, or nobody would make time clocks. But I've found that diligence is the rule," Richards said, "and not because we *make* it a rule"—except for that rule about what time you get to the office, of course. "Given the tools and the freedom they need to use their gifts, people enjoy working hard. . . . My experience around here has been that if people are imbalanced in their approach to work they are usually imbalanced on the side of working too much. . . . There may very well be some . . . with a disposition toward goofing off . . . but the culture pretty well takes care of that. . . . The diligent majority sets the tone and pace. . . . An open workplace is remarkably self-policing."[6] And yet he makes everyone punch in, and has chores for those who make a habit of missing the morning bell.

Whether this is a blind spot or a pragmatic concession to the habits of his industry is hard to say. It certainly sits oddly with Richards's talk, in his book and elsewhere, about trusting people to do the right thing. But Stan Richards is not a management philosopher. Some of the liberating leaders in this book are connected directly to one another or through a common intellectual heritage—McGregor's or Townsend's—arrived at independently. Richards is one of those who came to his views through a combination of a belief in his fellow man, as expressed above, and a desire to remove obstacles to doing the work that he loved. When we asked Robert McDermott or Rich Teerlink what drove them to do what they did at USAA and Harley, both men talked about their childhoods and their upbringings. Tom Quadracci explained the drive of his brother Harry as a reaction against bitter labor-management disputes he witnessed early in his career in the commercial printing business. Bill Gore, Bob Koski, and Gordon Forward all talked about the exasperation they experienced watching large corporations stifling people's initiative and creativity.

Stan Richards talked about advertising. "You know," he told us, "I've never thought that any of the things that I've done were radical. They just seemed natural." And then he delivered his bottom line: "I guess the thing that you need to understand is that my total focus is on our work. I was trained as an art director; that's where I worked for all these years. So everything is about the work. How good can it be? How good can it get? What can I do to keep making the work better and better and better and better? And so everything that I've done is for that purpose." In other words, if there are apparent contradictions between his emphasis on personal responsibility and tics like the obsession with 8:30 a.m., Richards justifies them as pragmatically necessary for "the work."

In *The Peaceable Kingdom*, we did find a passage that is the closest to a philosophical declaration as one can hope to get:

> I'd rather get burned now and then than to treat my employees like snakes. . . . Besides, experience shows that I'd be wasting my time as self-appointed corporate hall monitor trying to keep people in line all the time. My . . . colleagues are honorable men and women, and they prove it every day by their actions in a workplace where they're at liberty to run amok if they're so inclined. They're just not so inclined, that's all. The exceptions are so rare that to clamp heavy restrictions on the whole work force just to try to control the actions of the potential bad apples would be a colossal self-sabotage. We'd be robbing ourselves up front of the potential that people at liberty have.[7]

Richards has—effective upon his eventual death—given away his company to a foundation that is barred from selling it. Thus, the freedom environment Stan created for his people will never be destroyed by some Madison Avenue agency that might otherwise buy it.

For now, however, Richards owns 100 percent of the company. Even so, he is very open about company news—good and bad. Whenever "something comes up," whether it's losing a big account or winning a new one, he calls a stairwell to share the information throughout the company. He explained the openness this way: "The only way to defeat paranoia is by not keeping secrets, and so everyone is allowed to know everything." This is one reason that Stan Richards calls his five-minute stairwells.

"In most organizations," he explained, "the information goes to the important people first, and then it drifts down to the unimportant. There are no unimportant people here and therefore, information should go to everyone at exactly the same moment." A second benefit of the stairwell:

It is used to introduce prospects, clients, and visitors to all employees. Why is *this* a benefit? "A typical client working closely together will get to know twenty of us," Richards replied. "But the fact is there will be two hundred to three hundred others in this company who will touch and support their business in some way. And they will never meet [that client]. . . . But for them to see [the client] and to be a part of that experience that we have in the stairwell, makes us better at what we do because those people now feel connected to that client. . . . And this second benefit is far more important than the first."

Compensation is the one big exception to this openness. At the Richards Group, discussing your pay with your fellow employees is a firing offense. Asked to square this with his views on trusting people with information and being open, he said that it is "easier" this way. And certainly, it makes it easier on him, although his statement about paranoia, quoted above, would seem to apply in this area as much as in any other. Richards argued that people should decide for themselves whether they feel fairly paid, not by reference to colleagues, whose pay may reflect circumstances that don't apply to those around them. He may have a point, but the policy, like the time clock, is paternalistic in a way that Richards eschews in other areas.

But whether justified or not, these are exceptions. Most of what he has done at the Richards Group leaves people there far freer and more autonomous than their colleagues elsewhere. This satisfaction of their need for self-direction, as well as those for respect and growth, leads to both higher performance and employee happiness.

LOW TURNOVER, BOOMERANGS, AND OTHER SUPERNATURAL PHENOMENA

As at all liberated companies, the Richards Group's happy employees move on to other firms much less often than their peers do. Richards estimated a turnover rate of perhaps 7 percent annually—compared with more than 30 percent for the industry. "And I guess if you look at it from a practical standpoint," he said, "does it make the work better if we have turnover of key people in this agency? And the answer is no. It's not going to be better. It's going to be worse, and clients are not going to be well served." In this way, albeit without any of the religious overtones of McDermott, he is echoing Zobrist and the others: Employees who feel well treated are going to treat both colleagues and clients well in return. "I close every meeting with, 'Let's go have fun!' And that's the way it should be. Because if we are having fun, then the work is going to be better"— and the clients happier.

Stan Richards's approach is intensely pragmatic, and that does lead to anomalies. But the Richards Group nevertheless has managed to operate according to the same principles found at other liberated companies. It is, for one, deeply suspicious of controlling hierarchy and conspicuous perks of power. The seating arrangements are in some sense random but respect one principle: Within a room, those who have been with the company the longest, regardless of rank, sit the closest to the windows. A similar loyalty-reward program applies to parking spaces. Unlike many liberated companies, the Richards Group does have a small number of assigned spots near the entrance to the building. But these are not reserved for top executives. Rather, they have been awarded, again, to those with the longest service with the company, whether they are secretaries, account managers, art directors, or what-have-you. Moreover, if the holder of a spot doesn't need it or chooses not to use it, she is free to rent it to someone else in the company for whatever price she can command. In this way, what might otherwise seem an arbitrary perk can ultimately flow to those who value it the most. And in a final nod to loyalty, the company's conference rooms are not named after some luminaries but after those same long-serving employees—who, again, may not be senior in any other sense of the word.

Stan Richards himself has somewhat more space around his desk than most other employees, it is true, but even he doesn't get an office with walls and doors. All these steps are designed to replace the traditional privileges of power in a company with a different message: We treat our people with respect and dignity, and we value loyalty. And while this message may help explain some of the low turnover, we doubt very much that most Richards Groupers are hanging on at the firm for their shot at an eponymous conference room. Low turnover is another hallmark of all liberated companies. This is true even though none of the companies profiled in this book pay what could be called industry-leading wages. Stan Richards estimates that the base pay at the Richards Group is, on average, somewhat lower than at the competition—although he says that more generous bonus and retirement programs balance this out.

That may be true. But when it comes to talent retention, the psychic income—as McDermott liked to call it—of working in a free workplace is even more important than these alternative forms of financial compensation. This explains another universal feature of liberated companies: the "boomerang"—the employee who is offered a higher-paying job elsewhere, takes it, regrets it, and comes back. We met boomerangs such as Les Lewis at W. L. Gore & Associates at nearly every company we visited. The Richards Group, with some seven hundred people, had about one hundred of its own—one of the poets at the stairwell we attended read an ode in their honor. Pat Pelino, a consulting-practice leader at Vertex, insisted that she'd never seen anything like the way Vertex embraced its boomerangs. It has twenty-seven of them, or 4.5 percent of the total workforce—including three out of the company's top eight executives. At other companies where she'd worked, "It was like when you left, you left. There was no opportunity to come back, no matter how good the relationship was when you left."[8] Pelino had identified something that stands out about liberated companies. When Jeff Westphal tells his new hires "You're free to leave," the natural corollary is that you are *free to come back*. Forbidding either would be an affront to employees' personal dignity—it would suggest that they are either incompetent or not welcome to make the most personal of decisions and most individual of freedoms—what to do with their own lives.

At the same time, the fact that they come back in such numbers—and that nearly every company in this book has experienced the same thing—tells you something else. Those people found a real value in the way that they were treated and how they could grow and self-direct inside a liberated company that neither a higher salary nor a fancy title could fully replace. To put it into the language of psychology, they were having their universal needs met, even if *they* wouldn't talk about it in those terms.

Meanwhile, halfway around the world, another liberating leader has also made it her business—literally—to rearrange how her employees and her clients think about their office space.

12

THE SECRET OF LIBERATING LEADERSHIP

How Paradoxes and Wisdom Help Freedom

You can't fill a movie theater with a director. . . . The most important thing in the movie is the actors . . . and the decadence of the cinema comes from the glorification of the director not as a servant of the actors but as their master. The work of director consists of extracting from all of the actors the maximum human richness. So let us respect and love them and help them to be great because they are the people who make the cinema unforgettable.

—ORSON WELLES[1]

It's better to limp slowly along the right path than walk stridently in the wrong direction.

—MARCUS AURELIUS[2]

LIISA JORONEN IS the president of SOL, Finland's number two cleaning-services company, with eight thousand employees and

$212 million in revenue annually. And early one September morning she arrived to pick us up personally at our hotel.

The cozy hotel, it turns out, was once Helsinki's prison. The rooms are converted cells, with small windows facing the sky, so it was a bit of a shock to emerge into the lobby and find there the woman who has built the freest company in Finland, and possibly all of Europe. She was a short, slight blonde, waiting for us in a bright yellow raincoat and playing with a school-age boy, also blond. She smiled spontaneously.

"Hello, I'm Liisa," she said. "Do you mind if I first take my grandson to his school and then we go to the company?"[3]

We agreed.

"Do you mind if we take a tram? I have no car," she explained.

We knew from our email exchanges that she spends most of her time today on her farm in the south of France. "I need to give space to my children [her daughter and son, both key SOL executives]," she had written a couple months earlier. "It is not easy to be a child of Liisa Joronen. I have too often seen fathers who cannot give up and they 'kill' their children."[4] The meaning of this took us some time to understand. In the meantime, we were quite surprised to learn that she'd flown up from France to Finland for a couple of days specifically to show us her company.

After we'd traveled some way on the tram she told us it was time to get off. But the journey to the school wasn't over yet. "Now we need to change to another tram. You don't mind?" she asked, but the next tram took forever to come. So we took a taxi, dropped off her grandson, and finally arrived at SOL City, aka SOL Studio. The company's headquarters got this nickname because in 1991, when Joronen took over part of her father's business, the only place she could afford to rent for a head office was a deserted movie studio. It remains SOL's headquarters today, although its appearance has little to do with its movie days.

Joronen first joined the family business, Lindström, ten years earlier, in 1981, after fourteen years in banking. At the time, Lindström provided a range of cleaning services, from commercial cleaning to dry-cleaning and laundry. Her father anointed her CEO of Lindström at the age of thirty-five, and the trouble began almost immediately. Ten years later, it would culminate in the breakup of the company.

Joronen had strong convictions as to how a company should be run that she had not been able to put into practice as a bank manager:

> I had a dream of a company whose employees would be satisfied with themselves and their work, who could [have] influence on their own work and on their customer relations. I had a dream of a company without unnecessary rules and regulations, without unnecessary bosses and hierarchy that prevent people from doing good work. I deeply believe that people work well if they have the freedom to decide themselves many things concerning their work instead of their bosses [deciding for them.][5]

It turned out that the family business presented obstacles to realizing her dream. Her father was an old-fashioned, domineering type who would "not give up" and was still around most of the time, despite having officially handed the reins to Joronen. To avoid full-blown familial civil war, Joronen's father divided the kingdom. He offered Joronen the unprofitable cleaning and small waste-management activities, comprising one-fifth of the original company, while her brother and three sisters inherited the more robust laundry and linen-renting activities. Her father also told her and a key manager who followed her into the new company that both of them could return. "He was sure that it would never work. And we said, we will show ourselves, my father, and the rest of the world that we will succeed," Joronen later remarked.

The new company had no money. Joronen was not even sure how many of its former employees would stay—all of them did in the end—but it needed a headquarters. The studio space was hardly a traditional office, but it provided a blank canvas for the creative transformation SOL's new leader and employees immediately undertook. In their hands it soon started to look like no other company. In its audacity and bold colors, its interior design resembled the later offices of Google. Except at SOL, the interior design was conceived and carried out within five weeks by the people themselves.

From day one, Joronen organized the company according to her convictions, questioning traditional "how" practices: "Why should we have offices that look like offices? Why work from 9 a.m. to 5 p.m.?" The company's two hundred employees were asked to brainstorm and propose ideas about the workplace that they would like to have, and they responded with 1,146 suggestions. They also proposed the company's new name—SOL—with bright, sunny colors for the logo, symbolizing "positive spirit, happiness at work, creativity and courage."

Proposed workplace changes included getting rid of assigned desks for everybody—including Joronen herself. At the bottom left in the picture (see next page) are the bags people use to store their belongings after they've finished their work and cleaned up their desk. Two people, though, do have assigned desks: one at the entrance (in the far back in the picture) who is in charge of welcoming job applicants—and who still cleans up his desk for use by others when he's not around—and the union representative, whose desk is on the first-floor balcony. It's to this gallery that Joronen first brought us to tour the headquarters.

"It's very quiet now," observed Joronen, looking down. "There can be three hundred people here and sometimes it's like a circus or an amusement park."

We wanted to know what this depended on.

"It depends on the weather," replied Joronen and, seeing our surprise, explained. "Yes, of course. In summertime it is empty because people prefer their summer cottages. And if it's raining on Sunday evening, even Sunday afternoon, many people come here. And then on Thursdays . . . because we have free soup for everyone. They come for the soup and they arrange to have meetings that day. I always invite business

The interior of SOL's headquarters.[6]

partners or customers on Thursday because it is lively then and we have the soup."

We couldn't restrain ourselves from playing devil's advocate and asking, if people enjoy the soup so much, why not have it every day?

"It's too expensive," Joronen replied. And then she added, "And I don't want people to stay here. I want them to stay with the customers they want [to recruit], the marketing people to do marketing. . . . This is our headquarters. What do they do here? Very few people have to be here. . . . The more people you have here, the more you have internal problems. They create their own work and they create bureaucracy. Then you need more personnel managers and you need more people just to look after your own people."

We started to notice a puzzling pattern with this big-business-owning, tram-riding president. Having stepped aside as CEO in favor of her children, she professes to be reluctant to visit the company too often, but when she does, she clearly loves every minute of it (even flying to Finland from France for the opportunity).[7] She praises the free Thursday soup for employees and visitors alike but judges it to be too expensive to provide every day. In the first ten minutes of our conversation, Joronen told us—in the space of two sentences—that she "lives in chaos" but, at the same time, she insisted, "I don't go *there* and *there* and *there*," waving her hand in three directions, "I go somewhere." She also told us that once she "decides something," she'll "break through walls" to get it done—but she never "takes too big risks." She was, in a word, full of paradoxes.

And sure enough, she gave us another one a moment later. Returning to the question of corporate headquarters, we asked her whether companies that build large head offices are making a mistake.

"Oh, I love them," she said with her characteristic warm smile and just a hint of mischief. "I love them, because *we* clean them. And every time I give a speech to a client I end it, 'But don't do what we do here. I love you and your big headquarters because you are my client.'"

She was joking of course, but there was also something deeper in her attitude: Recall Harley's Teerlink saying "People don't resist change; they resist being changed." Beneath the humor, there was something of this wisdom in Joronen's remark. "It's not necessary for us" to have a big headquarters and all the support departments, she elaborated. "But, you know, it's their business. I always say, 'You can do good business in many ways. This is *our* way of doing things.'" But then she added, "I have to behave in society because I am the opposite of almost everything in the society. But I have to, because I still have the society, they are my clients."

So add "rebellious conformist" to the list of Liisa Joronen's paradoxes. We went back to the beginning: When her father offered her the most problematic, most unprofitable piece of the family business, did she hesitate?

"It was a big risk, but not too big, I thought," Joronen answered, adding: "I don't do any calculations, ever. I went to school for economics but [I never do them] . . . because if you've been running a business for five years, year after year, day after day, you know it." Then, to show she's serious about this approach to business, she added, "In 2009, for the first time, we have abandoned a budget. We don't do budgets anymore."

How do you run a business without a budget? From the start, she said, SOL's business philosophy was to avoid centralized corporate budgets and instead to have individual, supervisor-by-supervisor budgets. But now, SOL is leaving even those behind. In their place, supervisors will forecast only the end results: their "growth and profits." The goal, after all, is not to spend your budget, but to earn more than you spend.

That may sound too simplistic, but it recalled one conversation with Zobrist. Referring to the acquisition of the European steel giant Arcelor by Mittal, he asked us, "Do you know how many business indicators Arcelor had? One hundred and fifty. And how many does Mittal have? Four. Very clever company." And it's hard to argue with Joronen's results so far. In 2007, SOL grew 15 percent. Its profit margin was 8.7 percent, compared with an industry average of 3 percent to 4 percent. The profits continued even through the 2009 downturn, despite SOL's decision to charge less than the contractual price for many of its struggling clients, such as hotel and ferry companies.[8]

So, SOL's margins are very high because its costs are very low, we assumed.

"No, the costs are awful because the human costs are so expensive in Finland. Ninety percent of our costs are human," replied Joronen, adding another dimension to the puzzle.

So how does she explain the margins, we wanted to know.

"We don't spend money on overhead. Our overhead costs are very low. . . . Even if we are very profitable we do count every cent. We are very, kind of, lean. Lean, and stingy," Joronen explained, switching suddenly from company to family: "I mean, our family is stingy also." Not seeing what the family's stinginess had to do with keeping costs down, we asked instead how the company controls costs without an army of controllers.

"No, no, no. We don't control," replied Joronen forcefully. "I think if we, the managers, would have spent a lot on flights, good hotels, cars, the employees would follow our example. They understand the message we give here," Joronen continued. "We are a family company, 100 percent family company, we have always been. So what that means is that it belongs to the family, too, to set the example. I think that's very important. If I had a big office here, everyone would want to have one. I think the example is important."

A big business owner who flies only economy class? That filled our bag of paradoxes over the top. But before we attempt to resolve them, let's take a look at what Joronen achieved at SOL.

OUT WITH THE CLEANERS, IN WITH THE SERVICE AGENTS

The headquarters in the picture, which Joronen characteristically calls "awful, but . . . the cheapest and best place" available then—is still in use. But Joronen always wanted the action to be elsewhere. SOL is a cleaning

company, and you don't make much money cleaning your own offices—
and even less sitting in them. Joronen wanted her people out in the field,
exercising their "freedom to decide," as she put it, and dealing directly
with the customers. The first step was to build an environment in which
the cleaners were treated as equals. So, like Bill Gore before her, she began
by changing their title—from "cleaners" to "service agents." They also
asked for and got bright yellow and red uniforms, so they became highly
visible. While an ordinary office cleaner can be expected to dress in drab
colors, registering just barely above the office furniture in the awareness
of many of the employees around them, SOL's newly outfitted service
agents would be impossible to miss or to mistake—if you ever saw them.
Most office cleaners work at night, out of sight and mind. But not SOL's.
This was the big breakthrough in how SOL did business: SOL negotiated
with its clients to do the cleaning *during the day*, not in the evening or at
night. SOL was the first in Finland to do that. It started to clean during
the day not for its many business development benefits—more on those
in a moment—but because it wanted its brightly outfitted service agents
to be visible and proud of themselves and their work.

Once this groundwork had been laid, Joronen spent almost all of her
first year in a permanent tour of the regional studios—named after the
first one and, like the headquarters, designed by the people who worked
there. She repeated the same cheerleading message over and over: "We
are the best. You can do anything." But, of course, employees don't develop their skills and become able to "do everything" simply because
they are cheered on and treated superbly by their CEO. All service agents
were offered substantial training to acquire the skills to serve the customers for their full satisfaction—which they measured and collected from
the customers themselves. They were also trained in understanding the
numbers so they could grasp their own team's business rationale, profit
making, and even pricing, and to grow into service leaders.

Finally came the people's need to self-direct. The service agents were
organized into self-directing teams focused on specific clients and then

turned loose. Each team—based on the local knowledge of its market—decided what their growth and profit forecasts would be and created a budget to achieve them. Joronen admits to being "quite nervous" the first year, waiting to add up those numbers and learn what all those self-directing units had decided SOL's budget would be: "If the budget had been very low, what could be done? Or the reverse, if it had been very high?" Joronen remembered the budget game she had played herself at the bank, where everyone used to put down low growth targets because they always expected the higher-ups to add something on the top.

When the teams' budgets came in, she was surprised: Most of the teams put up ambitious forecasts, and, remarkably, they met their forecasts—despite a sluggish economy at the time. And these self-directed teams have never stopped since: From 1992 through 2008, they produced 15 percent average annual growth and 8 percent to 9 percent profit margins. But something more happened when these equally treated, highly trained people were turned loose on the customers. They did not merely provide cleaning services to the clients' full satisfaction—they even started to *sell* these services. While cleaning and interacting with the customer—recall, it's daytime—and while analyzing customers' satisfaction they often discovered new customer needs. It could be a customer unhappy with a wooden floor that needed waxing or with dirty windows that needed cleaning. Whatever the need, these service agents would then go to see the client's buyer, explain the newly discovered needs, and propose a price to do the job. This was possible in part because all the service agents were fully familiar with the company's pricing policies, margins, and finances. They also knew well that the margins on these extras are much higher than on the main cleaning contract itself, which must be won through competitive bidding.

So at least in SOL's free environment—"it's a company policy not to have policies"—there were no paradoxes: It was built on a consistent logic of self-motivating people through satisfying their universal needs. But what is the role of the CEO once the freedom environment has been built?

"Let's ask *her*." Joronen deflected the question to SOL's current CEO, Anu Eronen, Joronen's former right-hand woman, who replaced her in 2002. Eronen was coming out of the "summer cottage" built for meetings (in the picture's upper-left-hand corner), and Joronen asked her this question from up on the balcony where we were standing. Showing no evidence of surprise, the CEO thought for a moment and then replied, "Managing is organizing the success, organizing the kind of environment, [material and, more importantly] mental . . . and providing the tools to . . . activate all the success." Joronen added that when she was the CEO, Anu Eronen helped her, but today it is Anu who is "organizing the mental environment," stressing, for example, the company's focus on growth, profit, or what-have-you. "What you speak, you get," she concluded. This may sound deceptively simple, but it matches the importance placed by other liberating leaders on constantly sharing the vision with everyone in the company. The current CEO has maintained the freedom environment, so there is not much for President Joronen, retired to her French farm, to do. From time to time she'll fly from France to host visits like ours or to participate in external events. She has also continued to groom her children to succeed Eronen. (In 2011, they did. SOL meanwhile has grown into an 11,000-strong, $343 million company as of 2014.) But other than that Joronen stays away from the company. Yet when her son was asked how he feels about his mother's absence, Juppe Joronen was clear: "Liisa is all over the place, every day." This was the ultimate paradox: Joronen was nowhere and everywhere all at once.

These paradoxes are no accident. In fact, these apparent contradictions, found not only in the example of Joronen but of all of the liberating leaders, are not a sign of sloppy thinking, but rather of wisdom. To explain *that* paradox, a detour is in order.

THERE ARE NO CHINESE BILL BUCKNERS

Wisdom has a colloquial sense that we all readily understand. One recent psychological examination of wisdom described it, in part, as "excellence in judgment in matters of life combining personal and common good."[9] But research into the influences of how we make sense of the world gives us a better understanding of what makes somebody wise—as opposed to being smart, say, or knowledgeable. Wisdom properly understood is not about what we know—that's just information. Nor does it have to do with intelligence in the sense of IQ or intellectual horsepower. At bottom, wisdom is a function of *how* we think.

Some 350 years ago, French philosopher René Descartes put forward a simple-sounding proposition: If I can perceive something clearly and distinctly, it must be true.[10] But Descartes took for granted something that we now know isn't true—that our own minds are an open book to us, and that we can discover, by looking inward, all the possible errors to which our minds are prone.

The reality, however, is more complicated than Descartes believed. Our thought processes are influenced by a variety of factors of which we are often not even aware. Some of the intriguing research on what psychologists call "thinking styles" has focused on how they differ across cultures. These cultural differences are not of direct concern to us here, but the research in this field has illuminated aspects of how we think that we might otherwise take for granted or not see at all.

Take the case of the dire-sounding "fundamental attribution error," also known more mellifluously as the "overattribution effect." This is the tendency to assign too much credit and blame for a situation to a specific individual, without taking into account the surrounding circumstances or environment. Think of our desire to identify the hero or the goat when our favorite team wins or loses, and to place the burden for the win or the loss on their shoulders alone. Poor Bill Buckner, the Red Sox first baseman who allowed a weakly hit ground ball to roll between his legs in game six of the 1986 World Series, is a victim of the fundamental attribution error. A whole constellation of things had to go wrong for the Red Sox leading up to and after that play, but ask someone who Bill

Buckner is, and they'll likely tell you that he cost the Red Sox the World Series that year.

Psychologists once thought that the fundamental attribution error was, well, fundamental—a universal feature of how the mind works. But beginning in the 1980s, research revealed that it was, in fact, more of a cultural trait than a universal one.[11] In the 1990s, a team of psychologists tackled the hero-goat problem directly by comparing how Chinese and American sportswriters explained the same events.[12] What they found was that American sportswriters emphasized the actions of particular players in explaining the outcomes, while their Chinese counterparts focused on the context. Western thinking, in other words, tends to isolate actors and objects from their environments. In the East, however, context is king. Repeated studies have shown that East Asians are far less prone to the fundamental attribution error than Westerners are. This difference is the product of nurture, not nature, as people brought up outside their ancestral culture tend to adopt the characteristic thought patterns of the place in which they are raised. Chinese Americans, for example, fall in between the Chinese and the Americans of European descent. Studies of how mothers speak to their young children have uncovered an intriguing pattern: Mothers in Western countries tend to use mostly nouns in speaking to their babies, picking out objects and assigning words to them— "bottle," "diaper," "crib," and so on. East Asian mothers, in contrast, tend to use more verbs, focusing a young child's attention on the interactions between an object and its environment rather than on the object itself.[13]

Naturally, if these styles of thinking and habits of mind are learned, they can be changed, too. The wisest leaders are prisoners of neither of these dominant cultural milieus, but draw from the strengths of both. And in the past thirty years, developmental psychologists have shown that the best problem solvers think "holistically" and "dialectically" about the problems they face. That is to say, they consider all of the ways in which one problem may be related to its surrounding circumstances and environment—holism—and they are not afraid to entertain both sides of an apparent contradiction if it helps them move forward—that's dialectical thinking.

THE PARADOXES EXPLAINED

With that in mind, let's look again at Liisa Joronen's leadership style and her way of thinking about problems. She took a service—office cleaning—that is normally done as unobtrusively as possible, put her people in primary colors, and had them patrol the corridors of her clients' buildings in broad daylight in a way that they could not fail to be noticed. This was not mere contrariness, however. It emerged from the insight that visible employees would be *seen* doing their jobs, giving clients a perception of value. Visible employees would also act as the faces of SOL to their clients. Instead of scurrying about an office building at night like church mice after crumbs, they were encouraged not only to do their jobs with pride, but to seek opportunities to expand their business relationship with those clients.

The logic of it all is unmistakable and compelling—after you've set aside the prejudices about the nature of the work that kept you from seeing the opportunities the way Joronen did. *Dialectically*, she looked beyond the apparent drawbacks of having more-visible personnel at customers' sites and found the advantages that could result. And thinking *holistically*, she saw that higher visibility, liberated people, and unconventional work hours were all connected. Service reps who worked during the day but dressed like slobs would do her business no favors. And, even more important for our theme, none of these changes would likely result in any incremental business if those now-visible SOL reps did not have the power to act on their own and sell clients on new products and services as the opportunities arose in the course of their daily duties.

Joronen's business innovations were holistic—and wise—in another important sense. They took into account not only her needs as a business owner and leader, but her employees' needs as well. The uniforms and the daytime work schedules give them respect in a job that often lacks it. It encourages them to hold their heads high and take pride in their work.

Other paradoxes likewise become easier to understand once they are put into the fuller context from which Joronen approaches them. She flew from France to Finland to meet a visitor to her company, for example, but she escorted that visitor around Helsinki by tram. This is not mere frugality. It is part of the oft-repeated desire of all liberating leaders to avoid double standards. Just as Bob Davids speaks of "subordinating yourself to your employees," Joronen shows SOL's people that they are treated equally by not taking liberties herself or using a visiting "dignitary" as an excuse to be chauffeured around town while her employees take public transit. Single standards, however, do not necessarily mean thrift. What they do require is equity and fairness. For a long time, FAVI had a top-of-the-line Audi A8 among its company cars, and no special status or permission was required to use it for long rides to see clients. Sun Hydraulics has a beautiful, relaxing garden with a pond and fountain behind its plant—built at considerable expense. A large terrace opens up onto it so that everyone can enjoy the view while eating his lunch. And SOL's offices have dozens of sculptures and paintings from Joronen's collection—which she acquired with her own money.

Thus, liberating leaders' wisdom, with its holistic and dialectical thinking, helps to explain many paradoxes that so often strike a first-time visitor to a freedom-based company. But it can also explain one more paradox we encountered earlier: Liberating leaders such as Zobrist radically transformed their companies' managerial practices—and did so mostly through nonthreatening, often gradualist tactics. Yet Zobrist did not hesitate to take harsh steps against certain dictatorial managers, and to do so publicly.

This paradox, it turns out, is at the heart of why so few leaders attempt—much less succeed—to set their people free. There are many executives out there who have an inkling that they are not getting everything they could or ought to get out of the people in their charge.

But they are stymied as to how to begin, or else they charge forward with guns blazing—only to go down in a hail of bullets, leaving the old guard and their old ways firmly entrenched. It turns out that it takes the willingness to embrace a paradox—in this case, that of the nonviolent revolutionary—and the ability to always keep the big picture in view to eventually find the freedom solution.

"PLAN-ORGANIZE-EXECUTE" IS NO WAY TO RUN A REVOLUTION

Thousands of business seminars are conducted all over the world every year on the topic, "How to Be an Effective Change Agent," or some variation on that theme. They preach mantras such as "Plan-Organize-Execute." They teach managers how to lay out the steps, establish deadlines, and envision all the risks and how to handle them. This may be a great way to implement a new accounting or procurement system. But even here, the exercise in envisioning what could go wrong can easily fail to anticipate the biggest dangers. Some department will, unbeknownst to our change agent, feel it has been adversely affected by the change or was not appropriately consulted. When this happens, the resulting rift—or worse, the quiet insurgency—can drag on at the company for years. Even in relatively minor matters, it is impossible to prove logically to people that the leader's solution was right and that theirs was wrong. As everyone who has tried it knows, attempting to do so will only entrench people even deeper in their positions. These sorts of battles can last decades.

The stakes are much higher when it comes to transforming the way a whole company is managed, and the potential resistance is that much greater. Among the managers, of course, there may be some who won't resist at all, such as the minority at FAVI. Even in unionized, "how" companies such a minority often exists, as Adam Easter, billet yard and finishing manager at Chaparral Steel, observed: "I had over twenty years of steel experience [before] I came to Virginia in 2000, . . . both union and nonunion. I worked at one of the oldest plants in America and to the newest plant in America . . . and I never really had a problem managing in the union environment either because it boils down to the respect that you pay your people. Because if you show that you're concerned about their safety [and] their well-being, [if you stimulate] the mental portion of their lives to give that enrichment, [and they are doing] jobs where they can make a difference, you don't really typically have problems."[14]

This minority makes a great ally in the liberation campaign. But then there is the *other* group. Confrontation is ill-advised, and acquiescing to them will doom your hopes of liberating your company, as they will cling to their dual standards and their territorial claims and will make a mockery of attempts to reform management practices.

So a wise leader looks at the problem of intransigent managers holistically and moves dialectically to deal with it. To start, he will accept that these managers have legitimate historical reasons to resist the liberation—they have needs, too. Their position and status are threatened and their futures are made uncertain by the liberation campaign. Seen in that light, resistance is not only natural, it's rational. As Zobrist observed, FAVI seemed to be reasonably well run when he was named CEO. It was profitable and its practices were in sync with the times. As in most companies, the managers took comfort in this view of the company and had reason to believe their managerial approach was just fine. If not for some of Zobrist's accidental little discoveries, such as the exorbitant *true* cost of replacing a pair of gloves or the nightmare of repairing an imaginary lawn mower, even he might have continued to run the plant in the old way. Seeing the situation dialectically—from both sides—he started with changes that did not threaten those managers. Instead, he sent them to various seminars on alternative management approaches. Jacques Raiman did the same at GSI, sending his managers as far as the United States for it. Even later, when Zobrist took decisive action, beginning with his speech about FAVI-as-prostitute, he was adamant that a liberating leader should "never, ever leave anyone on the side of the road."

Rather than write somebody off because they've become a

counterproductive force or are resisting change, he said, "It's necessary to have the courage to say: 'I am ashamed, sorry. But during many years I let you do inept things that didn't allow you to fulfill yourself.'" And "courage" is the right word—rare indeed is the manager who will blame himself for the underperformance of a direct report. But notice what Zobrist gets as a result: He takes an impossible task—exhorting a suspicious and unconstructive employee to get on board—and transforms it totally by taking the blame on himself. "I let you do inept things"—if you mean it—puts the *listener* in the hot seat, because Zobrist has taken the blame on himself. Next, he suggests you make the following offer: "You have all the freedom and all the time to find in this company something much more constructive, first of all for yourself and then, for the common good." In other words, the one thing you *can't* do is to continue to stand in the way of other people doing their jobs. But the rest is up to you. Instead of, first, blaming the manager for doing a bad job, and, second, telling him how to shape up, Zobrist turns the whole encounter on its head: Take the blame yourself and leave the other guy free to figure out how to improve. Note, however, what he doesn't do in this hypothetical encounter: He does not pretend that unacceptable performance or behavior is acceptable in order to keep the peace, and he does not leave the preservation of the status quo available as an option.

In his twenty-five years with FAVI, Zobrist didn't dismiss any of the people whose bureaucratic jobs became useless in the freedom-based company. He did, however, fire three people—within a matter of hours—for bad faith and mistreatment of other employees. As Bob Davids would say, "The swift sword cuts clean," a mantra he employed when a person would become increasingly dictatorial and when he "realized that the rest of the people were waiting to see how long [Davids] will let this exist."[15]

Wisdom has also been helpful after the liberation.

Zobrist, who based his own style of dialectical wisdom on the writings of Douglas McGregor, Chinese tradition, and his own hands-on liberation experience, wrote that the overall principle guiding his action in the company after he achieved the "break" and built a freedom-based environment was that of the good Chinese prince mentioned in chapter 7: "To act without acting is a laissez-faire that does not mean doing nothing, but means creating conditions in which things happen by themselves."[16] How liberating leaders used yet another paradox—"acting without acting"—in order to *maintain* the freedom environment is the issue we turn to now.

13

THE ULTIMATE PARADOX

The Culture of Happiness as a Path to World-Class Performance

My job now is the keeper of the culture. That's my job. I do it by talking to everybody every day: "Hello, how are you, how's it going, what do you need?"

—BOB DAVIDS[1]

DAVID KELLEY—THE founder, chairman, and former CEO of the Palo Alto, California-based industrial-design company IDEO, has never met Bob Davids, but he unconsciously echoed him when he said, in answer to a question, "I view my job as maintaining the culture. That was the most important thing. . . . Everything else was a distraction."

We had asked him, "How much time did you spend building the environment—the culture—as opposed to running the business?" And when we asked whether he held this view of his job from the very beginning, he replied, "Absolutely."[2]

As an adult, Kelley built one of the most influential design firms in the world. As a young kid, he took his first full-sized bicycle, a bright-red Christmas present, and spent the day sanding the paint off so he could paint it green. Later he would build his own tandem bike by welding two bicycles together. He also made his own Halloween costumes, to rave reviews. As an engineering student at Carnegie Mellon University, and then again in Stanford's product design program, David Kelley's only passion in life was to design and build cool stuff. Today Kelley is a professor at Stanford's Hasso Plattner Institute of Design (the "D school"), where he spends most of his "free" time. And yet, when asked, he insists that everything besides maintaining IDEO's culture during his decades as a CEO was a distraction. Paradox again? Let's see.

It all happened, apparently, without a plan. While a doctoral candidate at Stanford, David did a lot of "creative engineering," working on projects spanning from medical equipment to a reading machine for the blind to computers.[3] In the late 1970s, Silicon Valley emerged as the place to be for young computer companies with an urgent need to develop innovative products. Many of them turned to Stanford students for help. Kelley was one of them, but he gleaned in these stints more than a simple way to gain extra money and creative design experience: "I thought this would make a great business." So, in 1978, together with a business partner, he started IDEO—then called Kelley Design—and soon had Steve Jobs knocking on the door to design an early Apple computer (and later Apple's first mouse). The company's reputation grew. In 1980, the partner—more interested in entrepreneurship, perhaps, than operations—decided to leave, and Kelley bought out his 50 percent interest. Kelley thus found himself not only without a partner, but more dramatically in his eyes, without a manager to run the business. Considering himself a creative engineer, his first thought was to hire somebody to run the place. But then the surprise came.

The company's fifteen employees, informed by Kelley about his intention, objected. "You're fantastic at taking care of us," they told him. "We love working for you." Kelley confessed that before that, he had never thought of himself as good at running the business and was surprised that his employees might see him as "good with people." But, obviously,

Kelley did *something* to warrant a unanimous recognition of his leadership skills. This "something" explains the paradox.

FROM CULTURE EXASPERATION TO CULTURE DESIGN

Unlike Bill Gore and Bob Koski, David Kelley didn't have a clear idea of the corporate environment he wanted to build. But, like Gordon Forward, Stan Richards, and Gore and Koski, he knew what he wanted to avoid at any cost: the exasperating environment he'd experienced at two big industrial corporations after graduating from Carnegie Mellon. At those firms, he says, "I felt like I was cattle, a sheep." Kelley explained:

> If you look at how these companies are set up, . . . you get hired, and [then] they say, "Here's your desk, you work for [A], you work with [B]." You are in a box! Well, I didn't get to choose them [A and B]. You wouldn't do that normally. I want to choose my friends, right? If I'm going to spend eight hours a day, or fifteen hours a day, working at something, I should choose who that is, rather than the company choosing who that is.

This didn't help Kelley formulate a vision for his new company, but it did allow him to make a statement that became legendary. When we visited IDEO, the company was preparing for its thirtieth anniversary, and Kelley's statement was emblazoned on the posters announcing the celebration: "I know that I want to start a company with all employees being my best friends." After he started to run the company by himself, one of his employee-friends complained that his chair was not comfortable. Kelley responded, "Would you like my chair?" He gave his friend his chair, making him so happy that he showed off the chair to his friends. In another company that would have been viewed as belittling the person, Kelley remarked, but at IDEO he considered himself as equal in status to his employees: "I never treated them like a boss."

He also instituted practices that would make sense among friends. One was Monday morning meetings. "Like the family sitting down at dinner on Sunday," Kelley explained, "the whole company gets together on Monday morning and we just talk about what's the most interesting thing that happened to [each one of us] last week." Kelley also systematically refused to formulate any policies and would refuse if some employees proposed them. "They [would] always want it," he said. "Well, I [would] answer them: 'Do what you think is right. Don't look in the book.'" At IDEO, leaders discuss decisions they are pondering with employees, giving them time to react. This included Kelley's decision to hire a new manager to replace his partner, which employees reacted to in an eye-opening manner. Indeed, it was these and some other practices that his fellow employees—and friends—appreciated and pointed to when they asked Kelley to "officially" assume the role of running the business. This, Kelley commented, "gave me the confidence to build the culture."

"Please meet my colleagues and, nevertheless, friends," is an old joke in academia, referring to the sometimes tense relations among professors, or between professors and their academic superiors. Though universities should be a harbor of peace, they—like any bureaucratic organization—foster individualistic interests that often lead to conflict-ridden, rather than friendly, relations among colleagues. Kelley did not introduce the above practices all at once—not, he said, "because I was smart [but] because that's the way I would want to be treated if I were them." In the beginning, he was inspired by the practices of one large company well-known in the Valley for its enlightened treatment of employees: Hewlett-Packard.

Hewlett-Packard was started in 1938 by two entrepreneurs in a garage in Palo Alto. The garage is still there, and today it bears a plaque that reads "Birthplace of Silicon Valley."[4] Their radical culture, called "The HP Way," was more renowned in the Valley than HP's product innovations. It was egalitarian, decentralized, and sported as its first principle "We have trust and respect for individuals." In a manner that would certainly please Zobrist, Hewlett once sawed a lock off a supply closet and left a note: "HP trusts its employees."[5] After that, no closet was ever left locked. At the time that Kelley was getting started, HP was still widely admired for its nontraditional culture. "I got the employee manual from Hewlett-Packard, tore the cover off it, and then I used it as my bible," he explained. But because at IDEO he had not merely employees but friends, he would improve on HP, adding, for example, an extra holiday to the number HP had. That lasted for some time, but Kelley wanted something better. Then one day, he had a "Eureka!" moment: "Geez, this is a design problem. I can be the one who designs a culture." At that moment, David Kelley transformed from a designer of cool products into a designer of cool culture and made that his "job." Paradox resolved.

DESIGNING FOR FRIENDS

One problem that Kelley did not share with leaders such as Liisa Joronen was how the office looked. From the very beginning IDEO employees had freedom to design their own workplace. When we visited IDEO, we saw an old brown Volkswagen microbus in the middle of one open space. Coworkers had bought it on Craigslist as an elegant prank for their colleague and friend. They removed the engine and gas tank, built a desk inside the van, and wired everything to make it a perfect office. The colleague was flattered and worked there for some time. Later, they redesigned it again, this time as a meeting space with an oceanside ambience. This unorthodox conference room echoes SOL's "summer cottage," designed by SOL's employees to add a lakeside ambience to their meetings. IDEO's workplace may, in fact, look something like a hippie hangout, and Kelley does nothing to disconfirm the impression, saying that some people have brought in not only dogs and turtles but snakes—big snakes. However, Kelley added, before making decisions that can affect a colleague—bringing in a huge snake, for example—the person consults with that colleague. If the colleague is affected negatively in his work, the envisaged decision is not carried out—a principle common to all freedom-based environments.

This principle of consulting with the affected applies not only to wildlife but also to moving, for example, to a different building. In the early days, IDEO occupied a series of small offices in downtown Palo Alto. As the company expanded, everyone agreed that it would be better and more economical to work in one bigger space. They moved into a four-story building, and then—surprise—employees didn't like it. Kelley laughed when recalling the episode: "It was too much like a corporate building. . . . Some of the freedom that people feel is that they can leave the building and walk around. And so if presently you walk between buildings, nobody says, 'Are you goofing off? Are you wasting your time?' 'No, I'm walking between buildings.'" But if you're all in the same building, you can't do that. So they moved back to the small buildings, nine of them today, in downtown Palo Alto.

At the time, downtown Palo Alto office rents were among the highest in the nation, which even for a successful company like IDEO, with clients waiting in line, was too expensive. So Kelley continued to look for more economical office space. Eventually he found a series of buildings renting for much less near the freeway. Happy with his discovery but following the principle of consulting on decisions that may affect others, he described his plan and added a sweetener. Instead of pocketing the savings on rent, he would distribute it as a significant salary increase to employees. At many companies, this would have been a no-brainer. But not at IDEO. Kelley's employees refused the move and the raise. They felt that it was important for their work as designers of consumer experiences to live among consumers: "We want to be able to see people: women pushing baby carriages; we want to be able to see moms, we want to be able to see everything." Then they added an argument that appealed to Kelley a great deal: They didn't want to move down by the freeway; that would make them too much like a traditional company. It takes guts to turn down a substantial raise for the sake of preserving your work environment. But Kelley's friends were not just any employees—they were liberated people who clearly felt they got more out of their jobs than simply a paycheck. And when they looked at what that raise would cost them—a cost that would never show up on any company balance sheet—they wisely turned it down.

FUN, HAPPINESS, AND THE GOOD LIFE AT THE WORKPLACE?

Kelley, in fact, touched upon the question of wisdom early in our conversation and without any prompting. He called the core of what he has built and is maintaining at IDEO "an attitude of wisdom," a notion coined for IDEO by two Stanford researchers. Robert Sutton and Andrew Hargadon studied the company's creative methodology back in the mid-1990s. Their view of wisdom—"acting with knowledge while doubting what one knows"[6]—derives from the Socratic view that a wise man knows the limits of his knowledge. Philosophers call this "epistemic humility."[7] As Kelley explained, IDEO's culture helps employees acquire this attitude of wisdom because it "supports people to allow them to express their ideas without being . . . hindered." It also helped them question the ideas brought forward by other people on the team. In contrast to the conventional notion of the lonely artist acting in isolation, Kelley's goal was "to move from an individual sport . . . to a team sport."

Kelley himself uses Socratic wisdom when he consults with his employees about his decisions—just as Jeff Westphal and other liberating leaders do. Yet the wisdom Kelley used in building and maintaining IDEO's culture went further. Socratic wisdom captures only part of what philosophers and psychologists today consider wisdom. We mentioned in the previous chapter the notion of wisdom as "excellence in judgment in matters of life combining personal and common good." That last aspect originated in ancient Greece, when Plato and Aristotle tied wisdom to happiness and the good life: "A man of practical wisdom [is] able to deliberate well about . . . what sorts of things conduce to the good life."[8]

This wisdom, sometimes referred to as Aristotelian wisdom, was also Kelley's cultural design focus: "Big companies . . . only have units to measure dollars. They didn't have any units to measure heart; social, emotional health. . . . This company is a reaction to [that] because it wasn't human." What he wanted instead was "a fantastic place to work, where you feel self-gratified"—or, in plain English, "have fun."

Kelley thought that a wise person should know not only how "to deliberate well" about things that "conduce to the good life," but also "how to construct a pattern that, given the human situation, is likely to lead to a good life,"[9] as some contemporary philosophers have suggested. He knew how to construct and maintain these patterns—IDEO's culture—that led employees to the "good life." But unlike Aristotle, his thinking was not simply analytical. Real wisdom takes holistic and dialectical thinking, and Kelley found his nonanalytical approach in IDEO's methodology of "creative design." This method has more in common with Socrates' dialogues than Aristotle's treatises.

First, a project's designers meet to share all they know about the product (or service).[10] Next, they split into small groups to observe consumers' real-life experiences with the current versions of the product. Back at IDEO, they share all they've learned and then brainstorm ideas for what a new product might look like. That done, every project member votes on all the ideas, which are posted on the walls, looking for those that are feasible and "cool." From there, the products enter a rapid prototyping phase, and mock-ups are presented to the client and other designers. As feedback is collected, improved prototypes are built and presented again, and so on until the product is perfected.

IDEO used this methodology to design hundreds of products, from Apple's mouse to a mechanical killer whale for the film *Free Willy* to P&G's squeeze toothpaste tube to, more recently, the Swiffer. It has also used this process to design services. IDEO, for example, redesigned AT&T's mMode wireless-data service—which led to a doubling of the membership in one year. The firm also designed the lingerie shopping experience for Warnaco Intimate Apparel, which had been seeing its sales in department stores brutalized by its rival Victoria's Secret.[11]

The methodology's power lies in *preventing* the participants from becoming analytical. It achieves this, first, by forcing designers into the field to immerse and observe—like anthropologists—how people actually work, play, and live. These are things that would go unnoticed or get buried in an analytical marketing research study or focus groups, but which are essential to intuitively grasping the consumer's real-life experience. Then, the methodology forces designers to come up with a very large quantity of ideas, including "crazy" ones, because brainstorming delays critique and analysis. Finally, after the initial selection, designers try out the surviving concepts with "cheap and dirty" prototypes. These are, in turn, presented and discussed with clients and colleagues because—as Socrates knew—one person's, or team's, knowledge is always limited. "Prototypes should command only as much time, effort, and investment as are needed to generate useful feedback and evolve an idea," IDEO CEO Tim Brown has written. "The more 'finished' a prototype seems, the less likely its creators will be to pay attention to and profit from feedback. The goal of prototyping isn't to finish. It is to learn about the strengths and weaknesses of the idea and to identify new directions that further prototypes might take."[12]

David Kelley used this same methodology to design solutions for IDEO's culture. He first proposed to have an extra holiday in the spring, which—after employee input—became an extra day off of one's choosing each year. It could be your birthday or anniversary or anything else—or nothing. This, in turn, evolved into a loose honor system about "day customization" because, as Kelley remarked, "we didn't pay much attention anyway." The move into that new four-story building proved to be a bad prototype, leading everyone back to their original office space. The building down by the freeway was another prototype, which the employees rejected without even trying it out.

The same holistic and dialectical thinking that underlies wisdom is integral to the "creative design methodology" Kelley used to design and maintain IDEO's culture. Observing employees (or customers) interacting with their environments—instead of isolating them and trying to influence their behavior through motivation (or attractive product features)—is holistic. Building quick prototypes while actively seeking outside input to improve them is profoundly dialectical. According to Kelley, it not only works, but "once you've had success a few times, you trust your creative . . . methodology . . . and you'll always use it." He believes so much in the power of his methodology that he views it as his life's legacy: "I've seen my whole life that my job, my dent in the universe, will be that everybody who comes in contact with me—employees, students—will become more and more confident in their creative ability." Kelley has even gone beyond influencing employees and students to change the thinking habits of some *clients* from an analytical approach to a more intuition-based one.

This, too, was not by design. It started as a way to get clients to stop bothering him: "Every client, every businessman who came in said, 'David, this is a very nice company. When are you going to really make it a company instead of a playground?'" So Kelley redefined the problem, "How can IDEO grow up?" into, "How can clients become less analytically serious and more intuitively creative?" The solution was a consulting activity focused on corporate transformation. Samsung, Kaiser Permanente, and Procter & Gamble, among many others, have benefited from IDEO-facilitated analysis-to-intuition transformation in their business thinking.

P&G, for example, first contacted IDEO to design new products such as the free-standing Neat Squeeze toothpaste tube and the Oral-B toothbrush for kids.[13] Later, in a bid to make P&G itself more innovative, CEO A. G. Lafley took his entire forty-person-strong executive team to IDEO's headquarters to learn about their design and innovation process. (IDEO promptly took them shopping for their own products.) Despite their enthusiasm, these executives were not able to reproduce IDEO's process back in Cincinnati in the face of resistance from the commercial side of P&G. It was then that, with the help of David Kelley, P&G executives realized that a deeper organizational transformation was required to make IDEO's innovation process work for them. In addition to transferring its design process to P&G, IDEO also trained more than one hundred P&G internal facilitators in it. IDEO also helped to create an "Innovation Gym" in Cincinnati, a physical space similar to that found in its own headquarters that is ideal for teams using the prototyping design process.

All of this has been beneficial to P&G, even though it falls well short of the thoroughgoing organizational transformation accomplished by Robert McDermott, Rich Teerlink, and others. P&G is a company with many virtues, but it is not a liberated one in the way IDEO is. But that was never IDEO's goal. "Our dent in the universe doesn't mean we have to do all the digging," explained Kelley. "We empower our clients. We teach them to fish,"[14] that is to say, to use less analysis and more creative intuition in their business thinking. And although—compared with the proprietary, carefully guarded approaches of most consultancies—Kelley sounds altruistic with his "open source" approach to fishing, he isn't worried: "I can give our methodology away because I know we can come up with a better idea tomorrow."

The culture that Kelley built at IDEO frees its designers both to do their best work and to have fun. And some of these designers have helped build similar, though more limited, cultures at client companies such as P&G, making it easier for *their* researchers and designers to produce and implement new ideas. But these clients aren't trying to radically restructure their whole corporate organizations—they are trying to develop environments and tools for a specific type of employee—one whose job it is to innovate and generate new ideas. And in "how" companies, this is a tiny subset of the whole. Even at IDEO, not everyone is a designer, so the question arises: Is IDEO a playground for its cherished designers, but *Dilbert*-land for everyone else? The litmus test of a liberated culture is whether it touches everyone—beginning with the receptionist and the janitor.

IDEO needs these people, too. But at IDEO these "support" functions have been organized into a work group called the "experience team." It's composed of several dozen employees responsible for receiving calls and visitors, accepting and shipping goods and mail, catering, setting up and breaking down project spaces, maintaining conference-room equipment, and even processing expense reports. In some companies "you see them feeling like victims," said David Haywood, IDEO's vice president for business development and a self-appointed guide to IDEO culture.[15] But at IDEO they work as a team with the mission of organizing co-workers' and visitors' experience of "living, working, and visiting here." What's more, they were trained in IDEO's creative design methodology to observe, invent, and prototype the best possible experience coworkers and visitors could have. One of the resulting ideas was to provide fresh bagels, cream cheese, coffee, and fruit every morning in the cafeteria. That way, people who came to pick up their mail—which is delivered to the cafeteria on purpose—would have a great experience while "talking to their friends." Every year the team even goes for a two-day off-site of the sort reserved for the big-time salesmen at some other companies. They rent a beach house, bring in meals and beer, and spend time brainstorming and designing unique experiences for coworkers and visitors.

Joani Ichiki is a member of the experience team who serves as a receptionist and food planner. When asked what makes working for IDEO different from other companies at which she's worked, she struggled at first with how to express her thought. "It's just different," she said. "I mean, I've worked at what, four other [companies], and it's just, I can't even explain it. It's *not corporate.*"[16] Was this because the people who worked at IDEO were friendly? "It's more than that," Ichiki replied. "I think here, if you have the initiative to try something different, they let you try and you can *do* it." IDEO provides all of its people—from Kelley to designers to the experience team—with a methodology for finding solutions that better the corporate environment. And then it gives them the freedom to build that environment.

IDEO is a design firm, so the interconnections between Kelley's activities as a designer of products and a designer of cultures are especially easy to see. IDEO's openness about how the company is run is clearly closely related to how the company designs for its clients—the same processes and the same sorts of interactions are required in both spheres. This relationship between organizational and professional openness is a vital feature of all liberated companies. In business terms, the open flow of information and ideas—from all corners of the organization—is without question the biggest single driver of innovation and financial outperformance. Every company in this book is, to some extent, applying their own version of Kelley's creative design process to building both their corporate environments and their products and business processes.

A HAPPY WORKPLACE, NOT A CULT

Even so, you may think that all this shaping of the corporate culture is simply an alternative and disguised means of employee control. And it is true that, instead of directly controlling their behavior through orders, policies, and motivational schemes—carrots and sticks—the freedom-based cultures use a number of norms—"unwritten rules"—that every employee must respect or face "soft excommunication." No culture is without norms, and some sense of "how things are done around here" is inescapable.[17] In a "how" culture, the norm may be "Always consult the hierarchy," while in a "why" company, it may instead be, "Inform and consult all persons potentially affected by your future decision," as it is at IDEO. This perception of the "social control" that a corporate culture exercises over behavior can be so strong that to outsiders, some liberated companies start to look like cults. And indeed, at Vertex, the Richards Group, and others, junior employees talk a little bashfully about how it must sound like they'd "drunk the Kool-Aid." But a liberated company's "rules of the game" are not imposed from on high. They grow up organically from people's own interactions with one another. And in keeping with their bottom-up nature, they are self-enforced; there is no managerial class authorized to enforce policy on those at the bottom of the pile.

The Kool-Aid drinkers are not in the grips of some nefarious cult leader; they are happy about where they work—and to their friends, this can be highly suspicious. To many people trapped in "how" companies, the very idea of being happy at work is unthinkable. But in this happiness lies one of the key differences between "how" and "why" cultures. "How" companies are never called cults because very few people are happy in them. And they're not happy because the cultural norms in these companies, instead of helping to meet people's universal needs, are designed to meet the corporate *nomenklatura*'s particular ones. As a result, many employees are not merely unhappy; they are chronically stressed out, with all the damaging health consequences that result from that. Seen in this light, it's the "how" companies that resemble real-life cults in the way they take advantage of new recruits for the benefit of the cult's leaders, and in which domination and stress are not far from the surface. Liberated companies, on the other hand, are built to meet people's universal needs so that they are self-motivated to act for mastery and happiness.

Finally, building a freedom-based environment is not a socially deterministic project. Unlike a "how" environment, which explicitly seeks to determine and control employees' actions, the freedom environment seeks to make employees free to act for their own and for their company's best interests—and to take full responsibility for it. Think again about Kelley's design process—it is a set of work practices intended to facilitate coming up with the best solution humanly possible. These practices exist to support the arena in which the best ideas come forward freely and can be acted upon.

One of the many good reasons that liberated companies all practice some form of IDEO's "consult with the affected" rule is that one never knows whose idea and feedback will be crucial to solving some problem.

So while a liberated company's norms and work practices constrain in some sense, they are liberating in another, far more profound, sense. Because these practices are "epistemically humble," they remain open to the contributions of all. "The goal," as IDEO CEO Brown put it, "isn't to finish. It is to learn about the strengths and weaknesses of the idea and to identify new directions [it] might take." The "constraints" are, in reality, "unwritten rules" that emerged to maintain that openness. The point of a bureaucracy, on the other hand, is precisely to be closed—to perform repeatable actions over and over in exactly the same way—and to "finish." To do what you "should do," in other words.

Bob Koski of Sun Hydraulics said that a liberated corporate culture is for "adults only"—for people who "are good judges of themselves ... [and] responsible for themselves ... [because here] they can't blame someone else for their nonperformance."[18] Liisa Joronen agreed that it is not for everyone and very tough on some because freedom comes with responsibility, and because a happy workplace demands self-discipline.

Not everyone is cut out for a liberated company.[19] Next we'll look at the challenge of sustaining a freedom-based culture over the years in the face of turnover among leaders and frontline employees alike.

14

BUTTERFLIES IN FORMATION

Sustaining Freedom Over Time

You can't step in the same river twice.

—HERACLITUS

OUR FOCUS ON liberating leaders may itself appear paradoxical, when freedom in the workplace begins with an understanding of the centrality of frontline people to a company's success and performance. This paradox arises because everything we have learned by studying these companies pointed in the same direction: The success or failure of the liberation campaign ultimately rested on the shoulders of the man or woman at the top—the leader's values, creativity, and wisdom were the key elements to the success of the project.

Even so, this reliance on a single, central figure does raise an important question: If it takes a leader with extraordinary qualities to build a free company, is it possible for that environment to outlive its creator? Can a liberated workplace be sustained, or is it the kind of happy accident that must invariably give way to bureaucratization over time?

This was, in a sense, Max Weber's bureaucratic ideal: replacing personal preferences with impersonal policies and procedures. Freedom in the workplace, on the other hand, harnesses all the information, insight, and actions that cannot be captured by rules laid down in advance. While a rule-bound mode of governance attempts to say, "*This has worked in the past, so this is how we will do it in the future*," a liberating leader knows that all kinds of valuable information had not been—and will never be—captured in those rules. She knows, moreover, that the desire to codify "what works" into rules is powerful and natural. Gordon Forward, the ex-CEO of Chaparral Steel, illustrates this danger with a story.

One day at Chaparral, a new employee stopped Forward to tell him how impressed he was with all the freedom he found in the company. Gordon thanked him. The employee went on, swept up by his enthusiasm. He thought it was great, for example, that nobody wore a jacket and tie in the office. "Let's have a policy that nobody wears a tie to work," the employee proposed.

"If we write that rule," Forward replied, "I'm going to wear a tie!"[1]

After telling us this story, he laughed and added, "It's such a stupid thing to write a rule." Stupid—unwise, even—but natural. This young employee liked Chaparral's company culture so much, he wanted to codify it. And this impulse—to turn one's preferences into rules for everyone else to follow—is a constant danger to be guarded against. This doesn't mean that there can be no rules. As Gordon Forward notes, Chaparral, a steelmaker, had lots of rules, particularly in the area of safety. These are vital in a business in which one is dealing with three-thousand-degree molten metal. And, as we've seen, all liberated companies have some unwritten rules, such as "Don't produce memos—inform orally" at GSI; or "Consult all the affected colleagues before making a decision" at Gore and IDEO. The key is to distinguish between the informal rules that arise spontaneously to signify some shared habit—a local tradition—and those that formally impose one person's preferences on everyone else. Forward was acting as a keeper of the culture in the sense described by Davids and Kelley, reminding his enthusiastic new recruit that the important thing was not whether white-collar employees wore ties, but their freedom to decide that for themselves.

Now, the freedom to wear a tie or not is hardly the most important business decision a company can make. That is precisely the reason that Forward likes to tell that story: The way he sees it, if you need to make rules about trivial matters, how can you trust employees to make important decisions on your company's behalf?

TIES, MIDRIFFS, AND THE DESIRE FOR RULES

This view of dress codes in particular was echoed at both Sun Hydraulics and Vertex. Greg Hyde, Sun's human resources director, connected dress codes with a theme we encountered earlier: the use of rules to avoid what would otherwise be considered normal human interaction. "Why have a dress code?" Hyde asked. If someone is offended by someone else's state of dress, "Aren't they the ones who should talk to them about it?"[2]

The dress code is a means of replacing that conversation—admittedly, a potentially awkward and tense one—with a formal rule. And a hierarchy to enforce it: "If you have a hierarchy," Hyde explained, "now you have to go to him [the boss] and say, 'Hey, he is violating the rule! Can you go tell him?'" Hyde added, wisely: "And now you create animosity between the people." A minor conflict that might have been resolved amicably becomes an occasion for one employee to wield the company's authority against another. That use of the hierarchy increases animosity, suspicion, and tension. A rule—in this case, a dress code—designed to maintain civility and decorum has, in practice, diminished both. And in the process, as Gordon Forward would put it, the appeal to rules has diminished everyone involved from responsible adults to rebellious children.

Now, again, dress codes are not the most pressing issue facing any business, and yet they came up repeatedly in our encounters. At the request of some employees, Jeff Westphal once let a committee meet to establish a dress code for Vertex. But after they had discussed such weighty questions as how much midriff exposure was too much, they returned to common sense and to the answer offered by Greg Hyde at Sun: If an employee is dressing in a way that makes someone uncomfortable, those two people should be able to talk without having to send the discussion through official "channels." Stan Richards had a formulation almost identical to Hyde's: "Dress so that you are comfortable, so long as it doesn't make someone else feel uncomfortable."

This topic came up spontaneously in the first hour of our visit to Chaparral Steel's mill—now owned by Gerdau Ameristeel—in Petersburg, Virginia. "The system Gordon [Forward] had implemented is of informality and of no symbolism," Gary Titler told us. Titler started at Chaparral's Texas mill in 1982 after a prior stint at a unionized plant in Michigan. When we met him in 2008, he was raw materials manager for the Petersburg mill. "The only time you'd see a tie other than a funeral would be in the case of a new-hire interview and that was it. At other times that tie was symbolic in the industry in the early days of the haves and the have-nots." Then, without pausing or even acknowledging the shift, Titler moved from talking about ties to talking about more profound freedoms. "So when I got to Texas, what I found was that the culture expected me to use my mind, to have ideas, expected me not to sit there and tell my fellow employees what must be done but tell my manager how I could help him."[3]

Quad/Graphics has taken a somewhat different approach, which relates to the nature of its business. Those working in the company's printing plants must dress in a certain way both for the sake of safety and because working around barrels of ink all day requires certain concessions in matters of fashion. But Harry and Tom Quadracci wanted to avoid creating an obvious distinction of status between the "suits" in the office and the printers, so they decided to institute a standard dark blue shirt for everyone. These are available in several styles, but all have the names of the company and the employee embroidered on them, and everyone from the CEO (and son of founder Harry), Joel Quadracci, on down wears them, with few exceptions.

This enforced uniformity would not sit well with all liberating leaders. But it is consistent with a principle that they would all embrace the need to eliminate outward signs of unequal status. The assault on status symbols was vital to the original liberation campaign at all the companies we studied. Some of them went farther than others in this respect: Quad, for example, has reserved parking spaces for some executives. Frontline people, when asked about them, told us that the reserved parking didn't bother them too much. It was an inconsistency with the single-status culture of the company, but not, they felt, a fatal flaw.[4]

By the same token, preventing status symbols from creeping back in over time—especially after a change of executive control or ownership—is critical to sustaining the free workplace. After such a change, these symbols are not by themselves enough to ensure that workers are both able to act freely and feel as if they are. As Gordon Forward's tale of the ties makes clear, it is all too easy for a new generation to accept the form of these changes while failing to grasp their real meaning. If this is not corrected, one of two mistakes is likely to follow: As in the case of Forward's enthusiastic young employee, a freedom can ossify into a formal rule. In that case, its benefits are lost. The enforcers of the once-informal rule become akin to the monkeys in the hosing experiment described in chapter 3. None of them knows any longer why you can't climb those stairs, but they do know to beat up any poor monkey who tries.

Alternatively, the practice in question is modified or abandoned because the underlying rationale for it is not understood by the next generation. Without that understanding, the natural tendency is to focus only on the accountable costs of the existing policy or practice.

MEANING OF WORDS AND MAINTENANCE OF TRADITION

Les Lewis of W. L. Gore & Associates spoke to us about this danger in a different and more serious context than mere clothing. Lewis, you will recall, had been with Gore almost since the beginning. And when we met him, he was perhaps the second longest serving employee still with the company. As such, he saw himself as "flag bearer," and he lamented that some of the relatively new hires didn't see the point of some of the "values," in Lewis's words, that the company's associates took for granted in the early days.

As noted in chapter 4, Bill Gore took on-time delivery seriously. So seriously, according to Lewis, that "he actually raised his voice" when someone suggested "that it was okay to have 85 percent on-time delivery." Many businesses, most in fact, view this question as an economic decision—a trade-off between the inventory costs and the delivery level. Zobrist's story of hiring the helicopter to complete a delivery is only the most extreme example of how costly it can be to insist on 100 percent performance. But for Bill Gore, delivering on time wasn't about the economics, at least not in the way the accountants would measure it. "Bill Gore was adamant," Lewis said, "that when you make a commitment to a customer, when you make a promise date for a delivery, it is a *commitment*. And the reason he was so adamant about keeping it was that it was a waterline decision. And it is waterline, because you jeopardize our reputation when you don't deliver on what you promised." Once you ruin your reputation, he said, "You never get it back."

This was one of the few topics that could really get Bill Gore "exercised," in Lewis's rather delicate phrase. It is no overstatement to say that it is the kind of question that, for Bill Gore, went to the core of what kind of culture he wanted W. L. Gore & Associates to have—a culture in which everyone kept his commitments. This had to be as true when it promised a delivery date as when it said that Gore-Tex was "Guaranteed to Keep You Dry." In the early days of Gore-Tex, in fact, Gore recalled all the Gore-Tex-lined apparel in the country because one Gore-Tex parka had leaked. The company then offered all dealers a total replacement program—at a cost of $4 million.[5] This also had to be true of the commitments one made to one's colleagues—as captured in Gore's notion of the "credibility bucket."

And yet, for all the passion that Bill Gore himself brought to this question, the bean counters seemed to be gaining ground in recent years. "I am, I have been, for the last fifteen years, the lone wolf, the lone voice on this," Les said. New hires—especially, in Lewis's view, those who had come from other large companies—saw Gore's commitment to 100 percent on-time delivery as quaint, not to say uneconomical.

Gore, the company, was approaching fifty years in business when we met Les Lewis. And in many ways the continuity of its culture—over three generations and counting—was remarkable. But for all that, here was Les Lewis fighting a lonely rear-guard action on an unwritten business principle that had once been central to the company's very identity. For Lewis, this was symptomatic of a certain drift in the younger associates' understanding of Gore's culture, and he spoke about bringing in old hands and retired associates to talk to the next generation, tell war stories, and try to imbue in them something of the spirit of those old days.

Everyone appreciates a good, well-told war story, so it wasn't surprising to hear Lewis say that younger associates were "hungry" for those tales. But whether they can be wholly effective in conveying the tradition is another question.

It would be strange indeed if a company that was founded by a man who liked to ask, "What mistakes have you made lately? None? You haven't been taking enough risks," stopped taking risks itself. So some evolution and reinterpretation of corporate tradition is not only inevitable but healthy. Each of these companies was founded or transformed based on the wisdom that the person at the top of the organization didn't have all the answers and that IDEO-style prototyping is necessary to pull in the ideas of others.

ETERNAL VIGILANCE IS THE PRICE OF FREEDOM

That said, when a company is doing things differently from what people may have experienced at other firms—or even throughout their upbringing and schooling—some sort of reeducation is needed to maintain the most important pieces of that culture. W. L. Gore & Associates has done that for more than fifty years, in part by the very words they use to talk about the company's culture. The "associates" and the "sponsors" and the "credibility bucket" and the "waterline" are all reminders that Gore is different. This language is off-putting to outsiders and newcomers—some of whom leave the company rather quickly—but this is not necessarily a disadvantage. Its goal is not to alienate outsiders, but rather to alienate everyone from traditional ways of thinking about responsibility and authority inside a company. The language Gore uses captures its culture's unwritten rules, key principles, and practices. If Lewis succeeds in explaining the principles of "fairness to the customer" and "commitment" to his younger colleagues, they will find for themselves the appropriate balance between 100 percent on-time delivery and the cost-reduction on inventory. It is not foolproof, of course. No tool is. And as the meanings of the words used can themselves shift over time, it requires eternal vigilance.

Gore's focus on language is just one possible technique for preserving and transmitting a company's culture over time, especially after a change of leadership or control. Not all of our companies share Gore's focus on using language to transmit culture. Some do it through social events and rituals, such as Quad/Graphics' annual musical, performed by all the top executives in front of the employees and their families. The executive cast of the show rehearses with professional singing and dance instructors for three weeks—during their free time, of course. Other companies transmit their unusual cultures in part through the radical physical design of the workplace itself, as at SOL, IDEO, and the Richards Group. But even these ways may not suffice after a company is sold or a key leader moves on.

When thinking about sustainability in the face of a change of ownership, it is helpful to distinguish among the different ways a company's ownership can change hands. At Gore, there is some employee ownership through an incentive stock program, but control of the company remains with the descendants of the founders, from Bill Gore's son Bob Gore to the current generation. Among the other companies we've studied, the Richards Group remains in the founder's hands, and CEO Stan Richards has no intention of handing ownership to his successor—or to his children. "Why would I want to ruin their lives?" he answered when asked why he wouldn't bequeath the business he'd built to his offspring.

Since Richards is still in charge and still owns the company, it is too soon to say whether his plans will work as he hopes. Recall that he has made arrangements to have the ownership of the agency put into a trust that is not allowed to sell the company. One of three named potential successors will be told that he or she is CEO when he steps aside, but not before.

Richards has taken the extraordinary step of putting his company into a trust upon his death because he doesn't believe that the agency's unique culture could survive an acquisition by a bigger firm. But as the experiences of other liberating leaders show, the transition of executive control can present as much of a challenge as a change of ownership—and sometimes more so.

Bob Davids grew Radica Games into an eight-thousand-person company from two people in nine years. When he stepped down as CEO in 1999, the board installed his handpicked successor. And yet, when asked what happened to the culture he'd built there, Davids said without hesitation that it is "totally gone."[6] His replacement, he said, "killed it in about six months." Asked *how* he destroyed it so quickly, Davids again didn't hesitate. "With dual standards," he shot back. "Dual standards are the cancer of culture. . . . It is absolutely the biggest killer of all." By this, he meant that his successor immediately began accruing all the perks of privilege that a liberating leader, if he is to be successful, must eschew. In isolation, taking over the corner office and other gestures may seem relatively innocent, but employees get the message immediately. The new man in charge is no longer subordinating himself to his employees; he feels he has arrived and is announcing it to the world.

Bob Davids relayed this fact—the swift dismantling of what he spent nearly a decade building—matter-of-factly. One of his favorite phrases is, "If you don't have an exit strategy, your job owns you." This is true, he argued, regardless of whether you or someone else owns the company on paper. In this respect Davids is very different from Stan Richards and Bill Gore. He has run a half-dozen companies in his career and measures himself by their performance *while he is in charge*, not by the standards of posterity. He would view the attempts of Gore and Richards to preserve what they built as quaint.

While at Radica, Davids said, he had a conversation with a promising employee who was resisting a promotion to plant manager. Davids asked him, "You want me to tell you the secret of being a CEO?"

"Yes," the reluctant manager said, and took out a pencil.

"Okay, write this down. [This is] the secret to being a CEO. You've got to—ready?—*make more mistakes than anybody else*. But never make the same mistake twice." Because you can only choose your successor once, the chances of making a mistake are high. But in the end, all you can do is try to groom the newcomer and leave behind the best person you can. If the new CEO—or the shareholders, if the CEO is not also an owner— takes the company in a different direction, there is really nothing that can be done about it. In this sense, Davids is justified in not troubling himself too much about Radica's fate. The company was eventually acquired by Mattel and became a division like any other in its new parent. Davids's ambition is to build world-class companies and to sell them—not to make them last and remain intact. But for those who do strive to leave something behind that stands a chance of outlasting their leadership, we uncovered plenty of evidence that it is possible.

TENDER, LOVING CARE TO MAKE
THE FREEDOM LAST

In 1996, David Kelley sold the majority of his stake in IDEO to Steelcase, which then went public. But according to Kelley, neither this change of ownership nor the transfer of his CEO duties in 2000 to Tim Brown ever prevented IDEO from operating as an independent unit and preserving its culture for the past thirty years. Rich Teerlink took Harley public in 1986 and then spent a decade liberating it. He stepped down in 1999 and today, Harley is on its third "liberating" CEO. Jim Ziemer, the current CEO, recognizes that "it takes initially a visionary to say that there is a different way."[7] But Ziemer is not shy about making a bold comparison to the culture Teerlink built: "It is like a religion, it is spiritual. You've got to believe in it and act like it's a religion. . . . Sometimes, maybe, command and control is great, but . . . if you don't have the same leader, then it does not sustain itself. If it is a religion, it can sustain itself."

Ziemer, who started at Harley as a union member, is not exactly a priest. But just like Kelley and Davids, he is a keeper of a culture that "needs maintenance and tender, loving care to keep it alive." He does forty town halls a year and walks through the shop floor asking what people need; he gets worried if he's *not* being stalked by employees: "I'd wonder if we had a new manager who said, 'Don't talk to Mr. Ziemer.' I'd be suspicious." Just as Les Lewis noticed in Gore, Ziemer is convinced that "you need continued care [for the culture] as well as the training" for new people coming from the "how" world. Harley puts every new hire though a six-month training program so that they have their own opportunity to doubt, ask questions, and absorb Harley's culture. Ziemer, by the way, started as a disbeliever. He admits now that at the beginning he didn't know why Teerlink's project was good and just went "along with the party."

Bob Koski, who founded Sun Hydraulics in 1971, took it public in 1998. The company's free culture persists despite the pressures of public ownership and two changes of the guard at the top of the company. His family still owns a minority stake. Koski himself passed away on October 11, 2008. But as of the middle of 2008, Koski, though ill, was still going to work regularly at Sun. He had equipped the company with a roster of executives who share his views about how a company ought to treat its people. The documents he left behind, from the original business plan reproduced in chapter 5 to his shareholder letters, offer a record of his vision for the company and its culture.

When we met him, Koski didn't like our use of the word "freedom." When asked why, he answered in a Socratic way, with a question: "How do you get the butterflies to fly in formation?"[8] Koski founded a high-precision manufacturing company. Its lifeblood is building hydraulic valves and manifolds that perform better and more consistently than the competition's. That means getting things exactly right, over and over. Sun is very good at that. It is so good, in fact, that even its rejects outperform most of the competition's parts. In other words, Sun lives or dies by consistency, reproducibility, and uniformity. So when Bob Koski asked about getting the butterflies to fly in formation, he was soft-pedaling his view: Sun can't afford butterflies in its plants, no matter how orderly they are. But that doesn't mean Koski wanted automatons, or Henry Ford's mythical "pair of hands," either. What Koski wanted were adults. When you go to work at Sun, he said, "You can't come as a parent and you can't come as a child. You have to build adult relationships." Relationships, in other words, in which each person treats the other as intrinsically equal.

That sounded familiar, so we pressed him further. How would Koski define Sun's essential characteristic, the thing that set its culture apart? At first, Koski said it was "hard to describe." He added, cautiously: "Some people understand it and some people don't, from day one." The "core thing," he said, is what he called "universal information," which sounds just like Stan Richards's idea that "there are no unimportant people," and so information should go to everyone at once. Universal information is intimately connected with Koski's idea of adult-to-adult relationships. It also echoes Bob Davids's warning that "dual standards" are a cancer. Dual standards can take the form of reserved parking spaces and other perks, but they can also show up in the flow of information within a company. And when information is wielded as a source of power, it is a clear sign that people are not being treated as adults or as equals.

That type of behavior is all too recognizable in most companies. But when Koski said you either get it or you don't, he was referring to something deeper than whether your manager treats every tidbit of information from on high as a state secret. This, in his words, was how he tried to illustrate the importance of "universal information" to Sun Hydraulics: "Take a look at what goes on on a factory floor, where all the problems are. The supervisor has two jobs. One is, a new employee comes in, he's got to teach him the job. So in that respect he's a mentor." But that supervisor, at most firms, is also the gatekeeper to the outside world. "When the work is coming in, he's getting the work, telling these people what to do and think." In the first role, as mentor, the supervisor gives the employee the tools, the knowledge, and the resources he needs to do his job. He helps him do it. But in the second role, he denies him some of those same things: information about order flow, deadlines, and scheduling. Koski continued: "Now this person, this worker, is being held accountable for something *he has no control over*. He can't pick what he does, how he does it, where he does it, or when." All these things are under the supervisor's control, and yet the worker is still held accountable for getting the job done on time according to a schedule being set by somebody else. The supervisor has his own goals and performance measures to meet, and so he, in turn, imposes requirements on those who answer to him in order to protect himself.

Koski said he didn't "have a good vocabulary" for talking about these workplace dynamics, and that he didn't know anyone who did. And he sometimes struggled with the words for what he was trying to express. But the strength of his grasp of the essentials was made clear by what he said next: "And that's where the problem is in terms of psychology: 'Hard' drives out 'soft.' And over time, the new supervisor, who starts out being mostly unmeasured, and then very soft with telling people what to do, becomes very eager, or impatient, I would call it, and more driving all the time, because he's being held accountable for the results. And that's the problem."

In other words, within a traditional, "how" system, the "soft" manager is either made "hard" or is driven off. If he goes easy on his subordinates, they will underperform because they lack the information and tools to motivate themselves to get their jobs done. A soft boss in a rigid system does not equal liberation. In fact, as Koski pointed out, it invariably leads to the opposite as that soft boss squeezes a little bit harder over time to meet his own targets.

"So how do you fix it?" Koski asked, and then answered his own question: "Provide all the information that anybody could want, and then teach them how to find out what they need to know."

"Universal information," in other words, is not simply about respect and equal treatment. It is a palliative for the destructive dynamic that Koski—much like Robert McDermott at USAA—described: The information deficit contributes to reduced productivity, because workers are operating in the dark. That leads to more control and less freedom for the people, necessitating still tighter control, and so on. As Hugh Osborn, a consultant working in education reform put it, you find yourself "chasing failure down."[9] Indeed, of all the ways to treat people as equals, providing them with abundant, "lavish" information is the most direct booster of their performance. Inversely, controlling and withholding information from people is the most direct way to chase failure.

Koski's insight was another version of creative problem redefinition. Instead of asking how to improve the mechanisms of employee and information control, Koski solved the problem of how to properly equip people with information about their jobs and the authority to act on that information. When you remove the need to have the supervisor detail how and when to get the job done by giving people the information they need to make those decisions themselves, you change the whole dynamic between the leaders and their people. Koski again: "Then the leaders, as I prefer to call them in the company, managers or whatever, are mentors. And they never have the drive to become hard. [Because] they're never holding anybody responsible for their performance, or not often." The workers' jobs have been "enriched," in McDermott's words, by both information and knowledge, and the managers' jobs have been made more fulfilling. And neither is being held responsible for factors that are outside their control and in the others' hands.

"One of the things we tell our boys," said Kevin Grogan, plant manager of Chaparral's Petersburg mill, "is that the best decisions are not always made at the top."[10] Jim Macaluso, in charge of melt-shop maintenance, added: "The people on the floor are making decisions in our mills worth millions of dollars. So we have to support them, give them tools and knowledge, and show them how to be better at that."[11]

Placing these responsibilities where they belong satisfies the needs of both the leader and the led to direct their own affairs and, therefore, eliminates stress. It also treats those frontline people like the adults they are. Another creative redefinition: The problem of "how to soothe relations between managers and subordinates to reduce stress" becomes *"how to transform the hierarchical relationship into one between equals in order to eliminate stress."*

It is no accident, then, that some variation on "universal information" came up with every liberating leader we met. It is an essential corollary, as Koski framed it, of altering the traditional "how" company dynamic. Perhaps butterflies can't fly in formation because they aren't well informed about their destination. Thus, they become—to use David Kelley's expression—sheep, herded from place to place by a sheep dog who is merely following the commands of a shepherd, who alone knows the destination. And we shouldn't be surprised, as Liisa Joronen remarked, that these sheep look unmotivated or just plain lazy: "Everyone wants to do good work. [People] are not lazy. . . . Everyone wants to be good. . . . It's like animals. They are not bad. We treat animals in a bad way," and you get bad behavior in return.[12]

Joronen, once she retired from her CEO position, achieved a result reminiscent of the peaceful Forest Troop baboons on her French farm. Having seen the film *Babe* five times, she gradually built a similar environment, acquiring several dozen domestic animals, including a pair of extremely smart piglets. But Joronen outdid *Babe*, and not only because her farm is real. Wild animals—deer, boars, rabbits, and foxes—moved onto the farm's land, too, and seem to coexist peacefully "because," Joronen explained, "we don't hunt and we give them food." Talk about the benefits of tender, loving care.

Employees, of course, are not sheep nor dogs nor wild animals, all of which have the rather simple need to be treated well physically. Ironically, it is to that need that for atavistic reasons many "how" companies still cater, although their environments more closely resemble George Orwell's *Animal Farm* than Joronen's. Employees are people with universal human needs. For them, being treated well includes access to "universal information," knowledge, and more. Indeed, what Koski didn't mention about information hoarding is the conceit implicit in it—that the information possessed at the top, or the center, is the most valuable, and is therefore worthy of protection and secrecy. Eventually, it is trickled down in meager drips and drabs to people on the frontlines on a need-to-know basis—a fetish at traditional "how" companies and a running joke among their frontline people. The flip side of this is that the information that only the frontline employee possesses—about the myriad ways in which his time or materials are wasted during the day, or the aspects of the company that most irk customers, driving them away—is deemed not worth knowing or listening to. Withholding information from people about decisions that affect them prevents them from offering input and a chance to improve the decisions made at the top.

If David Kelley hadn't informed everyone about his idea to move the company down by the freeway, he would certainly have done it, saving a buck but losing the immersion in the urban environment that his designers believed was critical to their work and success. He would also have had to herd them there. Instead, IDEO's leaders always inform and consult employees about important "destination" decisions. Once the decisions are accepted and shared, employees are invited to organize for themselves how to reach the destination. Most of the time they succeed, which means that, perhaps, a free environment does enable people "to fly in formation." Zobrist, for one, was convinced that they can. He compared FAVI not to butterflies but to birds:

> A cloud of starlings can be composed of hundreds of thousands of individuals. But when a hawk is near, the whole flock reacts instantly, as if it were one bird! A complicated system, with a boss, information relays, [and] even with decisions delegated close to the field, would not be able to react so swiftly. Indeed, two *simple rules* guide [the] cloud's functioning: (1) every bird constantly watches out to never collide with her immediate neighbors; (2) when the danger is near, the threatened birds dive into the cloud's center, provoking immediate movement of the whole flock.[13]

Zobrist cautioned, "But if one of these two rules is not respected, the system collapses into chaos." He concluded: "Chaos is characteristic of systems incapable of establishing complicated rules, or of respecting the simple ones." Indeed, complicated rules-based "how" systems do function, and sometimes they are so big that the drag the rules have on their forward progress isn't easy to perceive. But, as we've seen, the alternative to "how" systems is not anarchy or chaos. It's freedom, provided everyone—or nearly everyone—shares the destination and agrees on a few simple rules. Just watch a flock of starlings overhead.

HUMAN BEINGS ARE NOT RECTANGLES

There is no reason that "universal information" access cannot or should not be maintained over time and independent of changes of ownership. It clearly meets any reasonable test of a sustainable practice, one that is not dependent on personality or any particular leader within a company. While a new boss *can* decide to start withholding information that affects the people below her, the practice of sharing all information with the people who are affected by it can be embedded in any company's culture.

Of course, information access alone doesn't make a company or its culture sustainable. People must also be able to act on what they know to advance the company's goals. Some liberated companies, such as W. L. Gore & Associates, take a radical approach to ensuring this freedom of action *over time*. By eschewing titles and jobs in favor of commitments, Gore frees its associates in the present day as well as keeping them free over time. Here's how.

A job, especially when frozen in place on an organizational chart, takes on a life of its own. It's possible that, at the moment it is created, a job fills a vital business need. But those needs change over time, while the jobs and the org charts change much more slowly. Gore's concept of commitments is designed to mimic the way the company's actual needs evolve: Associates don't get reassigned all at once from one unit to another, or moved up and down in a periodic purging and reorganization. Instead, they migrate, moving from one commitment to another as their time allows and their interests dictate. This begins on a new hire's first day. When she asks, "Where is my job?" the answer she gets is, "Figure it out."

This organic system allows people to grow and direct their own work lives in a much more natural way than the typical agony of waiting for a promotion and worrying about getting passed up, with all the office stress that attends such moments. The feelings of many employees placed in that position are summed up in a bit of office black humor—or wisdom: "Where there is death there is hope." Those moments are stressful, of course, because they are largely outside our own control. But they are also stressful because they are so artificial—you might work for years to prove yourself in a job, trying to build up the case for you to get the next big promotion, only to face the equivalent of a coin flip by your boss that determines whether you receive the recognition you've sought.[14] Of course, in reality, the question of whether you have contributed effectively to your company's performance over those years is not an arbitrary one. But those rigid, rectangular "boxes and lines"—to use Rich Teerlink's mocking expression—of the organizational chart have a way of making us feel like it is.

Even as the boxes confine the people within them, they lock down the organization itself, too. Those periodic mass reorganizations that all companies undergo are the proof of it: Every couple of years, several units will be merged while others are broken up; this vice president will be relieved of some responsibilities while that one is given new ones. All the boxes below them are shifted around accordingly. The accompanying press release always includes a quote from top management about the necessity of realignment in "a changing marketplace." There is nothing new about this ritual. In *Up the Organization*, Robert Townsend quotes noted first-century Roman satirist and writer Petronius Arbiter: "We tend to meet any new situation by reorganizing; and a wonderful method it can be for creating the illusion of progress while producing confusion, inefficiency, and demoralization."[15]

Bob Koski described organizational charts, a little hyperbolically, as "casting in stone something that's going to change." It's not exactly stone, because these charts are frequently torn up and revised. But they are certainly static, while a world-class business—like the world itself—is not. That's why Townsend warned against printing and circulating organizational charts: They suggest that the higher-ups know more than they do. "It would not hurt to assume, in short," Townsend wrote for *Playboy* in 1970, "that every man—and woman—is a human being, not a rectangle."[16] And you never know when your company's fate may lie in the hands of a night janitor who answers the phone when she ought, really, to be mopping the floor.

Because of this adaptability, Gore's *lack* of formal organizational structure is not, as one might suppose, a hindrance to sustainability. Gore's fifty-year history testifies to that. As Koski argued, great companies are constantly reinventing themselves anyway, so at best an organizational chart provides an *illusion* of stability over time, while modifying it of-fers—as Petronius wrote—an *illusion* of progress. An organization that employees adapt on the fly—like butterflies reacting to a sudden wind gust—is less likely to build up, over time, anachronistic little fiefs that no longer serve a strategic purpose but are difficult to get rid of, because you can't reduce the number of people underneath so-and-so. Zobrist called organizational charts a company's stomach and asked: "How can a company be successful if it is totally focused on its stomach and totally ignores where the food comes from—the client?"[17] And in that sense, a liberated company has a sustainability advantage—those organizational rigidities, which might be allowed to build up for political reasons, don't do so if there's no chart by which to keep score. And without artificially imposed barriers, valuable information about clients, markets, and op-portunities will flow in lavishly—a key to sustainability of any business.

Not all the companies in this book have gone as far as W. L. Gore & Associates in this regard, although the distaste for documents such as org charts is a recurring theme at liberated companies, for good reason. But Gore's track record and growth performance show that it is not inevitable that a company's structure will harden too much over time if it is diligent about staying fluid. In Gore's particular case, the very language its associ-ates employ serves as a form of institutional continuity.

FREEDOM STRENGTHENS "WEAK SIGNALS"

None of which is to say that there can't be drift in the wrong direction—or even a catastrophic collapse of a relatively free culture, as seems to have happened at Radica Games after Bob Davids's departure. One long-serving employee of USAA, since retired, lamented privately to us that some things had changed for the worse since Robert McDermott retired in the early 1990s. It is still one of the great customer-service companies in the world, and it has the results to show for it. But he noted specifi-cally that it had fallen out of the ranks of the hundred best companies to work for in recent years, and he feared that some of McDermott's hard-fought gains were not completely understood by his successors at the top. USAA, perhaps in part because of its military heritage, never abandoned many of the privileges of rank, and its executive suite is both opulent and fortresslike. The overwhelming evidence is that the culture McDermott built at USAA remains largely healthy forty years after he came to the company and seventeen years after he left it. You have only to pick up the phone and speak to a representative or to speak informally with its people to appreciate what he accomplished. But whether those who succeeded him fully appreciate why he did everything he did is an open question. And sitting in their mahogany-lined redoubt on a company visit, it seemed easy to forget just how important those voices on the other end of the phone are to the company's success.

But even if USAA's culture were to collapse completely—which is unlikely—a forty-year run would be nothing to look down one's nose at. USAA has gone through several CEOs since McDermott's retirement, while maintaining a freedom-based culture that McDermott himself would still recognize. The same can be said in 2015 of Gore at 57, Sun Hydraulics at 44, Chaparral and Quad/Graphics at 42, and IDEO at 37— all having undergone at least one change of CEO since the original liberation campaign. To ask for more would be to risk tilting the playing field too far in favor of "how" companies.[18] At best, that method of organization offers an illusion of stability across generations and personalities. It is not without reason that Wall Street perpetually frets over succession questions even at their most beloved companies—perhaps especially so. All too often, the business press lauds the "system" put in place by a successful corporate leader, declaring it the model of the future—only to see it crumble when a successor is named or circumstances change. The "system" inside a successful company almost invariably gets more credit than it deserves, while the contributions of good fortune and great employees get overlooked.

Looked at in this light, freedom-based companies are actually *more robust* than their "how"-focused competitors. To some business-people, encouraging freedom seems like, at best, a very delicate dance between total anarchy and fruitful experimentation—even to Bob Koski, who worried about the butterflies in formation. Stories of rogue traders taking down banks and high-profile embezzlement cases are guaranteed front-page news, so it's little wonder that anxious CEOs—especially of publicly traded companies—might live in fear of being one clever thief away from total dissolution. It would be a mistake, however, to assume that this particular type of risk is greater in a free company than any other. If anything, the 97 percent or more who are basically trustworthy are likely to repay the faith vested in them. In any case, managing for the tiny minority—Gordon Forward's 3 percent—who might somehow pose a threat to a firm's safety, security, or finances has both costs and risks, too. A company in which people are accustomed to being treated as intrinsically equal and being able to act on their own initiative is, in fact, more likely to catch a rogue or a thief than one in which the dominant culture demands that everyone keeps his head down and minds his own business: Recall Stan Richards's comment in chapter 11 about goofing off and how the culture—people's peers, not the boss—disciplines such employees. Terry Holder, the manager of Chaparral's roll shop in Petersburg, says that peer pressure plays a big role in keeping steelworkers safe at the mill, too. "If you have a young guy," he says, "missing a step in safety, his peer is going to pull him aside and tell him: 'Hey, you did not follow a process or safety process. Get your act together and make sure you don't do this again.' You'll have his peer say that more than his manager."

In a liberated company, more people have more authority to make their own decisions on behalf of the business. This dispersed decision making understandably *feels* more dangerous—the fewer people there are who can make decisions for themselves, the fewer people, seemingly, can make a bad decision, right? Here, too, the advantages of a highly centralized system are overstated. In fact, they are nonexistent.

This decentralized decision making, which may be perceived as a weakness of a liberated company, is—on the contrary—a major source of strength. All companies, however rigidly organized, are inescapably dependent on everyone who works there. Concentrating authority at the center might appear to reduce the *number* of sources of decision-making risk. But even people without any authority to take helpful action on the company's behalf can still commit devastating blunders through incompetence, ignorance, or malice. Nobody has ever sought or granted permission to run an oil tanker aground or crash a train.

At the same time, dispersed authority to make decisions and take actions has enormous benefits. It is true that many people on the frontlines of companies will never see everything the CEO sees from his Olympian perch. But the converse is also true: The head of the company can never know everything that everyone on the frontlines learns every day about how his company and its customers are doing.

Management theorists have borrowed a term from physics to describe the sort of information possessed by these frontline people. They call it a "weak signal," which is the sort of information that is important—and might later prove vital. But by its nature, it doesn't rise to the attention of management because it never gets passed up the line or, if it does, it gets lost in the aggregation of data or in the noise of larger problems with stronger signals. One example is the design of the O-rings that sealed the booster rockets of the space shuttle. A NASA engineer knew long before the 1986 *Challenger* accident that their design was flawed, and he expressed his fear. But because there had not yet been an accident, the signal was weak. By the time it became strong enough for someone to act on, of course, the flaw had become tragically clear. It is the remote starlings, in other words, that are the first to see the falcon approaching. In too many companies, that knowledge deficit accumulates, showing up only after a big customer is lost, a major opportunity is missed—or worse. There is also no mechanism for self-correction when this happens: Mistakes are acknowledged, efforts are redoubled, control is stiffened, but still the information languishes because the only people who possess it aren't free to act on it.

BIRDS FLY AWAY FROM CAGES

This situation is, unfortunately, *also* sustainable for long periods of time, especially in very large "how" companies with a high capacity to both lobby and borrow. But in the normal course of events, talented people see opportunities that their employer is not acting on, and they leave to pursue those themselves, as Rich Teerlink's Dutch immigrant father did.[19] A foreman with International Harvester, he partnered with four other workers, bought his former employer's old equipment at the junkyard, and opened up his own shop. The partners quickly adopted all the ideas they had been unable to implement while at Harvester, and in ten years the company grew to become one of the top three in their niche industry and was written up in *Fortune* magazine. Some of these start-ups turn out, of course, to be dead ends, but a smaller number turn into blockbusters. And a few of these inadvertent spin-offs become monsters that eventually threaten the parent company itself. As is often said, these companies will ultimately hear their employee's ideas—when that employee has gone to work for the competition.

Sun Hydraulics, Quad/Graphics, Richards Group, SOL, and Gore are products of just this kind of attrition. No company can pursue every opportunity, and some people will strike out on their own just because they can and because it suits them. But yet another distinguishing feature of liberated companies, as we've seen, is their low rate of employee turnover. In every case in which data is available and meaningful comparisons can be made, these liberated companies have turnover rates well below average. Employee loyalty is a big advantage when it comes to sustaining a culture of whatever sort: It means more stable interpersonal relationships, institutional knowledge, and levels of expertise within the company. But this loyalty is an even bigger advantage for sustaining a *free* culture simply because the latter relies essentially on unwritten rules, on tradition, and on its keepers. Of course, very low turnover has a flip side: Companies need fresh blood. For liberated companies, though, it's less of a danger because they typically grow fast and hire a lot—still 15 percent annually at Gore, which already has more than ten thousand associates. And these companies make it easy for people to leave both because they genuinely want them to work at the place that best satisfies their needs and because they seek boomerangs, who are tremendous culture keepers, like Les Lewis at Gore. All the impartial rule making in the world won't sustain a company culture if you can't keep the people you need coming back to the office day after day.

When Max Weber wrote of the need for a bureaucracy to discharge the "official business of administration . . . precisely, unambiguously, continuously, and with as much speed as possible," he overstated the precision, lack of ambiguity, continuity, and speed of the bureaucratic system. It is possible to program a computer to run in the way that Weber described, but centuries of corporate organization have not yet succeeded in similarly programming people or organizations to behave as according to an algorithm.

People remain stubbornly human, despite the attempts of visionaries from Josiah Wedgwood to Weber and others to correct that fact or to design it out of our ways of running a business. A liberating leader—unsurprisingly—redefines this problem and takes the opposite approach. Rather than pushing against the impulses, desires, and needs that make us human and animate us in every other aspect of our lives, he tries to get them rowing in his direction. Men and women worked, invented, struggled, and strived long before the first business owner put the first foreman over their shoulders and a time clock on the wall. Sometimes they worked out of desperation, but they also worked out of the desire for growth and self-fulfillment. Ironically, the Industrial Revolution eventually led to the production of such vast amounts of wealth that the primordial needs for shelter and sustenance are largely taken for granted in the industrialized world.[20] And yet there remains something atavistic about our attitude toward the needs and motivations of our employees.

The modern entrepreneur exemplifies the ancient artisan's desires for recognition and self-direction; those needs are universal. And yet too often we treat our employees as if they were primarily driven by the need to satisfy their material wants. The liberated companies in this book have succeeded so fantastically because they have tapped into the higher universal needs—and not just of a few "great talents," but in every corner of the organization.

There are limits to how big an organization can be and still broadly tap into those universal needs. Both common sense and experience tell us this must be true. But whatever that upper bound is, it's high enough that easily 97 percent of all businesses in the world fall below it. In addition to the 10,000-plus associates at Gore, USAA employs 26,000 people, Quad/Graphics has 25,000 people, and SOL more than 11,000. There are companies that are larger than that, even a lot larger. (Since this book was first published, 138,000-strong Airbus, 111,000-strong Michelin, and 65,000-strong sport retailer Decathlon have joined the corporate liberation movement.) But not many, and what Gordon Forward said about managing for the 3 percent applies here, too—particularly given the fact that all large corporations are divided into smaller divisions and business units that enjoy a degree of autonomy to arrange their own affairs.

Experience tells us that those higher universal needs are felt more acutely in some people than in others. Bob Koski estimated that as many as one-fourth of the people who seek a job at Sun Hydraulics cannot adjust to the level of both freedom and responsibility that they find when they get there. Those people are "free to leave"—an expression that Bob Koski used, unwittingly echoing Jeff Westphal. But as we've already seen, oppressive, bureaucratic corporate environments also drive people out—birds hate cages. Kevin Grogan recalls how Chaparral's Texas mill would occasionally lose employees to unionized plants in the area offering two to three dollars an hour more. But, Grogan says, "they would come back and say 'Money isn't everything.' It's not what they're looking for."

The low employee turnover at liberated companies suggests that fewer people are scared off by "too much" freedom than are turned off by bureaucracy and lack of control over their own jobs.

Suppose, however, that this is not true—that some significant portion of the working population really prefers to be a cog in the wheels of corporate bureaucracy. Apologists for feudalism used to argue the same way about the average man and his ability to govern himself. But suppose that, when it comes to work, it is true for at least some people. If you are running a business, and you have to choose a system of organization, would you pick the one that would naturally self-select for people who wanted nothing more than to punch a clock and collect a paycheck, or the one that would self-select for those seeking satisfaction of their universal needs to motivate themselves to act for the best of the company? Which system would you choose? To put it another way, which group would you want your competitors to end up with?

KNOWING WHAT YOU DO NOT KNOW

There is no system of organizing or running a company that is foolproof. We mean that literally: Just as a fool with a tool is still a fool, a fool with a well-run company—liberated or not—can drive it into the ground with alarming rapidity. Even very smart people can act foolishly, and it takes a wise person *not* to do so occasionally. So we have declined to offer a seven-step plan for liberating any company, anywhere. It seems more useful to describe instead what successful liberators have done using their creativity and their wisdom.

The leaders in this book all shared common qualities: They all had a drive to build world-class businesses. But moreover, they all possessed a deep and sincere belief in the value of treating all their people as intrinsically equal, in helping them grow and self-direct. They were not seeking to embrace the latest management fad, though they used many management techniques—Total Quality Management and others—when those were compatible with their beliefs. This genuine commitment to satisfying people's needs is what convinced employees to join in. Employees, like children—an appropriate comparison in this instance—can smell a fraud a mile off. And nobody looking to sell their employees on "Freedom, Inc." just because it might add a point or two to company margins will win many converts. Human nature being what it is, some will try, but they will fail.

Freedom works because it embraces what Douglas McGregor called in 1957 "the human side of enterprise."[21] It engages people more fully in what they are doing, and so produces self-motivated employees in a way that no mere paycheck can. To succeed in engaging people more fully in their work, a liberating leader must, first, eliminate corporate signals that some employees are more equal than others. If you tell someone, directly or indirectly—say, by asking him to punch the time clock—that they are there only to be a pair of hands, one of two things will happen: They will comply, or they will leave. Either way, you lose the benefit of his brainpower, which could be solving problems invisible to you or finding opportunities—also invisible to you—for your business.

There is wisdom, as Socrates said, in knowing what you do not know. Of all the obstacles to casting aside the traditional corporate structures, Jean-François Zobrist's exhortation to do as little as possible may be the greatest in practical terms. The type of personality that "wants the keys" to the business is not often naturally disposed to adopt Zobrist's Zenlike, Taoist attitude. They worry, in fact, that only frantic activity can justify their position—and their pay.

To this point, Bob Koski said he was never the highest-paid person at Sun Hydraulics "because I never deserved to be." The impulse to appear to earn one's paycheck by frenetic activity is a natural one. But just as great manufacturers preach economy of motion, great leaders need to overcome the urge to act for action's sake. Action and decisiveness are needed to liberate a company, especially one established along traditional, top-down lines. Leadership is needed to ensure that employees *share the company's vision, understand their "charge," and know that they are free to act with those things in mind.* To this end, employees must also be equipped with *the information and tools they deem necessary to act.* But, by definition, a company that frees its people to act on their own initiative will leave less for the person at the top to do.

This need not make a would-be liberator too nervous, however. Judged by their financial performance, every CEO in this book is a standout. And judged by their ability to create and maintain an environment that makes their people both happy and highly productive, their record is even more impressive. All the evidence suggests that the latter—maintenance—task is harder, especially over years or even decades, than turning in good growth for a period of time.

The relationship between employee freedom and company performance is not merely a coincidence. Freedom works because we don't know what we do not know, and because some of what we think we know is wrong—or soon will be. There are no cures for those mental ills except help from our fellow man. If only we can harness the additional knowledge of more of our peers, we can even, *pace* Weber, move much faster than the bureaucracy can. And because the world around us and around our businesses is changing much faster than in Weber's time, the only way to harness that knowledge is to allow those who possess it to act on it when necessary, right away—*now*—without waiting for some boss to approve it.

A fragment survives from the famously cryptic pre-Socratic philosopher Heraclitus. It is quoted at the beginning of this chapter. Heraclitus's paradox was that, while the river may always be within the same banks, it is forever flowing and changing, and what is true about it in one moment may be wrong the next. Imagine trying to fish in that river under the rules of "how" corporate organization: Standing on the banks, an employee spots a fish amid the currents. If you're lucky, the employee asks his supervisor: "Can I cast the lure?" We say, "If you're lucky" because looking for fish might not be that person's job. Maybe he chops wood along the river or mows the lawn on the banks. But say you *are* lucky, and he asks his boss, who asks his boss, and so on up to the senior fishing committee. Even if that chain of command is relatively short and the answer delivered efficiently, the odds are that when the message is finally relayed back down to the water's edge, the fish will have moved on. That assumes that somebody else, who was free to fish and didn't have to ask for permission to cast his line, hasn't caught it in the meantime.

The CEO, the man at the other end of that chain of command who sees the river from afar out the window of his corner office, simply has no way of knowing how many fish swim past his company every day. There is no system of controls for ensuring that those opportunities are acted upon, or even that they are learned about in time. The river is constantly flowing, and nobody knows all of it at any one moment. As Jeff Westphal of Vertex put it, "My measure is the net performance of the organization, so we can either get an itty-bitty bit of leverage out of the incremental power of my little pea brain or we can get a ton of leverage by the incremental power of six hundred brains." Jeff's wisdom lies in knowing that however much the man at the top knows about the business, he knows less than all those people working for him put together. This is true even of the most knowledgeable, most qualified CEO there is—because the river is always flowing. Free your people, and you'll be surprised at what they fish out of it.

EPILOGUE: CORPORATE LIBERATION AND ORGANIZATIONAL PROCESSES

Since the publication of this book in the fall of 2009, we have never stopped reflecting on corporate phenomena. Some of the news was troublesome, such as reports about questionable control, safety, or motivational practices. Other stories were positive and showed how values could make a difference for the better in the corporate world.

The years since *Freedom, Inc.* first appeared have witnessed tremendous growth in the number of companies and organizations that embarked on their own corporate liberations. This growth has in turn led to questions about the nature of this liberation phenomenon. Is it a new fad? A new model that consultancies will soon implement cookie-cutter style? Or is it a leadership and organizational philosophy?

Tens of thousands are now discussing corporate liberation in media and on social networks. Some of the echoes of this debate—though not all—can be found on our blogs at www.freedomincbook.com (in English) and www.liberteetcie.com (in French). They contain, among other things, the op-eds we have published over the past six years. In this epilogue we reproduce some of that work, organized along key organizational processes.

This is not an exhaustive catalogue of corporate liberation applied to each and every organizational process. It couldn't be. To reiterate—corporate liberation is a philosophy, a set of convictions about people and leadership. Once articulated within a company's unique cultural context, it profoundly transforms most organizational process and practices, making them appropriate to our times. We show how it solves some challenges and we invite readers to embrace their inner "architect" or "winemaker" and craft their own liberating transformations.

CONTROL AND REPORTING

Instead of Stress, Worker Freedom:
We Are Micromanaging Our Employees to Death[1]
If President Nicolas Sarkozy wants Frenchmen to be happy, he might worry less about how many vacation days they get, and more about the crushing bureaucracies in which they work.

The French media is busy discussing the series of suicides at France Télécom. Since its trade unions started to track the data in 2008, 23 of the company's employees have committed suicide and 13 have attempted it.

The company's executives are no doubt chafing under the garish limelight, and critics of the coverage may have some points. As with airplane crashes, suicides are attention-grabbing but may be statistically unrepresentative. France Télécom has more than 100,000 employees, so perhaps if data were available on other companies, the suicide rate at France Télécom would not look exceptional. In their list, the unions themselves attribute some of the suicides to strictly personal causes. Like airplane crashes again, suicides can have a variety of combined causes.

But as the French say, there is no smoke without fire. A recent study reported that 52% of working French don't sleep well on Sunday night.

---

1. By Isaac Getz, *The Wall Street Journal*, Sept. 21, 2009.

But work-related stress is not a French disease, and is ubiquitous and severe in all developed economies. In the U.K. and U.S. 70% of employees don't sleep well on Sunday night either.

Unsurprisingly, work place stress is recognized today as a key contributor in 75% to 90% of all primary-care doctor visits. This, of course, has economic costs. Studies estimate costs for French businesses between €830 million and €1.65 billion per year, while for U.S. businesses these costs go as high as $300 billion per year, due to stress-induced absenteeism, lost productivity and health expenditures. Besides the costs, stress also leads to much human suffering.

If workplace stress lasts for a short period, it can lead to those mundane modern diseases, such as stomach disorders, back pain, musculoskeletal problems, headaches, skin problems, loss of sleep and energy, and emotional distress. If it persists over a long period, it often results in heart disease. Severe cases amplified by isolation may even lead to suicide.

The unions know it. That's why France Télécom's union called its branch tracking suicide data "Observatoire du stress et des mobilités forcées" ("Observatory of stress and of forced mobility"). But to analyze the root causes, one must understand the mechanism that generates stress in our lives.

It all begins with situations that we perceive as either physically or psychologically threatening. Psychologists call these "stressors." Stressors can include increases in one's workload, or work demands, or uncertainty about what needs to be done or where one will work (in France Télécom's case, see recent forced and sudden changes of employees' workplaces). In addition, stressors envelop all the constraints and inter-personal conflicts that prevent employees from doing a good job, such as being denied resources or information you need for your job.

All the big and small stressors trigger negative emotional reactions, most often anger or anxiety. From there, the road to stress symptoms is all downhill. Sometimes, stress leads to constructive actions aiming to cope with the stressor, such as getting the needed information from somebody else. But most often, the reaction is destructive: flight - hence, turnover and absenteeism - or fight, to include violence to ourselves.

Fortunately there is one extremely important potential ameliorating factor for workplace stress—the perceived control an employee has over his work. When a person believes he has a high degree of control in any given situation, he judges it as less stressful, sometimes simply as "challenging." Military fighter pilots don't typically report seeing their missions, even in combat, as stressful, because they have complete control over their job. This perception of control minimizes a person's emotional reaction to a stressor. For example, facing a sudden upsurge in clients, a salesperson who feels in control will be confident that she'll find a way to keep the workload manageable. Her emotions may even bring a positive feeling of challenge. High perceived control may even lead an employee to search for constructive responses to cope with the stressful event.

For a person with a low level of control over her work, the reaction is quite different. Not believing that she can change the way she does her work, she'll engage in the destructive actions of fighting or fleeing to reduce her emotional distress and feel better. Three psychologists, Hans Bosma, Steven Stansfeld and Michael Marmot, spent five years studying the stress levels of more than 10,000 British civil servants. They found that employees who feel they have little control over their jobs—whether that is true or not—are 50% to 100% more likely to develop heart disease than those feeling as if they are in control of their jobs.

High-level employees can of course find ways to escape bureaucratic procedures. But there is an alternative, much more dramatic way to reduce stress-related costs and suffering for everyone: Treat people as modern pilots, not as soldiers of the old wars. Give people real control over their work, stop giving them orders about how to do their jobs, and their stress will go down. With it, absenteeism will drop, and stress's hidden costs will shrink, while employee engagement goes up. All this, of course, is hard to accomplish in a traditional command-and-control company that often pays a lip service to autonomy but preserves the hierarchical chain of command—but it is possible.

Companies as diverse as French copper alloy firm FAVI or Finnish cleaning service provider SOL have accomplished it. There is more good news: Freeing a company's people to act not only eliminates hidden costs and human misery, it also dramatically boosts its innovation and organic growth. That's the sort of news for which any business would be glad to make the headlines.

The Obsession over "Reporting" Causes Managerial Ineptitude[2]

In early March, the media revealed that crime figures had been falsified for years by the Paris Police Headquarters. According to a report submitted to the Minister of the Interior, police superiors used various methods so as "not to make the figures skyrocket": They classified certain offenses as less serious offenses—for example, a burglary recorded as damage to a door. Some offenses were not even recorded at all. And finally, when the monthly target was in danger of being exceeded, for example in late February, offenses were recorded in March.

At the Ministry of the Interior, the report must have been a shock because it meant that the minister's policies had been based on fictional data for the past ten years or so. But in many private companies this news produced a smile. The police superiors' practices have been alive there for more than a century.

"Boosting the figures"? In a publishing house at which management requests weekly reporting on new business, the managers quickly realized that an old edition revamped with a new ISBN number counts as new. As for recording an operation in the following month, this is called "putting it in the fridge," a technique well known to all salesmen whose bonuses depend on monthly targets: Once the target is reached, they record end of the month sales the following month, thus increasing their chances of reaching targets that month as well.

As in the Ministry of the Interior, this means that the strategic and management decisions of most companies are based on fiction. But it's

---

2. *L'obsession du reporting crée l'inefficacité managériale*, by Isaac Getz, *Le Monde*, May 8, 2014.

much worse in the private sector. Indeed, no report is given to any CEO on this issue, and for good reason. Supervision and its instruments of reporting, plus incentives in the form of bonuses and sanctions—carrots and sticks—constitute the essence of the current management system in most companies.

In this system, the top management chooses strategies, translates them into targets and then makes use of incentives and sanctions to encourage the "troops" to achieve them. The latter understand the game: to avoid hassle they must produce good reports—not reality.

And it works. Senior management sees "good figures," the troops receive bonuses and this continues until someone discovers the uncomfortable truth. For example, a customer who ordered February 21 still has not received the goods on March 15; annual revenue comes in too low at the end of the year, while simultaneously many orders placed in December (to make the legendary end of year salesmen's bonuses) were cancelled in January; or simply that company shares plummeted by 20%. Not only does this system make the top management do its work while looking in a rear-view mirror (figures are always from the past), the mirror itself produces a distorted image.

This situation is omnipresent, but not inevitable. There are companies, all over the world, that have abolished this management system by replacing constant supervision and its "carrot-and-stick" by trust and self-control. Thus, they have no punch clocks or locked supply closets, they do not check whether employees work from their offices or at home, neither the employees nor the CEO have permanent offices, and they do not impose objectives. Those are set by the teams themselves.

Of course, there are people who take advantage of this lack of control. But unlike conventional businesses, where one tries to thwart bureaucratic control systems, here one must deceive one's own teammates. The latter trust you in principle, but if you are late for the second time, claiming again that your alarm did not go off, they stop talking to you. Trust does not mean anarchy; it means trust—within the team—in the quality of your work. If you haven't joined the team that then you have no place in it.

These companies are not only a place where the majority of employees are happy in their jobs, they are also continually at the top of their respective industries. Because they do have figures. But not too many: just what the teams consider useful for self-control. These constitute the minimum necessary for management to be aware of the current situation and make forecasts, for example for investment purposes.

Moreover, the top management of Poult, France's second-ranked cookie manufacturer, does not ask for even these indicators. Indeed, they do not look into the investment issue at all. Each year, a rotating group of 15 employees decides how to invest $8 to $9 million. No executive is present.

This today is an emerging trend in companies: training seminars take place in Paris on the "end of management reporting," and every week an article appears in the specialized or general press on "dehierarchization," "companies that trust," etc.

But not at Police Headquarters. They assure us that new software will make it impossible for superiors to falsify figures. But this certainly underestimates the creativity of the players in any organization where bonuses depend on good figures and sanctions result from bad ones. Creating more efficient control software will require more time and ingenuity to get around, which is to say, less time to deal with the real issue: How to improve the actual results—in this case, the reduction of crime in Paris.

"Those are the Rules" and Why We Should Get Rid of Them[3]

In 1903 Tolstoy wrote a short story, "After the dance," inspired by his brother's true life experience. The young hero is deeply in love with the

---

3. C'est le règlement et pourquoi s'en débarrasser, by Isaac Getz, LeMonde.fr, Aug. 5, 2014. http://www.lemonde.fr/emploi/article/2014/08/05/c-est-le-reglement-et-pourquoi-s-en-debarrasser_4466889_1698637.html

beautiful daughter of a colonel, whom he also admires. He is about to marry and is full of wonderful projects; in short, a happy man. One morning on the way home after a ball, he comes across a military ritual that changes his (and Tolstoy's) life. Hundreds of soldiers form a corridor down which two sergeants are dragging a half-naked soldier. Every time they pass one of the soldiers in line, the latter strikes the prisoner with a stick. At the end, the young man spots the officer presiding over the punishment. It is his fiancée's father, whose words, "those are the rules," spoken during the ball, now take on a sinister reality. The young man could never love his fiancée as before. It is the end of their relationship.

A company does not inflict corporal punishment on its employees. However, its world and its practices are reminiscent of those of the Tsar's army, with resulting disenchantment, if not worse. Each year, many young people enter their first job. What is the first thing they see? The employee handbook. In addition to some practical information—where to park your car, where to eat—they find work schedules, hygiene and safety rules and the inevitable internal regulations. Many do not read further than the table of contents. Thus, they continue to harbor hopes that their job will bring them fulfilment and enable them to contribute personally toward a large common project. If they had read it, they would have discovered that: 1.) The two most important actions in the day are clocking in and clocking out; 2.) They will now spend a lot of energy to avoid doing everything that is forbidden and regulated. That's when the disenchantment begins. And when one day, they witness a sanction imposed on a colleague by a superior or HR manager with the justification, "those are the rules," their commitment to the company will be over, and fear will replace it.

So why are companies doing something that destroys, a bit like a neutron bomb, the engagement of their own employees? Firstly, because without realizing it, they are practicing "management for 3%." Early in the life of a company, the dreaded internal regulations are small; just enough to comply with labor laws. But one day, one of the employees does some unacceptable thing. Rather than talk to them face to face, understand the reasons for their action, explain why it is unacceptable for the company and ask how they propose to remedy it, a line will be added to the regulations. As a result, the motives of the 3% have still not been understood and they will continue to harm the company—with more creativity next time. But above all, the company has punished the 97% of people who were faultless by prohibiting one more thing, by again pointing to an area in which the company no longer trusts them.

There are companies all around the world that have radically reversed this erosion of employee engagement caused by ever-increasing regulations and interdictions. They have reduced the internal regulations to the bare legal minimum and refused to add a single line, by clearly stating that the company trusts employees and that if isolated cases of abuse occur they are treated as such. It works.

But the proliferation of regulations and procedures has unexpected negative consequences not only for engagement: It also sends costs through the roof and torpedoes performance. In terms of direct costs, a group of employees that controls compliance with rules and procedures vastly inflates the payroll. Moreover, it results in further hidden costs. Although it forms part of a company's "support" functions, it actually does the opposite of support: it impedes. Indeed, the employees in the value-creation zone will have to try to circumvent many of these regulations and procedures to move forward. Thus, any salesperson faced with an endless purchasing process will hide in their expense account a $100 external drive they need to back up data, and a director of a subsidiary facing a long recruitment procedure will acquire a SME with the 10 employees he needs. Although hidden, the cost of those efforts spent fighting bureaucracy is huge. According to some researchers, these efforts consume up to 50% of the energy of employees who create economic value in the company.

Finally, there are indirect costs due to stress, depression, absenteeism and turnover. Seeing a colleague sanctioned without any real discussion and understanding, another forced to move, a third who has not kept their word and therefore whose probity is in question has important psychological impacts on any witnesses. It is the cause of insecurity, deep mistrust vis-à-vis the company, a reflex to "constantly cover one's tracks," "not to believe anybody." These behaviors violate the deeply held beliefs of most individuals. And when an employee experiences such events in person, the shock can be traumatizing.

Edward Deming, one of the greatest management thinkers, wrote that the bureaucratic organization is a modern invention and represents "a prison, in the way people interact" in it.

"Those are the rules" is at the heart of the management of any prison, but is it inevitable in business?

Tolstoy, in his essay "Shame," recounts the following historical case. In the 1820s, several officers in one of the most prestigious Russian military regiments decided they would no longer inflict corporal punishment on soldiers. When another officer, believing his colleagues—we would have called them "softies" today—revealed that a soldier in his regiment was drinking and stealing, they proposed to transfer the disruptive soldier to their regiment. Soon, the soldier stole another's boots. The commanding officer announced that the soldier would not be punished and requested that he change his behavior. The soldier stole again. The officer did the same. Amazed by the double lack of punishment, the soldier radically changed his behavior and became the best in the regiment. The officer in question did not stop at the application of these principles in his regiment: He was one of the five main leaders of the so-called "Decemberist" uprising of 1825, which sought to establish democracy in Russia and was repressed. But Tolstoy tells this story, not to speak of the impossibility of reforming Russia, but to recall that in 1895, corporal punishment was still the rule in his country, both in military and civilian life. He concludes that the arbitrariness of absolute power does not make it legitimate. It's the very opposite.

As for businesses, obviously it is not a question of expecting them to condone theft. At the same time, there are a growing number of business leaders who have renounced "management for 3%": regulations and other instruments of control and sanction. Instead, they have introduced trust as the fundamental principle of the company; trust in everyone's desire to do a good job together with firm treatment of isolated cases to the contrary. They have also demonstrated—some for decades now—that this principle works and that their businesses are most successful in their industries.

It's a Jungle Out There, Especially at Amazon[4]

Jeff Bezos has a problem. And the fact that he seems unaware of it is only part it. Last weekend's long and scathing *New York Times* piece on Amazon.com's corporate culture described a hard-driving, but also back-biting and burn-out inducing environment inside the company Mr. Bezos founded.

Some Amazonians have responded defensively. In a memo to his staff that subsequently leaked, Mr. Bezos himself wrote: "I don't recognize this Amazon and I hope you don't either." Mr. Bezos encouraged anyone who did recognize the culture the Times described—little respect for work-life balance, 24/7 demands on employees' time, sink-or-swim performance reviews—to write to HR, or to him directly (in that order, tellingly).

The wife of one former Amazonian took him up on the offer in an open letter published by Quartz.com. Beth Anderson described her husband's time at Amazon thus:

> As his one-woman pit crew, it was my responsibility to wake up
> with him when he was paged in the middle of the night, to pull over
> somewhere on the highway to find him WiFi if he was paged on

---

4. By Brian M. Carney, Acculturated.com, Aug. 20, 2015. http://acculturated.com /amazon

the road, and to make sure that our lives never involved traveling
anywhere more than 15 minutes from an internet connection.

As Ms. Anderson notes, there are surely many happy people who work
at Amazon and thousands who thrive on its culture. There may also be
departments in Amazon that look nothing like the relentlessly Darwin-
ian place that the *New York Times* and Ms. Anderson describe.

But Mr. Bezos should take only limited comfort in that. His problem
is real, and to the extent that it is, asking current employees to come forward may or may not flush it out. Many of them are probably too afraid
of the consequences, which is why Mr. Bezos had to learn about his problem in the pages of the *New York Times*.

Corporate cultures are, by their nature, self-sustaining and self-rein-
forcing. People who love a workplace stay—and because there's no accounting for taste, somebody probably loves it almost anywhere. The
questions Mr. Bezos should be asking are: What are the unseen costs of
a corporate culture that seems to drive off a significant number of otherwise talented and successful people? And are those costs worth it?

Nick Ciubotariu wrote a lengthy and hectoring LinkedIn diatribe that
Mr. Bezos encouraged Amazonians to read alongside the *Times* piece. In
it, he evinces a real love for and conviction about what Amazon does
and how it works. Mr. Ciubotariu may be lucky, or he may be part of the
problem. I don't know him or the people who work for him or for whom
he works. But his own writing leaves little doubt about how forcefully he
defends what he believes. In the terms of Amazon's leadership principles,
he clearly has "Backbone."

Still, another of Amazon's principles is that leaders should "work to
disconfirm their beliefs." So far, Amazon and its Amazonians seem more
interested in disconfirming theTimes' reporting than their own self-belief.
Interestingly, the admonition to disconfirm one's beliefs comes under a
heading that says leaders "Are Right, a Lot." One hopes that the last two
words are meant to underscore that they're also wrong (at least sometimes).

But I wonder whether that subtlety always comes across to the hard-driving and ambitious types that Amazon appears to both seek and cultivate.

When Isaac Getz and I were writing our book, *Freedom, Inc.,* we insisted on going inside the companies we were writing about. And whenever we could, we'd stop someone in the hall—someone who hadn't been prepped for the visitors, or told what the party line was—and ask them what they thought of the company's culture. This was a double test: In the best-run companies we found, those men and women on the street genuinely loved what they did. And the corporate bigwigs weren't afraid of our unscripted encounters with their employees.

In 14 years as a business journalist and five years doing field research on management philosophy, I never met a CEO who thought (or would admit) that his company's corporate culture was toxic. Most of the time, sadly, they have no idea what their front-line employees really think about working at their company. And for the most part, that's because those employees assume that the company runs the way the boss wants it too. If that's not true in Amazon's case, it will take more than a memo to fix what ails Amazon. That Mr. Bezos doesn't recognize his own company in the experiences of the people who used to work for him is evidence of a problem, not of the absence of one.

MOTIVATION AND ENGAGEMENT

Yes, You Should Eliminate Your Vacation Policy[5]

Henry Blodget at The Business Insider has posed a holiday question for his readers: Should his business have a vacation policy? (Full disclosure: My brother John works with Henry and would be affected by the answer to this question. I do not know what John's preference is. I write this from my own perspective.)

Blodget notes in his post:

---

5. By Brian M. Carney, businessinsider.com, Dec. 30, 2009. http://www.businessinsider
.com/yes-you-should-eliminate-your-vacation-policy-2009-12

In practice, therefore, our vacation policy seems to be "We're all adults here, so take as much time as you want. Just make sure you communicate clearly ahead of time and make sure your responsibilities are covered. And, of course, make sure that you do a great job."

That's the practice. The theory, as at most companies, is that employees get a specified number of vacation days, which they may or may not be able to "bank," or carry over into future years, and so on. I knew one long-time employee of Harvard who had accumulated close to a year of vacation time over several decades. She had gotten to the point that she was worried she might retire before she was able to use it all.

Some employers are quite strict about logging all this stuff, with forms to fill out and process and periodic statements sent to employees and the rest. But many, especially if they don't allow days to be carried over, don't pay a lot of attention. At other companies, it may vary from department to department, or even employee to employee, if a manager decides that certain people "need watching," while letting others get by on trust.

But Blodget has, as I suspect he's aware, hit on an even deeper issue than whether employees get 15 days, or 10, or 25, of vacation. Vacation policies are one of those class of policies that, while designed to set a floor under something–attendance at work in this case–become a ceiling as a practical matter. If employees can't save up their vacation days from year to year, they try to make sure they use them. In some cases, they do this even they didn't particularly want or need to use them. The psychology becomes, "They're mine, after all. I'm *entitled* to them."

Consider in this context the following from *Freedom, Inc.:*

A psychologist found himself disturbed by a group of kids that one day had come to play football under his window, making a lot of noise. So he went out and said: "You guys are really great. I enjoy watching you so much that every time you come to play here I will give you one dollar each." And he gave a dollar to each kid. The next day, when the kids were again enthusiastically playing football, he came out and said: "I really enjoy watching you but the thing is that I have no bills, just coins today. I can give you two quarters each." The kids were not delighted with this pay cut, but took the money and continued to play. The story continues until after two days, the psychologist offered them just a penny each, which one of them proudly refused and said: "We are not going to play here for a damn penny." And the kids never came back, much to the satisfaction of the psychologist.

Many psychologists think that this "experiment" is apocryphal, but it continues to circulate because it reflects what they know from hundreds of real experiments: If you take people who are deeply engaged in something because they enjoy it and then you offer them tangible rewards for doing it, a shift happens. Mentally, people establish a causal link between these rewards and the activity—something psychologists call a perceived locus of causality—and this link will undermine the initial, intrinsic cause they had for the activity, such as considering it enjoyable or important.

A vacation policy has a similar effect on employees' psychology. It becomes part of the baseline that they demand from their jobs, and so instantly ceases to be a motivating factor in their work.

Blodget touches on something even more profound at the bottom of his post, where he says:

> We don't want to end up with an empty office all the time (though, if we do, folks probably won't be satisfying the requirement that they do a great job–and we will have hired the wrong folks).

This sort of fear–that if no maximum is set, some people, and perhaps

even most people, will take "everything"–is, as Henry notes, both un-
founded and a symptom, if it were proved true, of a larger problem.
In *Freedom, Inc.* Gordon Forward of Chaparral Steel talks of the danger
of "managing for the 3%." In a large enough organization, there might
be a couple of people who would take two or three months' vacation–
but if a vacation policy is the only thing holding them back from that,
they're probably "vacationing" at their desks anyway. And so the policy is
concealing the problem with that "3%," not eliminating it.

The rest of your employees don't need a policy. Not only that, but your
policy, designed to maximize what you get out of your employees, may
well be encouraging them to take more time off than they need.

This is the sort of unseen, unaccounted-for cost of policy making and
top-down control that is rife in highly centralized companies. Vacation
policies are just the tip of the iceberg.

Free the Workers, Fix the Post Office[6]

This month's disruptive strikes at the Royal Mail are the fifth such industrial actions to hit the post office in the past 30 years. As we went to press
it was still possible that a last-minute bargain could avert the next round,
due to start today. But strikes are like repetitive fevers—symptoms of a
chronic inflammation. Avoiding the latest threatened strike may mask
the symptoms, but it won't cure what ails the Royal Mail. Let's do some
diagnosis.

In the early 2000s, on any given day, 10,000 of Royal Mail's 170,000
employees were absent without any valid reason—about twice the national average. Desperate to reduce absenteeism, the management offered raffle tickets to employees who bothered to show up for their jobs
for six months without missing a day. The prizes included 34 £12,000
Ford Focus cars and 68 £2,000 holiday vouchers.

We can assume that this lured back at least some of the malingerers.

---

6. By **Brian M. Carney & Isaac Getz**, *The Wall Street Journal*, Oct. 30, 2009.

But we're willing to wager that the managers of the missing 10,000 would have been just as happy if they'd stayed home. In offering enticements totally extraneous to their work—on top of, you know, paying them—the Royal Mail was engaged in an extreme version of treating the symptoms rather than the disease. It must have seemed far easier to the Royal Mail's top management to offer prizes than to examine why they had such a terrible absentee problem. But if management had wanted real insight into the root causes of the problem, Dave Ward, deputy general secretary of the Communication Workers Union, offered them some free advice: "The company needs to get to the root of the problem, which is low morale, poor pay and conditions. That is the cause of sickness and absenteeism."

Now, union officials always say that more pay will mean more productive workers. That's their job. But by bringing in low morale Mr. Ward was onto something, even if it is a subject that management wants to talk about even less than low pay. Increasing pay is, at least in principle, something management can easily do if it wants to. But improving morale is a lot harder than signing a check—especially because it requires management to examine their role and the structures they put in place that contributed to the problem in the first place. Far better then to ignore the causes and attack the symptoms—in the case of the Royal Mail, bribing employees to do what they had already legally contracted to do. Thus the inflammation stays untreated.

The Royal Mail's "medication" at that time was extreme—but most well-run firms never allow things to get quite that bad. This year was the first in 20 in which the post office turned an operating profit: £321 million. Compare that to absenteeism, which costs the Royal Mail £250 to £350 million a year. Few private firms can afford a deadweight loss like that—as even GM found out in the end. But all around us, every day, most of our organizations, large and small, instead of addressing the problem of employee disengagement, prefer to treat its "symptoms"—not through extravagant bribes but through the establishment of drastic rules and procedures aimed to catch the malingerers.

Gordon Forward, the former CEO of Chaparral Steel, calls this "managing for the 3%." Many managers have a tendency to address a small problem—sometimes a problem confined to a single employee, or a couple of them—by creating even more draconian rules for everyone.

"Management for 3%" is inevitable in "how" companies—those that focus on telling employees "how" to do their jobs—because simple control procedures are always outwitted by that 3%. So naturally, new, more severe controls are imposed to catch them. In addition to the ordinary bureaucratic overhead incurred through the accumulation of these corrective policies, managing for the 3% also imposes dramatic hidden costs on businesses by contributing to the disengagement of the 97%.

But this kind of rule-making, as silly as it looks from the outside, does have a number of advantages for the managers. There's no awkward confrontation with the pilfering employee, no embarrassed denials or outward resentment. Instead, the manager gets to fall back on the last refuge of bureaucrats everywhere—"That's the policy!" And so the regulations live on, far beyond whatever usefulness they ever once had, even years or decades after the single, awkward circumstance that they were designed to address has passed out of memory. All the while, these useless rules nevertheless reliably contribute to the malaise of the 97%, who find themselves treated with suspicion and crushed by seemingly arbitrary company policies. Meanwhile, the "why" question—why do employees do what they do, for what purpose do they wake up and go to work—is completely neglected in these bureaucracies.

You may suppose that disengagement problems such as those at the Royal Mail and GM are rare—that in the majority of traditional companies, a very small proportion of employees is disengaged. Otherwise, how can we explain the unprecedented growth that the developed world has experienced since the Industrial Revolution? The data we have on the matter tells a different story, however. Gallup regularly conducts broad surveys on the engagement of American workers. Its results are always very similar. In 2006, only 27% of employees at the average company were described as "engaged," while 59% were "not engaged" and 14% were "actively disengaged." To picture active disengagement, imagine that in an eight-man rowboat, you and another leader in the two front seats are rowing energetically. The five in the middle whom you can't see periodically dip their oars in the water just enough to make a little splash. The last man, meanwhile, is rowing energetically—but in the opposite direction from the rest of the crew. And you wonder why, for all the splashing, your company seems stalled?

So how to treat the root causes and make the corporate boat fly? Start by ceasing to tell your employees how to do their work and removing other symbols and practices that prevent them from feeling as intrinsically equal human beings—not human resources. Only then will they be able to answer the "why" question that should inform their jobs. Without that, a corporate vision is just a hollow, meaningless document posted on a bulletin board and universally ignored. Then provide an environment in which these employees have what they need to advance that vision through their own actions. All necessary information, knowledge and skills must be given lavishly to employees instead of rationed like food during a war. Finally, provide these willing and capable employees with the authority to act to solve the customer or production problems they face right away—without the frustration of working through the chain of command. Once such an environment is built, employees self-motivate themselves to embrace freedom and responsibility of action in the best interests of the company.

This is not a utopia. This sort of corporate environment has been successfully built in companies large and small, public and private, service and industrial—all steady leaders of their industries. And where there were strong unions, as in Harley Davidson, it has been built with the unions, in a true partnership. As a result, this company went from being in 1981 on the verge of bankruptcy and selling 30,000 motorcycles to selling 177,000 units in 1999. When Rich Teerlink—the liberating leader instrumental in building this environment—stepped aside that year,

Harley's profits surpassed the total revenue when he came on board and its market capitalization exceeded that of GM, even before the car maker's 21st-century woes.

Any company—the Royal Mail included—can choose which route to follow. When Mr. Teerlink first started to transform Harley in the 1980s, he began by setting aside all the ordinary management demands with which contract negotiations begin. Instead, he made an offer—give me a one-year contract, and spend that year working with me to figure out how to fix our company. It was a dramatic offer, and it helped change the tone at Harley-Davidson. Given the state of labor relations at the Royal Mail, its management could do worse.

Google's 20% Mistake[7]

Recent reports indicate that Google has been effectively zeroing out employees' "20% time"—the policy of letting Googlers spend a fifth of their time working on whatever innovative, maybe even crazy, projects they wished.

The news is a shocker. Google had widely touted its 20% time as a cornerstone of its "innovation machine." Larry Page and Sergey Brin also cited 20% time as leading to many of Google's "most significant advances." These include Gmail, Google News and Adsense—and that last one accounts for a quarter of Google's $50 billion-plus in annual revenue.

Founders Page and Brin, together with ex-CEO Eric Schmidt, reportedly used it personally. So what explains Google's push to reduce the number of such projects, to put "more wood behind fewer arrows"? The short answer: ignorance. Google's top brass seems not to understand the reasons for their company's success.

Continuous innovation is one of the hardest tricks in business. Sustaining it over decades has proved impossible for all but a select few, such as 3M or W.L. Gore & Associates. One can't just throw money and bodies

---

7. By Brian M. Carney & Isaac Getz, *The Wall Street Journal*, Aug. 27, 2013.

at innovation—there is no correlation between the size of a company's R&D budget and its innovation rate. Most ideas are bad ones, so you have to entertain a lot of them to find the real gems. On average, a company needs 3,000 ideas to get 300 of them formalized, 125 of them into small experimentation, ten of them officially budgeted, 1.7 launched—and one that makes money.

Those are long odds. So naturally many executives seek to "optimize" these dynamics. Looking from the top, they decide on, say, 10 official projects to favor. This kills most of the informal ideas, which employees just keep to themselves—or bring to a competitor. What's more, it is extremely unlikely that people at the top know in advance which ideas are going to be the big winners.

At 3M and Gore, it is their employees' initiatives that have introduced them to new markets. Take Gore's Elixir guitar strings—which started as an employee's informal idea for an innovative bike gear cable. Today Elixir is a market leader, and one of 1,000 new products the company has successfully launched since it invented Gore-Tex.

Seen in this light, this 20% time is not just another on-the-job perk. Within a culture in which employees are free to act and believe that their ideas will be taken seriously, it is a token of respect that offers room for personal growth and a degree of autonomy to every employee, regardless of what their "day job" is. On paper, eliminating it might look like it saves money. But the signal it sends is that management, not the workers, know what the most productive use of your time is. It's a step down the road to a company of clock-punchers.

The freest, most innovative companies we know were coherently built to produce a corporate culture that nurtures those universal needs of intrinsic equality, growth and self-direction. In such a culture, the vast majority of people are self-motivated and decide for themselves what initiatives are best for advancing the corporate vision.

Google has never consciously built such a culture. And as it has now made clear that its 20% time was not—unlike at Gore—part of a freedom-of-initiative culture, but a perk. Google has a legendary collection of those, from free gourmet food to, most recently, a death perk: As Chief People Officer Laszlo Bock explained to Forbes, an employee's surviving spouse gets a 10-year pay package, with all stock vested immediately, while any children receive $1,000 monthly until 19 (or 23 if a student).

Adding perks is a business decision. They are powerful retention tools, and reducing turnover by several percentage points saves a lot of money.

But scrapping perks is also a business decision. At some point, some executive will demonstrate that a given perk's cost exceeds its benefits. Paradoxically, as soon as a perk becomes established, it loses its motivating power and becomes a potential liability. Ex-Googlers tell us that the crackdown on 20% time began during the post-crisis recession, as the company's revenues declined. This suggests that 20% time has long been viewed by management as just another expensive indulgence.

When 20% time isn't a perk but part of the freedom-of-initiative culture, it stands as an acknowledgment of the higher-ups' ignorance—that they don't know what the next Gmail or Adsense is, and so they're counting on you to find it. A company that wants to put "more wood behind fewer arrows" is a company that believes it has already found all the targets worth aiming at. Such a company risks leaving its best growth in the past, and exporting its best ideas to its competitors.

SAFETY AND SECURITY

Put People at the Center of the Nuclear Safety[8]

The fact-finding mission of the French Parliamentary Office has published its interim report on the safety of nuclear installations. It makes valid points about the lack of accountability when multiple levels of

---

8. *Reconnaitre l'homme au cœur de la sureté nucléaire*, by Isaac Getz, LeMonde.fr, July 7, 2011. http://www.lemonde.fr/idees/article/2011/07/07/reconnaitre-l-homme-au-c-ur-de-la-surete-nucleaire_1545122_3232.html

outsourcing are involved, as well as less valid ones claiming that the government is the guarantor of safety in our nuclear power stations.

Imagine the driver of a bus that is approaching a railway crossing too fast and tries to slow down, but doesn't realize that his brakes have failed. Then he sees the barrier coming down and just when he smashes into it the train arrives. Nobody wants such an accident to happen, but it is easy to imagine. It's also easy to imagine the reactions of a government.

Indeed, public opinion will always demand that action is taken to prevent such "human error." The authorities will do so in the only way they know: more drastic regulations (speed limits, roadworthiness tests for vehicles and automation of railway crossings, for example). This will reassure public opinion because we have the impression that technology is more reliable than humans. But we should investigate this a bit more. Rather than protect the safety of people via such safety measures, these new regulations and automation weaken it even further.

Unfortunately, this type of reaction by the authorities is common following accidents in all areas of risk—road and air traffic, oil rigs and nuclear power plants—and is at the heart of the current debate following the Fukushima accident. But common sense and in-depth examination show that the quest for safety is in vain unless it puts people at its heart. Common sense tells us that expanding procedures and producing ever more precise rules is useless: the unexpected inevitably arises. And the further people are from the problem, the more likely they are to have inappropriate reactions to the situation.

As for in-depth examination, such as the investigations following serious accidents, most often they find that there are systemic causes of "human error." Thus, Lord Cullen, chairman of the U.K. Commission of Inquiry into the Piper Alpha platform explosion (167 casualties) wrote: "The quality of safety management by operators is fundamental to the safety of platforms. Regardless of the level of detail in safety regulations, they could not compensate for deficiencies in the way safety was managed by operators." And HSE, the new British safety regulator, used that conclusion when advising businesses to adopt a more effective approach to managing safety: "A 'humanist' approach to management that consisted of managers giving increased consideration to the problems of operators or personnel at work."

The establishment of a "humanist" approach to management is not simple for oil and nuclear companies: It is very different from their prevailing business culture (without mentioning the culture of conflict and mistrust that exists between clients and contractors revealed after the huge oil spill in the Gulf of Mexico). Here are some key aspects of this corporate culture.

First, within these companies people always communicate directly, face to face, and without concerns for hierarchy. Why is this better for safety than memos and respect for hierarchy? Many incidents and accidents happen because of weak signals spotted on the ground but not shared in real time. Moreover, information transmitted face-to-face is much richer in terms of interpretation and reliability. This is vital to understanding ambiguous situations, which in turn is essential before any preventive action is taken.

Second, processes and procedures are developed by or with the essential participation of field teams, which then are responsible for following and improving them. This is important because the teams integrate all their informal tacit knowledge in these procedures, appropriate them, and therefore respect them unfailingly without supervision. As these procedures are "theirs," they do everything they can to constantly improve them to ensure that they remain relevant in ever-evolving conditions.

Lastly, within these companies people create stories and games. The stories about past incidents are essential for learning from and sharing the often unspoken logic of errors, their consequences and preventive actions. No abstract procedure can codify this wealth of knowledge. And when serious consequences have not occurred, games stimulate the imagination of various scenarios that will help develop responses to these numerous virtual situations.

Some observers have found evidence of this culture in nuclear power stations in France, the largest nuclear energy producer in Europe. We also had the opportunity to meet their highly dedicated skilled teams, always on the front line when problems arise. But there is concern that rather than ask the nuclear industry to strengthen the "humanist" culture within, the authorities will regulate even more.

Why do the vast majority of drivers respect speed limits? For fear of the police or radars? No, they do so because they understand the importance of not exceeding the speed limit (too much) for their safety and especially because they have a simple means of self-monitoring: a speedometer.

Can we imagine a situation where the judgment of the person at the wheel is replaced by GPS automation or by a police officer in every bus who would monitor their speed constantly? The regulating authorities must decide whether to put people at the heart of safety measures by requiring companies to strengthen the "humanist" culture in them, or remove them from it. They cannot do both at once.

How to Avoid New JP Morgan Breakdowns[9]

Last week, Bruno Michel Iksil, a trader at JP Morgan Chase, cost his company close to $5 billion. Previously, traders at Société Générale (over $6 billion), Sumitomo Corporation (over $3 billion) and Barings Bank (over one $1 billion, causing his bank's bankruptcy) have committed similar acts. The measures proposed after each of these disasters are always the same: more regulations. Yet these new regulations always fail to prevent future disasters.

This prediction arises from a long-established finding by systems researchers: For a complex system to prevent most accidents, the

---

9. *Pour éviter de nouvelles affaires JP Morgan…*, by Isaac Getz, LaTribune.fr, May 21, 2012. http://www.latribune.fr/opinions/tribunes/20120521tribo00699472/pour-eviter-de -nouvelles-affaires-jp-morgan.html

organization overseeing it must be at least as complex...in terms of human relations.

When the organizational mode is primitive—based on hierarchy and procedures—people ignore the warning signals, interpret them erroneously, withhold information or avoid solving urgent problems. Can we imagine that none of the office colleagues of Bruno Michel Iksil, Jérôme Kerviel, Yasuo Hamanaka or Nick Leeson noticed any of their bizarre and excessive behaviors? What were the organizational practices in their companies that encouraged obscure rather than transparent communication; a "not-my-job" reaction, rather than personal action in the face of imminent risk?

Since the fall of Barings in 1995, the complexity of banking and financial systems has continued to increase. However, the organizational modes overseeing these systems—hierarchical bureaucracies—remain as primitive as ever. In fact, they have worsened. Indeed, the strictest regulations have never prevented an underhanded employee from circumventing them. However, they did manage to promote caution—even fear—in the 99% of employees who have always respected the norms and have never contemplated transgressing them.

To reduce the likelihood of future disasters, companies must find a way of continually increasing the complexity of their organizations in terms of human relations. But we're not there yet. Even worse, our organizations have continued to reduce this human complexity. In bureaucracies, people are fundamentally treated as robots or simple beings whose behavior the bureaucrats seek to control... and employees behave as such. Even the most enthusiastic and intelligent are "digested" by the bureaucracy and turn into frustrated or even cynical employees.

A well-known apocryphal experiment helps explain why. Five monkeys are in a cage. A banana is suspended from the ceiling and there are steps to climb up to it. When the most enterprising monkey starts climbing up toward the banana, the experimenter splashes him and the other monkeys with cold water. Once they have understood the lesson, the experimenter replaces one of them with a new monkey. The enthusiastic newcomer notices the banana and heads for the steps—where he is abruptly stopped by the other four, who are afraid of the cold water.

Once the newcomer has understood the lesson, another one with direct experience of the cold water is removed and replaced by a new recruit. The process is repeated, with the first replacement participating in the violence toward the newcomer without even knowing why he must not let the former go up the steps. One by one, the original monkeys are replaced, but every newcomer learns the rule—do not attempt to take the banana—even though none of them, at the end of the experiment, has been a victim of the cold shower that the first group underwent. If the monkeys were endowed with speech, they would explain that trying to take the banana is against company policy.

We are not insinuating that banking systems and their safety are in the hands of monkeys. Just bureaucrats. And bureaucracies lead initially enthusiastic and intelligent people to look away when they notice suspicious behavior. The rules on which any bureaucracy is based are vital in some areas, particularly for security, safety, and quality. But here, the bureaucrats commit two errors.

Firstly, they believe that rules are needed in all areas. Secondly, they think they know what the right rules are better than the people who will ultimately work according to them. The first error leads, for example, to the policy requiring a formal approval for all purchases, even to order a USB stick. Consequently, most people have the impression they are not trusted. Paradoxically, they learn to break the rules in order to be able to achieve results. But it's the second error that interests us more here.

When procedures are drafted by security bureaucrats, it is the fear of punishment that drives employees to respect them. Employees don't know why the procedure exists, what dangers it addresses or how this danger could jeopardize the entire system they are in charge of. However, they know that if they mess with what does not concern them, in this case, a security problem, they will be slapped on the wrist by a security bureaucrat. Therefore, people quickly learn to look away from alarm signals.

However, there are companies, some of whom are in the financial sector, who are distinctly un-bureaucratic and where security is taken very seriously; "taken seriously" not by the security bureaucrats, but by employee teams who have elaborated their own effective security procedures. Based already on human complexity of their organizational mode, these companies increase it even further. They make their employees understand why security is important, what kinds of dangers exist and where they occur, and let them devise by themselves practices to face these dangers.

All this is without any bureaucrats to monitor security. However, as security is strategic, the leaders of these companies contribute a lot thereto. They meet with the teams regularly and discuss security issues. At the same time, they share the vision and strategic information they possess by contributing even more to the human complexity of their organization. It is therefore possible to ensure the security of banking systems while avoiding bureaucracy.

For this, financial sector companies must dismantle their bureaucracy and replace it with an organization that fundamentally trusts employees, that continually increases the human complexity of teams and hence, drastically reduces the likelihood of new disasters. These companies will also become the most sustainable leaders in their sectors. Thus, "security or performance" gives way to "security and performance."

GOVERNMENT AND ADMISITRATION

Obama's Federal Suggestion Box[10]

President Barack Obama is proposing what amounts to a giant suggestion box for government workers: "We'll establish a process through which every government worker can submit their ideas for how their agency

---

10. By Brian M. Carney & Isaac Getz, *The Wall Street Journal*, May 1, 2009.

can save money and perform better," he said in his Saturday address to the nation. He described the idea as a "bottom-up" effort to "make your government more efficient and effective."

The president's intention is admirable, and he's right to say that "Americans across the country know that the best ideas often come from workers—not just management." But American workers also know that even in the private sector, management often does little to implement their ideas. If the president really wants to take government workers' ideas seriously, he should know that there's a lot more to it than setting up an email address and telling workers to fire away.

There are good reasons the suggestion boxes at most companies collect more chewed-up gum and recommendations to "fire my boss" than valuable ideas. Workers know that the bureaucracy will strangle even good ideas with "suggestion-review committees" and rules on who is eligible to offer ideas, what kind of ideas will be considered, and how to decide what constitutes a "good" idea.

It doesn't have to be this way: Toyota's plants in Georgetown, Ky., and Fremont, Calif., benefit from a continuous flow of their employees' ideas. But copying this model isn't easy: GM co-owns the NUMMI plant in Fremont and has tried to emulate its culture -- with little success, as the administration is well-aware.

Creating a process for gathering employee ideas and implementing them isn't enough to change an organization, just like doing 50 push-ups every morning so you can overeat the rest of the day won't get you in shape. In between the president, or a CEO, and all those frontline workers stand decades of rules and regulations and layers upon layers of accumulated management tasked with enforcing them.

Those managers, by the way, have their own personal and institutional interests. In some cases, the best ideas of those frontline workers will threaten the authority—if not the very jobs —of the people in the middle of the government's organization chart. And in a bureaucracy, arguing for your boss to be deprived of some perk or some tool of control is professional suicide, whether the president asked you to do it or not. It doesn't take many rejections—usually one is enough—to convince a worker that his ideas aren't welcome by the management. So what can be done?

For starters, don't blame managers for the accumulated weight of bureaucratic regulations. Though management enforces the rules, it didn't create them. Managers are fellow victims of what Gordon Forward, the former CEO of Chaparral Steel, calls "management for the 3%." Under management for the 3%, rules are slapped on the honest 97% in the hopes of clamping down on the tiny minority who might abuse their freedom.

To start "managing for 97%," a CEO or president has to reject this top-down approach. He has to punish the 3% and start trusting and showing respect to the 97%. This means removing time-clocks and breaking down the myriad symbols of status that signal to workers that they are lazy and untrustworthy.

Even if this can be done within the restrictive confines of government agencies, there are still all the rules and regulations that tell people *how* to do their jobs and which tell them, implicitly, that they are stupid and incompetent. This message, delivered to workers daily, is much stronger than a suggestion, even from the president himself, that they have «the best ideas.» To overcome this would require a broad cultural shift in how the government does business. Managers would have to stop telling workers to «do it by the book,» and start asking, «What do you propose?»

Only when you stop telling your employees how to do their jobs can you start building a freer, more efficient and effective "why" organization. If a company or a government agency wants ideas from everyone, the CEO or president has to spend a lot more time explaining to people "why" they do what they do, and leave the "how" to them.

This freedom has the advantage of giving workers responsibility for their jobs. And once they own their work and feel that they are trusted, employees will come up with ideas and initiatives and act to put them in place. Without being asked. There are companies around the world that do this today, including W.L. Gore & Associates, the San Antonio-based insurer USAA and Sun Hydraulics in Sarasota, Fla., among others. And their performance is nothing short of astonishing. But they didn't get there using a suggestion box.

How to Liberate the NHS[11]

Health Secretary Andrew Lansley's NHS reform, announced this week, is the biggest decentralization of decision making ever undertaken in any organization. The idea of liberating front-line employees is a powerful and exciting one. The bureaucracy of the NHS is not just a nightmare for patients, but also for the doctors, nurses and other workers too. Patients only have to contend with it when they're sick. NHS employees confront it every day.

But trying to set the NHS free is also fraught with peril in an organization so large and bureaucratic. Announcing to staff that they will enjoy freedom and responsibility in their decisions without building a workplace that makes it possible is a formula for failure.

Building a workplace in which people are free and responsible to make decisions that they—not some bureaucrats or rules—deem to be the best isn't an ideological issue. It's an organizational issue that involves finding a form of workplace that delivers the best results for the clients, users, or patients. According to the early 20th-century German sociologist Max Weber, the "bureaucratic organization" was the best. He claimed that only a "strictly bureaucratic organization" was capable of discharging its "official business . . . precisely, unambiguously, continuously, and with as much speed as possible."

But the unprecedented economic and social growth achieved by traditional bureaucratic organizations has come at a price—both human and economic. British psychologists Hans Bosma, Steven Stansfeld and Michael Marmot, for example, studied the stress levels of more than 10,000

---

11. By Isaac Getz, *The Wall Street Journal*, July 16, 2010.

British civil servants and found that men who feel that they have little control over their jobs are 50% more likely to develop heart disease than those who feel that they are in control of their jobs (for women, it's even worse—the risk is 100% higher). Mr. Bosma and his associates suggest that such control and freedom of choice may be a universal human need. There is a reason, in other words, that the television show "The Office" resonates with so many people on two continents.

Economically, Columbia University professor John O. Whitney estimated that about 50% of activities in a bureaucratic organization are performed because of the lack of trust in employees, constituting a costly waste and distracting resources from servicing customers and users as well. More, Mr. Whitney claims, "wasted activities and unnecessary complexity sap creative energy and the motivation of the people doing the work. A cost that is not measurable."

In writing the book "Freedom, Inc.," my co-author and I studied a several dozen liberated workplaces, many in the service industries, including health care. If their leaders could change the culture inside companies that had been dysfunctional for decades and set their people free then there are lessons here for the leaders of any workplace—the NHS included.

One thing we learned is that success or failure is always decided locally—in the workplace. No matter what the politicians say, it is the leaders on the ground who have the power to allow front-line employees the freedom to make decisions they deem the best. In introducing his reform, Mr. Lansley said, "The NHS remains stifled by a culture of top-down bureaucracy, which blocks the creativity and innovation of its staff." This is certainly true. But in an organization the size of the NHS, the danger is that Mr. Lansley only manages to replace one bureaucracy with another, in which the heads of his new doctors' consortiums simply replace the old managers and continue to stifle GPs.

It's thus the liberation carried out by the leaders at each of these local workplaces—and the maintenance of it thereafter—that will make or break the NHS reform. Here are some lessons from the liberating leaders that NHS units' leaders may use to succeed.

Stop telling your frontline people how to do their work and start listening to their solutions. Then, remove all the other symbols and practices of bureaucracy that prevent your people from being treated with trust, fairness, and equity. For NHS units, that means reducing to a minimum the rules, regulations, and policies that broadcast daily to frontline people that they are not trusted to do their job well and, basically, considered stupid. But there's more. All kinds of privileges for the higher-ups—reserved parking spaces included—have to go too. As legendary basketball coach John Wooden said, "It's hard for second-class citizens to do a first-rate job—to take pride in their work or the organization that treats them poorly." He also added: "This is not their fault. It's your fault." So, change this reserved lot's sign from "Directors" to "Visitors."

Start openly and actively sharing your vision of the organization so people will "own" it; but don't do this before the first step because people who are not treated as equals will leave you alone with your vision. For NHS units, that means actively sharing the new NHS vision—the best health-care options for patients at reasonable costs—with all stakeholders. Doctors are one such constituency, but an equally important one is other NHS employees. And if they are represented by unions, that means sharing the vision with unions so that it becomes theirs too. For freedom to work to the advantage of the organization—and patients—NHS employees have to "own" the criteria by which they are making decisions with their newfound power. Having a performance indicator for the vision's advancement helps too. For the NHS, it could be the percentage of patients' needs solved during the first contact with the service provider—an indicator used by the world's best service organizations.

Stop trying to motivate people. Instead, build an environment that allows people to grow and self-direct—and let them motivate themselves: If they understand the vision from the previous step, they'll take care of the rest if only you let them. For NHS units, that means that the Shadow

Health Secretary Andy Burnham's remark to the Health Secretary Andrew Lansley "you are demoralizing NHS staff at just the time you need them at their motivated best" is partly correct. If government has to avoid demotivating its employees, it—or the NHS units' leaders—also have to avoid trying to motivate them (usually with handouts). Only self-motivated employees can make the best decisions, those that will make the new NHS vision advance. But most NHS employees hate the bureaucracy too. If you can take it off their backs, you might be surprised at how little motivation they need to do the right thing.

Stay alert. To keep your employees free, become the culture-keeper. For NHS units, especially the new GP consortiums, that means that its staff—often unwillingly—will always try to solve problems by establishing new procedures instead of doing what's best for the new NHS vision. Liberating leaders have to be vigilant not to let the bureaucracy virus back into the workplace. The price of liberty is eternal vigilance.

Liberating a large organization with many stakeholders is long and complex: There are no shortcuts in changing the way people work. It helps to know that people want to work well and suffer from not being able to do so. More, people don't resist change; they resist being changed. But it takes time to transform a workplace to where people are self-motivated to continuously make the best for the vision decisions. In case of Harley Davidson it took 10 years. Finding the leaders for such liberation and allowing them the time to carry it out will decide on the success of the NHS transformation—or the failure. In case of the second, it would be a tremendous waste of opportunity to build the health care of the future. The whole world will be watching.

Trust as a Basis for Government Innovation[12]

Can we go beyond the simplification of government and foster innovation there? In companies, innovation—products, processes, economic

---

12. La confiance comme base pour innover l'Etat, by Isaac Getz, LesEchos.fr, May 19, 2014. http://www.lesechos.fr/idees-debats/cercle/cercle-98023-la-confiance-comme-base-pour-innover-letat-1006992.php

models, even management approaches—is a priority for most leaders. Can it be this way in the public sector? Welcome to the Belgian Ministry of Social Security.

This ministry was reputed to be the country's worst, always ranking last in the number of civil servants applying to it. And deservedly so. Its 2,100 employees, 80% of them low-skilled, would go there to spend 7 hours and 36 minutes every day in austere buildings and provide poor service to citizens. But everything changed in 2002 with the arrival of the new President of the Ministry (the highest ranking civil servant), Frank Van Massenhove. He began—with his new team—by implementing new working methods, improving processes to better serve users. But three years later, in 2005, the organization and the administrative structures still remained intact.

It was during an internal survey that the ministry's employees, answering questions such as "what makes you happy or unhappy at work," stated that they preferred having more time than more money. Though startling, Frank Van Massenhove was not surprised by this result. Since 2002, he had been meeting bi-weekly with personnel for open discussions and knew that on average the employees spent two hours a day commuting. With the hour taken for lunch added, it made a total of three hours wasted each day just to come to work at the office. From this emerged the President's idea of letting employees choose *where* and *when* they wanted to work—at the office or at home. Participation in this new working mode was voluntary.

In 2008, 70% of employees responded positively and started to work at home up to three days per week—the legal maximum. In addition, the relocation of the ministry in 2009 was accompanied by a complete digitization of all archives, which further simplified working from home. This move proved to be the least expensive in the history of the Belgian Administration: as there were no papers or furniture to move, each employee took only a box of their personal belongings by subway to the new building. The new building had furniture and spaces specially designed for a novel collaborative working mode. There were no fixed offices, but instead "flex" open space offices, always clean and adaptable. Many semi-open and soundproof spaces for meetings and discussions were also installed. With many working at home, teams came to the office mostly to coordinate rather than to carry out their work.

Once the consequences of this major change had been measured, the skeptics smiled with satisfaction: Employees worked an average of 6 hours at home instead of the supposed 7 hours 36 minutes at the office. But there was an upside: They were 20% more productive. Moreover, as 70% of employees chose to work up to three days weekly at home, 7 "flexi" desks sufficed for 10 employees. This saved about $8 million reduction in annual rent.

Encouraged by these initial results, Frank Van Massenhove surrounded himself with other leaders, notably Laurence Vanhée, HR Director, and began a truly radical transformation of the ministry. Now, all ministry employees were allowed in a free and responsible way to take any action to improve the service provided to its citizen-users. This involved nothing less than the dismantling of hierarchical bureaucracy—the heart not only of the ministry, but also of all institutions and companies as we know them today. Here is what Mr. Van Massenhove had to say about them:

"Hierarchy makes the organization blind to problems. Nobody signals them because they are seen as a criticism of the manager, who always 'knows better.' Traditional managers are afraid to let go of control, to abandon the trappings of power. Here, nobody has an office, including myself. Managers have become coaches, facilitators. This stirs debate, but I want to make the employees happy. Not because I like humankind so much! Simply because happy people work better and thus deliver better service to our customers—the citizens."

The conviction of the President is therefore not that managers are useless, but that common sense clearly indicates that it is the frontline employees who deliver services and are therefore the most important. All other collaborators—those in support functions, managers and executives up to the President of the Ministry—are in service of the frontline employees. This is also the common sense that led the President to give up his 540 square foot office. He requested the amount of time he spent there to be calculated: it turned out to be 3%! The savings–more than $22,500 in annual rent. The same common sense prompted him *not* to ask his Minister's authorization for these transformations.

When the latter finally learned—through the media—he was not offended. Instead—common sense again—he was pleased because the transformation results were good for the citizens and the national economy. Today, offices designed for "employee happiness" are comparable with those of Google. But paradoxically, 900 of the ministry's 1,300 employees prefer to carry out their work at home, "where, when and how they want," as Frank Van Massenhove likes to repeat. It is precisely because of the trust and freedom that they enjoy that these employees set extremely ambitious targets and have distributed them fairly among the members of each team. As Laurence Vanhée explains, "it is not because one is a civil servant that one is content with doing a minimum at work." Trust also means open access to stationery supplies—a culture shock in this government administration that, not so long ago, required forms to be filled out for each new pen or marker. An economic shock too, since the cost of supplies plummeted by 35% in one year. Further cost reductions have followed, such as a 30% reduction in energy costs. In all, the Ministry has reduced its spending by 8% in one year. The Belgian Government had only asked for 4%! Trust is always less expensive than control.

All this has generated great excitement in the media. The ministry was voted the best work environment in the country for two consecutive years, Frank Van Massenhove was voted manager of the year and Laurence Vanhée the country's best HR Director, although that is not her official title. It's "Chief Happiness Officer," because HR, she says, does not mean Human Resources, but "Happiness Rendering." It is not surprising, therefore, that this ministry is now the most in demand by civil servants. It is also visited by thousands of companies around the world, including neighboring French ones, who come for inspiration for radical transformation. Government administrations come to visit too. Even the Ministry of Finance of South Korea visited Brussels for inspiration. But the example also spread to the rest of the Belgian administration. The Belgian Ministry of Mobility and Transport began its transformation based on trust under the leadership of its new President, Laurent Ledoux. Another ministry, which defines the HR policies for all Belgian governments, was greatly inspired, as well as the Minister for the Government Simplification of Administration. In fact, he set up his office on the 6th floor of the same building as the Ministry of Social Security, in which he finds much to learn and to adopt for other government branches.

After having studied organizations based on the trust and freedom of employees for over seven years, we can confirm that the Ministry of Social Security is one of the most successful of such organizations in the world, government and private companies combined. Perhaps the time has come to learn from the Belgians?

LEADERSHIP, VISION AND VALUES

Welcome to a World without Distrust or Supervision—Japan[13]

The business press has spoken a lot recently about companies based on trust. In some American and European companies, employees choose how long their vacations are and decide when and where—office or home—they wish to work. In some American and Brazilian companies, employees fix their own compensation. None of this is new. Businesses based on trust have existed in the world for several decades. At the same time however, their mode of functioning has always seemed so unusual that some refer to them as…sects.

Something strange must be happening for people not to take advantage

---

13. *Bienvenue dans le monde sans méfiance, ni contrôle... au Japon,* by Isaac Getz, LeMonde.fr, Nov. 6, 2014 http://www.lemonde.fr/emploi/article/2014/11/06/bienvenue-dans -le-monde-sans-mefiance-ni-controle-au-japon_4519748_1698637.html

of the situation and cheat. That said, it is a legitimate fear—all the more so as the hierarchical bureaucracy of traditional business is a manufacturing machine for cheaters. If these companies can survive despite all the imaginary illnesses, shirking, fake numbers and reports—all this magnified by the hidden costs of supervision—it is clear that companies based on trust can survive the trickery of the 3% of free riders. They above all manage to avoid adding a new layer of control each time someone abuses the trust. They prefer to get rid of the free rider rather than punish the honorable majority.

A sect? Maybe, but certainly not "softies." Arguments in favor of trust, like those mentioned above, will never suffice, but the fact is that these companies continue to draw the attention of players in traditional companies, as if to compensate for a lack of something—of trust, in fact. Yet psychoanalysis tells us that one can never truly compensate for a lack of something: one can only transform it into something else to be free of it. Recently, a business leader going on an assignment in Japan, and deeply intrigued by businesses based on trust, asked me if I knew one in Japan. I advised him not to benchmark Japanese companies, but rather Japanese society.

Many Westerners return from Japan expressing great surprise at what they saw on Japanese trains; a ticket inspector enters the car, bows to all the passengers, and then, when leaving, turns around and bows again. That's nice, you may say, but they inspect the tickets too, no? You're right, but in light of the following they might as well not bother.

Here is Nara Station, the historical capital of Japan, which attracts crowds of tourists. Judging by the traffic, the station must have a large supermarket. Up to this point, nothing unusual. Except that there are no real doors or even walls between the station hall and the supermarket. You are walking and suddenly there you are in the aisles. To pay you have to move to the front of the store. So there must be hidden security guards somewhere? No, because—as Western expatriates will explain to you—the Japanese do not steal...and they think that tourists don't steal either.

I didn't do it on purpose, but I have tested this claim. On a recent trip to Japan, I took a Shinkansen, the Japanese bullet train, and when I got out in Kyoto, I realized on the platform that my Samsung Galaxy 4 had probably slipped out of my pocket on the train. I went to see the station master, with my thoughts on the purchase of a new phone. No one spoke English of course, but since this is inconvenient for many tourists, retired Anglophones volunteer there next to a big "WE SPEAK ENGLISH" sign. They helped to translate my problem.

I scanned the face of the station manager. He was clearly embarrassed. His apology for my mishap was translated and he asked if I remembered my seat numbers. Yes, I remembered them. He called the train manager immediately and told us that he had gone to look for the phone. After a short wait, his phone rings and I see the sad face of the station master: "Nothing found." But that wasn't the end of it. He told me that if I was sure my phone had fallen out in the train—I was sure of that—the cleaners would find it at the terminus near Osaka. "Come back tomorrow at noon," he said.

The next day at noon, neither the manager nor the retired volunteers from the day before were there. But different translators relayed my situation to a new station master and his face lit up. He handed me my phone. Accustomed to distrust, I asked him if he needed me to describe the phone, such as the home screen, to prove that it was indeed mine. I saw on his face that he didn't have a clue why I was asking that.

I told this story to a friend, the boss of a small business and admirer of Japanese society. I concluded: "This is a people that cannot imagine a lack of trust." His reaction was: "And that changes a lot about everyday life!" Indeed, we supervise because we do not trust. With this comes all the delays, procedures, hassle, and hidden costs of supervisors—plus the energy used trying to get around them. But if you do not have suspicion of others there is no need to supervise.

Just imagine how much easier it makes life: how much more fluid all transactions and exchanges are. The energy that is devoted to supervision—and its circumvention—is suddenly available for doing really useful things for others: an employee, a customer, a supplier, a stranger. The companies that I mentioned at the beginning understand this. They have decided to trust their employees and use the freed energy to create value. Of course, not everything is rosy in the land of the Rising Sun. However, it is not my aim to discuss here all the particularities of this country, but simply the role played there by trust.

Liberated Companies: Their Philosophy and their Anti-bureaucratic Creators[14]

In 1787, Thomas Jefferson, then ambassador of the United States in Paris, wrote a letter to his friend James Madison, who was busy elaborating the U.S. Constitution. Rather than commenting on a specific system for the balance of power, Jefferson outlined for him three different philosophies for governing society. The first, which he associated with the Continental European countries of the time, was that of government by force. The second, which he associated with America and the U.K., was that of a government accountable to the people. Finally, the third, which Jefferson associated with Native American societies, was that of self-government built on the values internalized and shared by all members of small communities.

Jefferson stated his preference for the third philosophy, before conceding its impracticability for large populations. In all discussions on the subject of liberated companies, I prefer to avoid comparisons with political systems (autocracy vs. democracy etc.). Here, to emulate Jefferson's approach, I will discuss the philosophies that underlie businesses, rather than their systems or their supposed models.

In 1957, Douglas McGregor laid out the philosophy on which

---

14. *L'entreprise libérée est une question de philosophie, ses créateurs des anti-bureaucrates.* By Isaac Getz, LeMonde.fr, June 5, 2015. http://www.lemonde.fr/emploi/article /2015/06/04/l-entreprise-liberee-est-une-question-de-philosophie-ses-createurs-des-anti -bureaucrates_4647696_1698637.html

so-called traditional companies are based, with their central belief that: "The average employee has an intrinsic aversion to work and prefers to be directed, thus avoiding any responsibility." Liberated companies are founded on a different philosophy, namely that human beings aspire to satisfy their universal needs of intrinsic equality, self-realization and self-direction: universal needs, though expressed differently in each cultural context. Different organizational modes stem from these two philosophies.

The first philosophy poses the problem of how to manage employees. The solution—as explained by the physicist and philosopher Marc Halévy—is a hierarchical model because it constitutes a mathematical solution for supervising the maximum number of employees with the minimum number of managers.

The second philosophy may not involve any particular model. Indeed, if an organization is to meet the needs of employees in a manner relevant to their cultural context (profession, sector, region, etc.), they alone will know how to design a unique and appropriate organizational mode.

That is why at the beginning of a "corporate liberation," employees must be asked about the values/rules by which they wish to live in their company. The answers vary from one company to another because the need for intrinsic equality, for example, may be expressed through values like respect, trust, goodwill, listening, good humor or fairness.

Once these values have been unanimously agreed, the following question arises: "What practices and symbols must be removed because they are contrary to our values, and what other practices and symbols must we adopt to foster them?" Thus emerges a diversity of organizational modes that each reflects a unique cultural context.

For example, the single, standard value in SOL, a liberated Finnish service company, guarantees that no one—including the CEO—enjoys "privileges" such as personal offices, company cars, reserved parking lots or business class flights. However, the same egalitarian value in Richards Group, the largest privately held American advertising firm in Dallas, results in reserved parking lots and open-plan offices, with better views granted according to seniority.

Though each liberated company's organizational mode is unique, one aspect is found in virtually all them: the limited size of operational units. Known as mini-plants, villages, speedboats or self-directed teams, they never exceed 250 people. The reason is not only the difficulty of sharing values between too many individuals, but also that of maintaining organizational practices that continue to satisfy fundamental needs. For example, how can employees communicate with respect and trust—directly and orally—with more than 250 people when they don't even know each other's first names? That's when the writing of emails starts.

In view of the above, the philosophy of liberated companies seems to resemble the one Jefferson associated with Native American tribes in the late eighteenth century—but with several caveats. The main difference is that these tribes were not built but emerged historically, whereas the organizational mode of liberated companies is the result of a transformation launched and carried out by a leader. The leader accomplishes this by articulating the universal corporate liberation philosophy within an inherited human and cultural context, resulting in a unique organizational mode. Therefore, the liberating leader has nothing in common with the Native American tribal chief.

Furthermore, for the above-mentioned reasons, there can neither be a model for corporate liberation nor a recipe for setting it up. None of the liberating leaders we studied have said they applied a particular model. Some, like Liisa Joronen, President of SOL, recounted that researchers had tried to model SOL's organizational mode. Yet others, such as Jean-François Zobrist, leader of FAVI, an icon of liberated companies in France, despite being wary of theories, subsequently attempted to model FAVI's organizational aspects. While at W.L. Gore, a liberated company since 1958, four employees began to codify their 40 year-old organizational culture in the early 2000s.

To draw an initial conclusion, the only thing all liberated companies share is a philosophy that each one of them expresses within an inherited cultural and human context and which results in a unique organizational mode. This is also why corporate liberation is not a revolution—which by definition ignores heritage and imposes on diverse reality a single theoretical model—but an evolution, albeit radical.

So what is the role of liberating leaders in corporate liberation? At first glance, one could compare them to architects. Like an architect beginning an architectural creation, a liberating leader initiates a company's liberation, and like an architect, a liberating leader possesses no recipe to guarantee the result. This is also why liberation, like any creative process, is not simple but complex, risky and often frustrating. However, like most analogies, this one too has its limits.

Unlike an architect, who typically isn't involved with the future building's occupiers, the liberating leader co-creates the main pillars of the liberated company *with* its employees: a vision—though some entrepreneurs have given birth to their vision independently and then shared it—and above all, common values. That's why a liberated company is inseparable from the liberation process conducted by the liberating leader in conjunction with the employees.

The other difference is that most architects work—understandably— to become well-known and indispensable. This is not the case of the liberating leader, who has no ego and seeks to become dispensable. This is the price of victory for the organizational practices that aim to satisfy people's needs for trust, self-realization and self-direction. It is also at this moment that a leader can claim to have built a liberated company; a company in which employees have complete freedom and responsibility for actions that *they*, not their bosses or procedures, have decided are best for the company's future. Accordingly, every three years, Jean-François Zobrist asked employees if they wanted to keep him as the head of the company. Robert Townsend, who liberated Avis in the early 1960s, advised CEOs to remain no longer than five years in their posts, while Alexandre Gérard, who liberated his company ChronoFlex, simply left to tour the world with his family for a year.

The liberating leader is therefore an anti-chief and anti-bureaucrat. His aim is to ensure that problems are resolved by employees so he becomes dispensable, whereas the bureaucrat seeks to deal with problems, thus continuing to be indispensable.

The Love that Liberates the Greatness of Vineyards and Companies[15]

Imagine you have just tasted a great wine. If you are an amateur, it has delighted you, helped you to enjoy a marvelous moment. But if you are a connoisseur, you will try to learn more about the wine. Your questions will focus on its region, the variety of its grapes, its soil and the winemaking process. Are the grapes from the entire vineyard or from one specific plot? How old are the vines? Have the vines been chemically treated, or are they the result of organic or biodynamic winegrowing? Then come questions about the winemaking: are the grapes picked manually or mechanically? Are the tanks stainless steel, cement or wood? Are grape varieties fermented separately or mixed prior to fermentation (in the case of blended wines). Was the wine aged in barrels or not?

An amateur would quickly tire of these questions. Conversely, connoisseurs and professionals would like to go even further in learning the "how." Connoisseurs believe that technical information helps them to *understand* the wine (there is debate on this last point: should wine be understood using knowledge, or intuition?) As for the professionals, they seek the method: the magic recipe.

It is certain that much technical expertise is involved in the creation of a great wine. I remember the huge fans in a great Pessac Léognan vineyard in Bordeaux. The vintner used them in autumn to circulate the cold morning air to prevent freezing. Surprisingly, great vintners share their expertise easily, not only with connoisseurs, but also with other vintners. I still remember a former entrepreneur, the new owner of a vineyard in the Languedoc region in France, who had come to visit a great vintner in

---

15. *Cette affection qui libère la grandeur des terroirs et des entreprises*, by Isaac Getz, Huffington Post, Sept. 2015.

the Loire region. He asked dozens of technical questions, such as how has the vintner treated the barrels' interior, and so on. The vintner answered readily. There was something paradoxical in his sharing all his secrets after so much hard work and experimentation.

However, a small detail showed that this did not bother him in the slightest. While answering all the technical questions, the vintner appeared absorbed by other thoughts. However, as soon as he tasted his wine, his face lit up. Sometimes he looked surprised: "this one is not bad one," or, "should I work more on this one?" Each remark implicitly expressed the fondness he had for his wine: some would say, love.

What is the recipe for love? Ever since Ovid wrote *The Art of Love*, numerous poets have devoted themselves to the subject. More prosaically, the Beatles sang "money can't buy me love." They could also have sung "consultants can't buy me love." The technical aspects of winegrowing and winemaking are of course indispensable. A great deal of knowledge is necessary to master biodynamics or meticulous blending. There are a number of excellent wines that consultants in viticulture or winemaking have helped produce for their owners. If a connoisseur tastes a wine, he will say: "this is a great Médoc" or "it is a superb Santa Inez Pinot." Rarely, however, will he recognize the domain or name the specific wine. This is not their fault.

Inevitably, good wines from the same region produced with the same techniques are similar. In other words, they are not unique, whereas a great wine *is* unique. And it is the fondness of its creator, a great vintner that made it so. It is possible that he was helped to acquire certain techniques, especially in the beginning, but the fondness, the love of their terroir and its wine, were innate. They were not acquired. The Beatles were right.

What is the link between these winemaking considerations and liberated companies? I believe it to be strong.

A leader liberates his business because he has the ambition to make a world-class and unique— great—company. Such a leader will of course be inspired by other liberated companies. What great vintner has not tasted others' great wines? But the leader will not look for recipes. Like a vintner with his terroir, he knows that his company is like no other. The people who work there, their customs, their history —all this is unique. This leader is attached to this legacy. He could have chosen another company but he has fondness for this particular one. And it is for this company that he dreams of greatness through the liberation of its full potential.

So the leader will try to discern from the experiences of other leaders—who have already liberated the potential of their businesses —what their beliefs and their philosophy are. Soon enough, he will realize that they are close to his own convictions; that certain fundamental principles are recurrent.

Firstly, the principle of respect. Like the vintner who respects his land, its vines and grapes, the liberating leader has a deep respect for people. He will not try to change employees' behavior by applying this or that method. Rather, he will create a natural and conducive environment that will encourage the employees to do the best job they are capable of. He is just like the great vintner, who respects and listens to his vines, creating the natural environment conducive to giving birth to the best possible grapes and later, to the best possible wine.

Secondly, liberating leaders use the principle of trust to enable employees to achieve their potential. As the great vintner who believes in the potential of his vineyard, this leader believes in the potential of every person. For him, each person has a gift, a talent. Therefore, he creates the conditions for this potential to be unleashed: potential of which, sometimes, the person herself was unaware. Just like for wine. Look what some vintners have managed to make from grapes like Melon de Bourgogne in Muscadet region in France. Great wines.

Finally, there is the principle of self-direction. As with the great vintner, who believes in the intelligence of his vines, the leader believes in the intelligence of each person, in their ability to find solutions to the problems they face. The vine roots know how to sink deep into the ground to find water. Similarly, employees with the intelligence of "those who do the things," find solutions to their problems.

However, through these observations of others' experiences, liberating leaders do not seek techniques. They are aware that other leaders have relied on their philosophy and their beliefs to invent unique solutions to the many challenges they face when liberating their companies.

What does a liberating leader do, once armed with his philosophy and his beliefs? He implements them by articulating them within the human and cultural heritage of the company he is fond of. Proposing neither recipes nor models, he will ask his employees to propose the unwritten rules they wish to see applied in the company. Past experience shows that these rules are all close to values such as respect, self-realization and self-direction, as mentioned above. Then, the leader will ask his employees to indicate the business practices that do not correspond to these unwritten rules and ask them to suggest new practices to shape the new organizational mode. Unique, this working environment will free the initiative and potential of employees, and with it the greatness of the company.

Liberating leaders are, indeed, like great vintners. Great vintners "listen" to their terroir so as to transform all the practices that are incompatible with their beliefs: respect for the land, faith in its potential and its productive ability. Similarly, liberating leaders reinvent the company according to their beliefs. The two results—vineyard and company—may not be perfect, but they will be unique; created to unleash potential and greatness.

How long can a vineyard remain a great vineyard? Let's say that if it is great for at least a decade, there is a reason. But what are the events that can cause it to lose its greatness?

Firstly, there is the vintner who created it. One day he will leave. Who will replace him? Someone who views himself as a simple "guardian" of the terroir, just "there to pass on the vineyard one day" as Aubert de Villaine, the great vintner of Domaine Romanée-Conti in Burgundy, said.

Or conversely, by someone sure of his intelligence, who will say that they must produce the natural wine of the land of which they are in charge.

Then there is the new owner. Will he trust the vintner, like the previous owner? Or, if not, will he ruin the treasure he has acquired? Is it not said that the best way to make a small fortune is to invest a large one in a vineyard?

The wine will not rebel, but it will change. One day, an amateur, a lover of this wine, will taste it and say: "this is not the same." Fortunately, this is not the only wine he loved, because has tasted others, and each year, new wines will delight his palate.

"To your good health!"

ACKNOWLEDGMENTS

This book has two names on the cover, but it could not have been written or published without contributions, large and small, from a great many people.

Our thanks and gratitude go out first to Brian's young family. Without the patient support of Samantha, Luke, James, and Aletheia through the long years of this project's incubation, research, and writing, you would not be reading this now.

We also owe a great debt of gratitude to all of the people who work at the companies we write about in this book. While that group is too large to list by individual names, we could not have written it without the access, insights, and wisdom that they all provided in great abundance.

Unique acknowledgement is due though to a special group that became the focus of this book: Bob Davids, Gordon Forward, Liisa Joronen, David Kelley, Jacques Raiman, Stan Richards, Richard Teerlink, Jeff Westphal, Jean-Francois Zobrist. The acumen and perspicacity of these liberating leaders helped crystallize our own thoughts and very often gave us the vocabulary to put them on paper.

Two of the liberating leaders we met, Bob Koski and Robert McDermott, passed away before we could finish writing 2009 edition of this book. The world is poorer for their passing; we only hope that in some small way we have done justice to their memories. In 2015, Jacques Raiman passed away too, a man who loved his people and was loved in return by them. Each of the three men was a prince among men, generous of spirit, abounding with good humor and good sense. May they rest in peace.

Two other liberating leaders—Bill Gore and Harry Quadracci—passed away before we started working on it. We'd like to thank Burt Chase and Les Lewis of Gore and Joel and Tom Quadracci and Karl Fritchen of Quad, who shared with us their memories and their thoughts on leadership.

Any frailties in relaying the insights of all these people are due entirely to our own shortcomings, and where credit is due it is due mostly to them and to everyone else who appears in this book, whether by name or not.

We often had occasion to remark to each other, in the writing and production of this book, on the myriad ways in which good luck seemed to intervene to drive it forward. But truth be known, it was the goodwill of others more than pure chance—in every case we benefited from the intercession of a worldly angel of fortune who appeared at just the right time to help us over some obstacle. Heather Bushong, Roe D'Angelo, Annette Godart van der Kroon, and Jason Riley, were all, wittingly or not, there at just the right moments to help when we needed it.

The 2009 version editor, John Mahaney, pushed us to make what we thought was a good book even better. Both he and our indispensable agent, Kris Dahl, believed in this book and gave us the courage and the opportunity to try to realize our vision for it. Kris, together with Caroline Eisenman, continued and oversaw this 2015 edition. They are the godfather and the godmother of this book and we could not have written it without them.

Last but not least, Brian could never have finished this book without the support, encouragement, and understanding of his colleagues at the *Wall Street Journal*, especially Paul Gigot, Robert Pollock, Bret Stephens, and Taylor Buley. Isaac, likewise, would like to thank his institution, ESCP Europe Business School—established coincidentally almost two centuries ago by the business leader and great proponent of freedom Jean-Baptiste Say—for its support. Many of Isaac's research assistants helped with often tedious tasks during this project. However, the efforts of Marie Elisabeth Holm, who tirelessly read and reread the manuscript as we drafted it, are especially worthy of recognition. Lucy Carney's eagle eye also caught many typos and omissions throughout the process.

We owe all of you more than we can ever hope to repay. Thank you.

NOTES

INTRODUCTION

1. Quoted in Richard Florida and Martin Kenney, *The Breakthrough Illusion: Corporate America's Failure to Move from Innovation to Mass Production* (New York: Basic Books, 1990), p. 157.

2. Personal interview, May 17, 2008.

3. Robert Townsend, *Up the Organization: How to Stop the Corporation from Stifling People and Strangling Profits*, commemorative ed. (San Francisco: Jossey-Bass, 2007), p. 59.

4. In Tom Peters and Robert Townsend, *Winning Management Strategies for the Real World* (Niles, Illinois: Nightingale Conant Corp, 1986), audio-cassette.

5. Douglas McGregor, *The Human Side of Enterprise*, annotated ed. (New York: McGraw-Hill, 2006), pp. 45–46.

6. Ibid., pp. 65–66.

7. Warren Bennis, foreword to McGregor, *The Human Side of Enterprise*, p. xx.

8. Seminar given at the ESCP Europe Business School, February 18, 2009.

1: "HOW" COMPANIES AND "WHY" COMPANIES

1. Alan Deutschman, "The Fabric of Creativity," *Fast Company*, December 2004, pp. 54–60.

2. Personal interview, March 1, 2006.

3. Peter Marsh and Stefan Stern, "The Chaos Theory of Leadership," *Financial Times*, December 2, 2008.

4. Deutschman, "Fabric of Creativity."

5. Jean-François Zobrist, *La belle histoire de FAVI: L'entreprise qui croit que*

l'homme est bon (Tome 1: Nos belles histoires) [The Nice Story of FAVI: The Company Which Believes That Man Is Good (Vol. 1: Our Nice Stories)] (Paris: Humanisme et Organisations, 2007), pp. 24–25. The book's back cover explains that its author is a "Favien" who only "kept a quill" for the stories told by other "Faviens." In fact, the author is Jean-François Zobrist, who compiled the stories he wrote and distributed them to all the company's employees every week for a dozen years. We thank Zobrist for granting us permission to reproduce some excerpts of his writing in our book.

6. Ibid., p. 26.

7. Personal interview, April 8, 2005.

8. The name "Zobrist" comes from the Swiss-German word *zu oberste*, which means "one who comes from the top"—presumably of the Swiss Alps. FAVI's CEO, however, rejected this etymological heritage and determined, instead, to put his employees on top—and leave them free to act.

9. Personal interview, April 8, 2005.

10. Rich Teerlink and Lee Ozley, *More Than a Motorcycle: The Leadership Journey at Harley-Davidson* (Boston: Harvard Business School Press, 2000), p. 28.

2: ARE YOU MANAGING FOR THE "THREE PERCENT"?

1. Between 1500 and 1820, per capita income in western European countries and their offshoots (North America and Australasia) rose by 60 percent—although it rose a mere 7 percent in the rest of the world (population growth was similar in both regions). This means that, minuscule elite aside, the vast majority of people lived at a level of mere material subsistence, if not hunger. However, from 1820 to 2001, per capita income rose twentyfold in the West (sixfold in the rest of the world). See Angus Maddison, *Dynamic Forces in Capitalist Development* (Oxford: Oxford University Press, 1991); and Angus Maddison, "Contours of the World Economy and the Art of Macro-measurement 1500–2001" (Ruggles Lecture, IARIW 28th General Conference, Cork, Ireland, August 2004).

2. Max Weber, *Economy and Society* (Berkeley: University of California Press, 1978), p. 227.

3. James Hoopes, *False Prophets: The Gurus Who Created Modern Management and Why Their Ideas Are Bad for Business Today* (New York: Perseus Books, 2003), p. xv.

4. Most leading management thinkers since Weber—including Mary Parker Follett, Peter Drucker, W. Edwards Deming, Tom Peters, Russell Ackoff, Sumantra Ghoshal, and Gary Hamel—disagreed with him and took a very negative view of bureaucracy.

5. See Hoopes, *False Prophets*, for a skeptical discussion of the views of some of the leading management thinkers.

6. Isaac Getz and Alan G. Robinson, *Vos idées changent tous!* [Your Ideas Change Everything!] (Paris: Editions d'Organisation, 2007).

7. Rahul Jacob, "TQM: More Than a Dying Fad?" *Fortune*, October 18, 1993, pp. 66–72.

8. Jeffrey K. Liker and Michael Hoseus, *Toyota Culture: The Heart and Soul of the Toyota Way* (New York: McGraw-Hill, 2008).

9. Ibid., pp. 381–82.

10. Reported by Rich Teerlink, personal interview, August 15, 2005.

11. Christine Buckley, "Turn Up for Work and Bag a Prize," *Times* (London), August 5, 2004.

12. Personal interview, September 25, 2007.

13. Gallup's State of the American Workplace, 2013.

14. Isaac Getz and Alan G. Robinson, "Innovate or Die: Is That a Fact?" *Creativity and Innovation Management* 12, no. 3 (2003): pp. 130–36.

15. G. A. Stevens and J. Burley, "3,000 Raw Ideas = 1 Commercial Success!" *Research-Technology Management*, May–June 1997, pp. 16–27.

16. D. Harhoff, F. Narin, F. M. Scherer, and K. Vopel, "Citation Frequency and the Value of Patented Inventions," *The Review of Economics and Statistics* 81, no. 3 (1999): pp. 511–15.

17. "The TR Patent Scorecard 2001," *Technology Review*, May 2001, pp. 48–49. Lately, IBM admitted that patenting is not only unhelpful for innovation but even hampers it; "Why Technologists Want Fewer Patents," *Wall Street Journal*, June 15, 2009, p. A13.

18. Florida and Kenney, *Breakthrough Illusion*, p. 171.

19. Personal interview, August 19, 2005.

20. Personal interview, September 25, 2007.

21. "Gallup Study: Engaged Employees Inspire Company Innovation," *The Gallup Management Journal*, October 12, 2006, http://gmj.gallup.com/ (accessed July 3, 2008).

22. The November 2015 Gallup engagement study's results are slightly different from the previous survey: in 2013: 32 percent are engaged and 68 percent are disengaged or actively disengaged.

23. Jeffery McCracken, ' "Way Forward' Requires Culture Shift at Ford," *Wall Street Journal*, January 23, 2006; and Dee-Ann Durbin, "Ford's Restructuring Plan Calls for 30,000 Job Cuts," Associated Press, 2005,http://www.staugustine.com/PalmPilot/stories/012406/new_3595454.html (accessed May 25, 2007).

24. "'Churn': How to Reduce Customer Abandonment," *The Marketing Intelligence Review*, no. 6, December 2005, http://www.daemonquest.com/en/the_marketing_intelligence_review/6/1192 (accessed December 14, 2008). Only 24 percent of customers attributed their abandonment to high prices. Remarkably, when these companies' directors were asked about the main cause of their customers' abandonment, 50 percent attributed it to price and only 21 percent to their awful customer service.

25. G. Gitelson, J. W. Bing, and L. Laroche, "The Impact of Culture on

Mergers & Acquisitions," *CMA Management*, March 2001, http://www.itapintl
.com/(accessed May 15, 2007).

26. Towers Perrin-ISR, "Engaged Employees Drive the Bottom Line,"
http://www.isrsurveys.com/(accessed April 20, 2007).

27. The following pages on workplace stress and its health consequences draw
from: William Atkinson, "Managing Stress," *Electrical World* 214, no. 6 (November-December 2000): pp. 41–42; Hans Bosma, Stephen Stansfeld, and Michael
Marmot, "Job Control, Personal Characteristics, and Heart Disease," *Journal of
Occupational Health Psychology* 3, no. 4 (October 1998): pp. 402–9; S. Cartwight
and C. L. Cooper, Managing Workplace stress (Thousand Oaks, California:
Sage, 1997); "Are You Working Too Hard? A Conversation with Herbert Ben-
son, M.D.," *Harvard Business Review*, November 2005, pp. 53–58; L. M. Cortina,
V. J. Magley, J. H. Williams, and R. D. Langhout, "Incivility in the Workplace:
Incidence and Impact," *Journal of Occupational Health Psychology* 6 (2001): pp.
64–80; R. S. Lazarus and S. Folkman, Stress, Appraisal, and Coping (New York:
Springer, 1984); J. H. Neuman, "Injustice, Stress, and Aggression in Organiza-
tions," in *The Dark Side of Organizational Behavior*, ed. R. W. Griffin and A.
M. O'Leary-Kelly (San Francisco: Jossey-Bass, 2004), pp. 62–102; Anne G. Per-
kins, "Medical Costs," *Harvard Business Review* 72, no. 6 (November-December
1994): p. 12; Oakley Ray, "How the Mind Hurts and Heals the Body," *American
Psychologist* 59, no. 1 (2004): pp. 29–40; Paul E. Spector, "Employee Control and
Occupational Stress," *Current Directions in Psychological Science* no. 4 (2002):
pp. 133–36; and Joanne Wojcik, "Cutting Costs of Stress," *Business Insurance* 35,
no. 13, March 26, 2001, pp. 1–2.

28. "Gallup Study: Engaged Employees Inspire Company Innovation."

29. Sample items from the "Workplace Aggression Research Questionnaire,"
as described in Neuman, "Injustice, Stress, and Aggression," p. 66.

30. Bosma, Stansfeld, and Marmot, "Job Control, Personal Characteristics,
and Heart Disease," p. 406

3: FROM ARTISANS TO AUTOMATONS

1. The description of Birmingham and its Lunar Society is based on Jenny
Uglow, *The Lunar Men: Five Friends Whose Curiosity Changed the World* (New
York: Farrar, Straus and Giroux, 2002).

2. We owe the term "horsepower" to Watt and Boulton, who didn't simply sell
engines. The key to their business model was to collect a fee from the businesses
to which they sold their engines. The fee was calculated based on an estimate of
how much the mill or mine had saved by replacing teams of horses with an engine. The more powerful the engine, the more horses it displaced and the higher
Watt's and Boulton's royalty.

3. Uglow, *The Lunar Men*, p. 199.

4. *Encyclopaedia Britannica Online*, s. v. "Work, history of the organization
of," http://www.britannica.com/eb/article-67037 (accessed February 15, 2008).

5. David Mckie, "Last Train to Etruria," *Guardian*, November 16, 2005.

6. Richard Weaver, *Ideas Have Consequences* (Chicago: University of Chicago Press, 1948).

7. *Encyclopaedia Britannica Online*, "Work, history of the organization of."

8. Tim Lambert, "A History of Northampton," http://www.localhistories.org /northampton.html (accessed January 28, 2009).

9. The description of primates' studies in the following pages draw on Robert Sapolsky, "Culture in Animals: The Case of a Non-human Primate Culture of Low Aggression and High Affiliation," *Social Forces* 85, no. 1 (2006): pp. 217–33; Robert Sapolsky, "A Natural History of Peace," *Foreign Affairs* 85, no. 1 (January–February 2006); and G. Hohmann and B. Fruth, "Intra- and Inter-Sexual Aggression by Bonobos in the Context of Mating," *Behaviour* 140 (2003): pp. 1389–1413.

10. F. B. M. de Waal and D. L. Johanowicz, "Modification of Reconciliation Behavior Through Social Experience: An Experiment with Two Macaque Species," *Child Development* 64 (1993): pp. 897–908; and F.B.M. de Waal, "Peace Lessons from an Unlikely Source," *PLoS Biology* 2, no. 4 (2004): pp. 434–36.

4: FREEDOM IS NOT ANARCHY

1. Personal interview, September 24, 2007. Bob Davids credits this approach to Robert Townsend, from whom he borrowed it.

2. Personal interview, September 24, 2007.

3. Personal interview with Kris Curran, September 24, 2007.

4. Personal interview, March 1, 2006.

5. Personal interview, March 3, 2006.

6. Telephone interview, August 7, 2008.

7. The preferred term of Max De Pree, who, by his own account, built a freedom-based environment while CEO of the furniture and design company Herman Miller, the maker of the iconic Aeron office chair, among other things.

8. In 1999, Bob retired as CEO of Radica to focus exclusively on Sea Smoke Cellars. In 2006, Mattel acquired Radica for about $230 million.

5: WHY THEY DID IT

1. *Online Encyclopedia*, "Wilkens, Lenny (1937-). Basketball coach, basketball player, Early life, Chronology, First taste of intolerance, Another shot at the Olympics," http://encyclopedia.jrank.org/articles/pages/4513/Wilkens-Lenny -1937.html (accessed January 22, 2009). In 2010, he was surpassed by three wins by Don Nelson.

2. Personal interview, March 3, 2006.

3. Robert K. Greenleaf, *Servant Leadership* (New York: Paulist Press, 2002), pp. 24–25. Emphasis in original.

4. Albert Camus, *The First Man* (New York: Penguin, 1996), p. 256 for the first sentence, then, p. 241; emphasis in original.

5. The technical term for this business strategy is the "George Costanza," after the eighty-sixth episode of the hit television series Seinfeld, titled "The Opposite," which originally aired on NBC on May 19, 1994.

6. Sun Hydraulics, *Observations from Bob Koski and Clyde Nixon*, no. 7 (2003).

7. Personal interview, May 20, 2008.

8. Linda A. Hill and Jennifer M. Suesse, "Sun Hydraulics: Leading in Tough Times (A)," Harvard Business School case study, 2003, p. 1.

9. Sun Hydraulics, *Observations from Bob Koski and Clyde Nixon*, no. 7.

10. We thank Bob Koski for his permission to use this image.

11. Sun Hydraulics, *Observations from Bob Koski and Clyde Nixon*, nos. 1–2 (2003).

12. Ibid., no. 1; the word "investor" is put by Koski in quotation marks because for Sun Hydraulics "investors" are not only stockholders, but also its customers and suppliers.

13. There is no paradox in the coexistence of the "how" culture and freedom environments at DuPont, as well as at AT&T and a few other research-based companies in those days. Facing a shortage of scientists and engineers and high turnover in their R&D departments, these companies created an "island of freedom" in R&D. Inspired by the university lab culture, people were free to decide what projects they wanted to pursue and how they wanted to go about their business. These "freedom islands," however, were never meant to be expanded to the rest of the companies—to the sorrow of Bill Gore. (See also note 7 in chapter 9.)

14. The following remarks are based on Bill Gore's internal memo "The Lattice Organization—A Philosophy of Enterprise," May 7, 1976. On the cover his wife and business associate Vieve wrote, "Attached is a write-up Bill has made of the talks he has given at various times. Many of you have heard this before but may be interested in reading it. For those to whom this is new, it outlines many of the basic principles of our Association."

15. Ibid., p. 4.

16. Ibid., p. 5.

17. Richard Arter, email communication, January 30, 2009.

18. Personal interview, September 24, 2007.

19. Personal interview, September 24, 2007.

6: WHAT'S YOUR (PEOPLE'S) PROBLEM?

1. All the stories in this chapter on Harley-Davidson and Rich Teerlink are based on our August 15, 2005, and September 27, 2007, personal interviews with Teerlink, as well as on Rich Teerlink and Lee Ozley's book *More Than a Motorcycle: The Leadership Journey at Harley-Davidson*. Quotes that are not footnoted are from our personal interviews.

2. "Telluride Town History," Mountain Studies Institute, http://www.mountainstudies.org/databank/history/Towns/Telluride.htm, (accessed September 29, 2008).

3. Harley's York, Pennsylvania, plant has remained a staunch pocket of resistance to Harley's new culture. In February 2007, the union there launched a two-week-long strike that affected production throughout the company.

4. Robert Townsend, "Further '*Up the Organization*,'" Playboy, July 1970, pp. 86, 89.

5. Townsend, *Up the Organization*, p. 66.

6. Ibid., p. xxviii. Interestingly, there is a parallel between blocking back in the American football and "water boy" in European football, where the expression is applied to the defensive midfielders. Their visibility is low, but they are so important to making others play better that the sports press often designates them as the MVPs of the greatest teams, such as Claude Makelele of the French 2006 World Cup runners-up, and Marcos Senna of the Spanish 2008 European Cup champions.

7. The idea of leader-as-servant was invented by Robert Greenleaf. A servant-leader does not merely treat his employees as equals. Because their role is to satisfy customers, to add value, the leader's role is to serve them; see Greenleaf, *Servant Leadership*.

8. Bob Davids, "How Robert Townsend Talked Me Out of Getting an MBA," preface to Townsend, *Up the Organization*, p. xx.

9. Ricardo Semler, *Maverick: The Success Story Behind the World's Most Unusual Workplace* (London: Random House, 1993), p. 68.

10. Teerlink and Ozley, More Than a Motorcycle, p. 54.

11. Ibid., p. 19.

12. Ibid., p. 16. Interestingly, there is a recent liberation case in the most "chief-dependent" US organization—the military. David Marquet, describes in his book Turn The Ship Around how he liberated a nuclear submarine turning it in one year from worst to first.

13. Ibid., p. 49.

14. Ibid., p. 137.

15. Ibid., p. 129.

16. Ibid., p. 135.

7: LIBERATING AN ESTABLISHED COMPANY

1. The following descriptions of Zobrist and FAVI are based on our personal interviews on April 8, 2005, and January 25, 2006. They also make use of materials from Zobrist's book La belle histoire de FAVI and notes available on FAVI's website, http://www.favi.com/. We have translated all of the materials. For more of Zobrist's material translated and synthesized in English, see Shoji Shiba et al., *Transformation Case Studies* (Salem, New Hampshire: GOAL/QPC, 2006), pp. 3–20.

2. Zobrist, La belle histoire de FAVI, p. 26.

3. Zobrist would later tell us that this way of speaking to his people was tailored to the tastes of the local population in Picardy. He does not necessarily advocate crude speech as a management technique generally.

4. Douglas McGregor, *The Professional Manager* (New York: McGraw-Hill, 1967), pp. 67–68.

5. David Montgomery, *The Fall of the House of Labor: The Workplace, the State, and American Labor* Activism, 1865–1925 (New York: Cambridge University Press, 1987), p. 251.

6. Here Zobrist uses his favorite expression, "faire en allant," which means "doing while walking." He elsewhere explains his admiration for a cinema hero who, when his car breaks down in a desert, takes a jerry can and starts to walk. When his more intellectual companion inquires where he is going, the hero replies, "I prefer one advancing idiot to ten sitting intellectuals." Zobrist never believed in the radical models, but in finding FAVI's own unique way.

7. Jean-Christian Fauvet, Comprendre les conflits sociaux (Paris: Editions d'Organisation, 1973).

8. Vasily Grossman, Life and Fate (New York: New York Review Books Classics, 2006), pp. 82–83.

8: FROM MOTIVATION TO SELF-MOTIVATION, PART ONE

1. Thomas Jefferson to Richard Price, 1789.

2. Thomas Jefferson to Joseph C. Cabell, 1818.

3. The description of the University of Virginia project is based on Virginius Dabney, *Mr. Jefferson's University: A History* (Charlottesville: University Press of Virginia, 1981); Joseph J. Ellis, *American Sphinx* (New York: Knopf, 1997); Daniel Walker Howe, "Religion and Education in the Young Republic," in *Figures in the Carpet: Finding the Human Person in the American Past*, ed. Wilfred M. McClay (Grand Rapids, Michigan: Wm. B. Eerdmans Publishing, 2007), p. 382, and a personal interview with John T. Casteen, president of the University of Virginia, May 21, 2008.

4. Nevertheless, in order to earn a degree, a student would have to pass examinations in at least three fields, called "schools." Alternatively, a student could seek a "certificate of graduation" by completing the requirements of one or more schools, which today we would think of as academic departments.

5. Dabney, *Mr. Jefferson's University*, p. 8.

6. Obviously, not all of America's inhabitants were treated as intrinsically equal in Jefferson's time, although in 1819, he claimed that "no man on earth wanted an end to slavery more than he did" (Ellis, *American Sphinx*, p. 317). He would never find, though, a way to abolish slavery without causing what he saw as the economic destruction of the South.

7. The debate about tangible rewards is not entirely settled among the psychologists (see for example, R. Eisenberger, W. D. Pierce, and J. Cameron, "Effects of Reward on Intrinsic Motivation—Negative, Neutral, and Positive: Comment on Deci, Koestner, and Ryan," *Psychological Bulletin* 125 [1999]: pp. 677–91). Some researchers point out that the argument in the football story and similar research experiments is not about the damaging effect of tangible rewards but about the

damaging effect of first promising and then withdrawing these rewards. This, however, is exactly what almost always happens with bonuses and perks in companies once bad results or times hit, as they always do. More important for our purposes, though, is that the vast psychological findings on the tangible rewards' damaging effects on self-motivation is essentially ignored by traditional "how" companies.

8. Personal interview, September 24, 2007.

9. John Dewey, *Later Works*, 1925–1953, ed. Jo Ann Boydston (Carbondale and Edwardsville: Southern Illinois University Press, 1985), 12, p. 112.

10. D. L. Rubenson, "Art and Science, Ancient and Modern: A Psychoeconomic Perspective on Domain Differences in Creativity," in *Creative Intelligence: Toward Theoretic Integration*, ed. D. Ambrose, L. M. Cohen, and A. J. Tannenbaum (Cresskill, New Jersey: Hampton Press, Inc., 2003), pp. 131–46.

11. Robert Sternberg, *Intelligence Applied: Understanding and Increasing Your Intellectual Skills* (San Diego: Harcourt Brace Jovanovich, 1986).

12. Robert J. Sternberg and Todd I. Lubart, *Defying the Crowd: Cultivating Creativity in a Culture of Conformity* (New York: Free Press, 1995), pp. 93–94.

13. Douglas McGregor, *The Professional Manager* (New York: McGraw-Hill, 1967), pp. 10–11. The emphasis is McGregor's.

14. McGregor, *The Human Side of Enterprise*, p. 265.

15. Townsend, *Up the Organization*, p. 96.

16. Blaise Pascal, *Pensées*, trans. W. F. Trotter (New York: P. F. Collier and Son, 1909–14), p. 347.

17. The description of Deci, Ryan, and associates' views and research is based on Edward Deci and Richard Ryan, "The 'What' and 'Why' of Goal Pursuits: Human Needs and the Self-Determination of Behavior," *Psychological Inquiry* 11 (2000): pp. 227–68; and M. Gagné and Edward Deci, "Self-Determination Theory and Work Motivation," *Journal of Organizational Behavior* 26 (2005): pp. 331–62.

18. It can be argued that the highest need in Maslow's hierarchy—self-actualization—is never fully satisfied and so continually motivates people to new action to satisfy it. Though this may be true for a small portion of human beings, even for them Maslow's view of an unsatisfied need is that of a tension that one strives to reduce, which is very different from Deci and Ryan's view of needs as nutriments.

19. We are not ignoring the importance of physical and security needs. A chronically hungry or hurt child obviously won't enjoy playing. At the workplace, whether the majority of employees have their essential physical and security needs satisfied or not is, of course, debatable. Regarding employees in developed economies, Angus Maddison has shown (see note 1 in chapter 2) that the satisfaction of other than material-subsistence needs was no longer limited to a tiny elite but was available to the majority of the inhabitants of developed countries.

20. Deci and Ryan define relatedness as "desire to love and care, and to be

loved and cared for"; competence as a "propensity to have an effect on the environment as well as to attain valued outcomes within it"; and autonomy as a "desire to self-organize experience and behavior and to have activity be concordant with one's integrated sense of self"; Deci and Ryan, "The 'What' and 'Why' of Goal Pursuits," p. 231.

21. We prefer intrinsic equality, growth, and self-direction to denote people's universal needs rather than Deci and Ryan's "relatedness," "competence," and "autonomy" for two reasons. First, terms such as "competence" and "autonomy" have acquired specific meanings in management. "Competence" is often used as an HR term, as in rather command-and-control "competency management," and autonomy is often discussed in "balance" with control within a company. Second, we want to stay close to McGregor, who talked about treating people as if they are good and about self-direction and self-control.

22. Dabney, *Mr. Jefferson's University*, p. 6.

23. Ellis, *American Sphinx*, p. 338.

24. Ibid., p. 310.

25. Dabney, *Mr. Jefferson's University*, p. 21.

26. "History of the Honor Commitee," University of Virginia, http://www .virginia.edu/honor/intro/honorhistory.html (accessed June 12, 2008). Tucker's beliefs in freedom and responsibility may well be the product of family education. His father, judge St. George Tucker, known as "America's Blackstone," was the author of the first commentry on the Constitution in 1803, in which he wrote: "A bill of rights may be considered, not only as intended to give law, and assign limits to a goverment about to be established, but as giving information to the people. By reducing speculative truths to fundemental laws, every man of the meanest capacity and understanding may learn his own rights, and know when they are violated," quoted from *View of the Constitution of the United States with Selected Writings* (Indianapolis: Liberty Fund 1999).

27. The case is based on the following sources: Lars Kolind, *The Second Cycle: Winning the War Against Bureaucracy* (Philadelphia: Wharton School Publishing, 2006); N. J. Foss, "Selective Intervention and Internal Hybrids: Interpreting and Learning from the Rise and Decline of the Oticon Spaghetti Organization," *Organization Science* 14 (2003): pp. 331–49; N. J. Foss, "Internal Disaggregation in Oticon: Interpreting and Learning from the Rise and Decline of the Spaghetti Organization" (working paper, Department of Industrial Economics and Strategy, Copenhagen Business School, 2000); Pernille Eskerod, "Organising by Projects: Experiences from Oticon's Product Development Function," in *Managing the Unmanageable for a Decade*, ed. Mette Morsing and Kristian Eiberg (Hellerup, Denmark: Oticon, 1998), pp. 78–90; Tom Peters, *Liberation Management* (New York: Ballantine Books, 1994), pp. 201–4; and email interviews with Lars Kolind, January–May, 2007.

28. Kolind, *Second Cycle*, pp. 195–196

29. Ibid., p. 197.

30. Ibid., p. 207.

31. Ibid., p. 115.
32. Eskerod, "Organising by Projects," p. 87.
33. Kolind, *Second Cycle*, pp. 209.

9: FROM MOTIVATION TO SELF-MOTIVATION, PART TWO
1. Warren Bennis and Robert Townsend, *Reinventing Leadership* (New York: Quill, 1995), pp. 66–67.
2. Ibid., p. 67.
3. Ibid.
4. Ibid., p. 68.
5. Ibid., p. 75.
6. Personal interview, August 15, 2005.
7. As Warren Bennis wrote in the editors' note to McGregor's *Professional Manager* (p. 14, note 5): "In . . . the scientific research laboratory . . . management has gone a considerable way toward [building a freedom-based environment]. The reasons for doing so have been largely connected with the problem of obtaining and keeping competent scientists, rather than with the acceptance of new ideas about human nature." Indeed, freedom aspects have been built in R&D centers such as DuPont's Experimental Station and AT&T's Bell Labs to attract and keep a particular talent pool. The environment has not been built elsewhere in these companies, though. Today, approaches similar to DuPont's and AT&T's are used by top consulting and software companies that rely heavily on "knowledge workers." SAS Institute has long been known for outstanding conditions and for extremely low turnover of its software developers. Google, which studied SAS carefully, seems to have adopted a similar approach.
8. Personal interview, March 2, 2006.
9. Personal interview, September 26, 2007.
10. John Fennel, *Ready, Fire, Aim* (Pewaukee, Wisconsin: Quad Graphics, 2006), p. 182.
11. Personal interview, March 2, 2006.
12. Personal interview, August 15, 2005.
13. Personal interview, October 18, 2007. Since the time we've written these lines, both Jacques Szulevicz and his president Jacques Raiman, to our great sorrow, passed away
14. While Milton Friedman is often credited with this coinage, and he did write a best-selling book of that name, the phrase appears to have originated in the press in the 1930s. Its exact origins are shrouded in mystery.
15. Fabienne Gambrelle and Félix Torres, *Générale de Service Informatique* (Paris, France: Albin Michael, 1996), p. 122.

10: IN SEARCH OF LOST BOOTS
1. Our interview took place on March 6, 2006. General Robert McDermott died at the age of eighty-six of complications from a stroke on August 28 of that year.

2. Personal interview, March 7, 2006.

3. Personal interview, February 4, 2008.

4. Avishai Margalit, *The Decent Society* (Cambridge, Massachusetts: Harvard University Press, 1996), p. 217.

5. It's interesting to note that in his book, Townsend advises the following approach on making budgets with regard to outside company stakeholders: "Most lenders, directors, and owners look at the monthly report to see if you made your budget. If you did, into the file with it. If you didn't, the report goes to an uninformed nitpicker who dreams up a lot of stupid questions. To save yourself this agony, put some arbitrary safety factor into the top statements that go outside the company. You haven't distorted the figures by which you and your managers are trying to measure trends, but you have something you can use to offset unforeseen setbacks without missing the budget as far as your investor/lenders are concerned." Townsend, *Up the Organization*, p. 9. The head of operations in Grenoble most likely read it, because a copy was given to every GSI manager.

6. The French *aimer* means both "to like" and "to love" and here denotes a stronger affection than simple liking.

7. Personal interview, May 20, 2008.

8. The French word Raiman uses is *justice*. In the context of his other statements, we translated it as "fairness" as the following discussion of the fair—in French *justes*—managers shows.

9. The French *bonheur* can be translated both as "joy" and "happiness."

10. Personal interview, November 21, 2008.

11. Quoted in Joel Cutcher-Gershenfeld, "Introduction to the Annotated Edition," in McGregor, *The Human Side of Enterprise*, p. xlii.

11: THE ANTI-MAD MEN

1. Personal interview, March 6, 2006. All of Stan Richards's quotes, unless specified, come from this interview.

2. Stan Richards, *The Peaceable Kingdom* (New York: John Wiley, 2001).

3. Ibid., p. 9. Richards often compares Madison Avenue firms' atmosphere to U.S-Soviet relations during the Cold War.

4. Ronald Coase, "The Nature of the Firm," in *The Firm, the Market and the Law* (Chicago: University of Chicago, 1990), p. 33–56.

5. *The Peaceable Kingdom*, p. 20.

6. Ibid., p. 142.

7. Ibid., p. 143.

8. Personal interview, March 3, 2006.

12: THE SECRET OF LIBERATING LEADERSHIP

1. Conference for l'Institut des Hautes Etudes Cinématographiques, Paris, 1982. We thank Jean-François Cottin for having pointed us to this video.

2. Cited in P. B. Baltes and U. M. Staudinger, "Wisdom: A Metaheuristic

(Pragmatic) to Orchestrate Mind and Virtue Toward Excellence," *American Psychologist* 55 (2000): p. 133.

3. Personal interview, September 8, 2008. All the quotes from Liisa Joronen, unless specified, come from this interview and will not be referenced separately.

4. Personal communication, July 18, 2008.

5. "The SOL Story," SOL internal document, February 2006.

6. Photo by Anne Nisula. Used with SOL's permission.

7. In 2000, Liisa Joronen distributed 90 percent of the ownership of SOL to her three children, keeping just 10 percent for herself. But she retained a "golden share" giving her veto power over many corporate decisions. She kept the deciding vote for herself, she said, "in order to keep the children happy."

8. Personal exchange with Liisa Joronen, May 10, 2009.

9. P. B. Baltes and U. Kunzmann, "The Two Faces of Wisdom: Wisdom as a General Theory of Knowledge and Judgment About Excellence in Mind and Virtue vs. Wisdom as Everyday Realization in People and Products," *Human Development* 47 (2004): pp. 295–96.

10. René Descartes, "Meditations on First Philosophy" in *The Philosophical Writings of Descartes*, Vol. II, trans. John Cottingham, Robert Stoothoff, and Dugald Murdoch (Cambridge: Cambridge University Press, 1984), p. 24.

11. M. W. Morris and K. Peng, "Culture and Cause: American and Chinese Attributions for Social and Physical Events," *Journal of Personality and Social Psychology* 67 (1994): pp. 949–71; and R. E. Nisbett, K. Peng, I. Choi, and A. Norenzayan, "Culture and Systems of Thought: Holistic versus Analytic Cognition," Psychological Review 108 (2001): pp. 291–310.

12. F. Lee, M. Hallahan, and T. Herzog, "Explaining Real-Life Events: How Culture and Domain Shape Attributions," Personality and Social Psychology Bulletin 22 (1996): pp. 732–41.

13. A. Fernald and H. Morikawa, "Common Themes and Cultural Variations in Japanese and American Mothers' Speech to Infants," *Child Development* 64 (1993): pp. 637–56; and T. Tardif, M. Shatz, and L. Naigles, "Caregiver Speech and Children's Use of Nouns versus Verbs: A Comparison of English, Italian and Mandarin," *Journal of Child Language* 24 (1997): pp. 535–65.

14. Personal interview, May 22, 2008.

15. Personal interview, May 18, 2008.

16. Zobrist, La belle histoire de FAVI, p. 1. The principle opens Zobrist's book.

13: THE ULTIMATE PARADOX

1. Personal interview, May 18, 2008. Other Davids quotes in this chapter are from this interview and our interview on September 24, 2007.

2. Personal interview, September 15, 2008. All other Kelley quotes, unless specified, come from this interview.

3. This paragraph is partly based on "Designed Chaos: An Interview with David Kelley, Founder and CEO of IDEO," Virtual Advisor, Inc., http://www.va

-interactive.com/inbusiness/editorial/bizdev/articles/ideo.html (accessed July 7, 2007).

4. Peter Burrows, "Hewlett & Packard: Architects of the Info Age—The Founding Fathers of Silicon Valley Steered Tech Away from Hierarchy," *Business Week*, March 29, 2004.

5. Ibid.

6. R. I. Sutton and A. Hargadon, "Brainstorming Groups in Context: Effectiveness in a Product Design Firm," *Administrative Science Quarterly* 41 (1996): p. 685.

7. The various philosophers' views and quotes on wisdom in these paragraphs are based on Sharon Ryan, "Wisdom," Stanford Encyclopedia of Philosophy, http://www.science.uva.nl/~seop/entries/wisdom (accessed November 26, 2008).

8. Aristotle, *Nichomachean Ethics*, (Stillwell, KS: Digireads, 2005), p. 66, VI, 1140a–1140b.

9. J. Kekes, "Wisdom," *American Philosophical Quarterly* 20, no. 3 (1983): p. 280.

10. This description of the methodology is based on "The Deep Dive (at IDEO)," a *Nightline* segment that originally aired on ABC on July 13, 1999.

11. Bruce Nussbaum, "The Power of Design," *Business Week*, May 17, 2004, p. 96.

12. Tim Brown, "Design Thinking," *Harvard Business Review*, June 2008, p. 87.

13. See Linda Tischler, "A Designer," *Fast Company*, February 2009, pp. 78–101; and A. G. Lafley and Ram Charan, *The Game-Changer: How You Can Drive Revenue and Profit Growth with Innovation* (New York: Crown Business, 2008).

14. Tischler, "A Designer," p. 78–101.

15. Personal interview, September 15, 2008. The following quotes on the "experience team" are from this interview.

16. Personal interview, September 15, 2008.

17. See, for example, C. A. O'Reilly III and J. Chatman, "Culture as Social Control: Corporations, Cults, and Commitment," *Research in Organizational Behavior* 18 (1996): pp. 157–200.

18. Personal interview, May 20, 2008.

19. This does not necessarily mean hiring the "best" in the traditional sense. When Robert Townsend toured Chaparral Steel in the 1980s, he said to Gordon Forward, "Gordon, you are cheating. You have good people here!"; personal interview with Gordon Forward, September 25, 2007.

14: BUTTERFLIES IN FORMATION

1. Personal interview, September 25, 2007.

2. Personal interview, May 20, 2008.

3. Personal interview, May 22, 2008. All the quotes in this chapter from

employees at Chaparral's Petersburg mill were gathered in personal interviews on that day. In July 2007, Gerdau Ameristeel bought out Chaparral Steel for $4.2 billion, and at the time of our visit, Chaparral was still being "integrated" into its new parent company. The fate of the culture that helped make Chaparral such an attractive prize to Gerdau cannot be predicted as of this writing.

4. Harry Quadracci was strongly opposed to unionization of Quad/Graphics, having witnessed divisive strikes at an earlier employer. For this, Quad has earned the attention and ire of organized labor, but so far no one has succeeded in organizing a Quad facility, which speaks to the Quadraccis' success in maintaining a fruitful relationship with their employees.

5. Frank Shipper and Charles C. Manz, "Employee Self-Management Without Formally Designated Teams: An Alternative Road to Empowerment," *Organizational Dynamics* 20, no. 3 (1992): pp. 48–61.

6. Personal interview, May 18, 2008.

7. Personal interview, August 17, 2005. Ziemer retired in early 2009.

8. Personal interview, May 20, 2008.

9. Personal interview, November 26, 2008.

10. Personal interview, May 22, 2008.

11. Personal interview, May 22, 2008.

12. Personal interview, September 8, 2008.

13. Zobrist, La belle histoire de FAVI, pp. 107–8.

14. One Gore associate, a first-generation immigrant from India, joked with us that his status-conscious family back in the old country was very concerned that he'd been at the company over a decade and was still a mere "associate."

15. Townsend, *Up the Organization*, p. 111.

16. Townsend, "Further '*Up the Organization*,'" pp. 86, 89.

17. Jean-François Zobrist, seminar given at ESCP Europe Business School, Paris, February 18, 2009.

18. A study of 6,772 large "how" firms from 40 industries showed that only 2 to 5 percent sustain a competitive advantage over a 10-year period, and only 4 firms sustain it over 20 years. More, about 99 percent of firms—large and small—disappear over the first forty years of their life (C. I. Stubbart and M. B. Knight, "The Case of the Disappearing Firms: Empirical Evidence and Implications," *Journal of Organizational Behavior* 27, [2002]: pp. 79–100.)

19. Personal interview, August 15, 2005.

20. See Angus Maddison's finding, note 1 in chapter 2, that beginning in 1820 and up to 2001, per capita income rose twentyfold in the West. This meant the satisfaction of needs beyond mere material subsistence was no longer limited to a tiny elite. The majority of inhabitants of developed economies could now concern themselves with "higher" universal needs whose pursuit is unique to humans.

21. Title of a paper presented at a conference at MIT on April 9, 1957; reprinted in McGregor, *The Human Side of Enterprise*, pp. 341–56.

INDEX

ABOUT THE AUTHORS

BRIAN M. CARNEY is Senior Vice President for Corporate Communications of Rivada Networks.

Brian was a member of The Wall Street Journal's editorial board from 2004-2014 and editor of The Wall Street Journal Europe's editorial page from 2004-2005 and 2009-2014. His interview with Nestle Chairman Peter Brabeck-Letmathe was included in the Columbia Journalism Review's "Best Business Writing 2012."

In 2009, Brian won the Gerald Loeb Award for Commentary, America's most prestigious business-journalism prize, for his coverage of the financial crisis. In 2003, he received the Frederic Bastiat Prize for Journalism for his writings on the European economy.

ISAAC GETZ, with Ph.D.s in Psychology and Management, is a professor at the top-ranked ESCP Europe Business School operating in Paris, London, Berlin, Madrid and Turin and has been a visiting professor at Cornell and Stanford Universities and at the University of Massachusetts. His research on the liberating leadership has won the Syntec Award for the best academic article in 2010. Isaac's work has been featured in all the main US and French media. He is also an author/co-author of three other books translated into dozen languages, many articles and op-eds and is an active public speaker. Isaac has been instrumental in creating the corporate liberation movement involving hundreds of companies and organizations of all sizes and industries.

For more information about Brian M. Carney's and Isaac Getz's work, visit www.freedomincbook.com.

Lightning Source UK Ltd.
Milton Keynes UK
UKHW03f1940240418
321588UK00001B/130/P